THE GOSPEL
ACCORDING TO

LENNON

D0756269

THE GOSPEL
ACCORDING TO

LENNON

ALAN CLAYSON

BOBCAT BOOKS

LONDON / NEW YORK / PARIS / SYDNEY / COPENHAGEN / BERLIN / MADRID / TOKYO

Order No: BOB 11528R
ISBN 13: 978.1.86074.656.7
ISBN 10: 1.86074.656.X

Exclusive Distributors
Music Sales Limited,
14/15 Berner Street,
London W1T 3LJ.

Music Sales Corporation,
257 Park Avenue South,
New York, NY 10010, USA.

Macmillan Distribution Services,
53 Park West Drive,
Derrimut, Vic 3030,
Australia.

Printed and bound by Gutenberg Press Ltd, Malta

A catalogue record for this book is available from the British Library.

Visit Omnibus Press on the web at www.omnibuspress.com

To Robert Bartel

'For it was inside that all the magic was, the kind of magic that only a person raised by the water's edge can understand – but this magic quickly disappears when one realises that it was but a summer's dream that did not last.'

– Tomas O Criomhthain

CONTENTS

Introduction

What You Got

Following a biographical resume, *The Gospel According To John Lennon* takes the form of a pot-pourri of incidents and events in the subject's life and death which draw attention to aspects of his extraordinary musical, literary and visionary talent. Far more than any mere pop star, John Winston Ono Lennon is now accorded the kind of acclaim afforded to a small handful of spiritual leaders, a state-of-affairs that certainly never existed in his lifetime, whether as unofficial leader of The Beatles or in the years after their demise.

On the face of it, the showbusiness sensation of the 20th century had no visible 'leader', which meant that fans could be fickle in their affections towards individuals yet still maintain overall loyalty to the group in its entirety. With uniform stage suits, impenetrable Liverpool accents and haircuts as distinctive as Hitler's toothbrush moustache, the coherence of the quartet's corporate image presented what seemed at first glance to be a single focus for worship. Ridiculous as it seems in hindsight, especially now that their individual characteristics are so apparent, there was a time when commentators couldn't tell one individual Beatle from another. However, it was surely always the case that the crucial balance within the group that led to their success was a direct result of the inevitable differences between them.

Musically, the crux of The Beatles was the self-contained songwriting team of John Lennon and Paul McCartney which had become formidable by the time the group impinged on national consciousness with the chart entry of their debut single, 'Love Me Do', late in 1962. Very much the junior partner, George Harrison was to make tentative explorations as a writer, but he found John and Paul's head start a tough yardstick. Furthermore, the careers of many other famous acts – including The Rolling Stones – were launched or stabilised by the gift of a Lennon-McCartney song.

Although the myth continues to propagate of 'raw' John and 'melodic' Paul, it was only their public personas that suggested diplomatic McCartney's responsibility for ballads, leaving the ravers to rough old Lennon. On the likely conjecture that the principle composer was also lead vocalist, their most memorable numbers show an even split – for nearly every 'Yesterday', there is an 'In My Life'; for every 'I Feel Fine, a 'Can't Buy Me Love'; for every 'Why Don't We Do It In The Road', a 'Revolution 9'.

In general, Lennon was the most experimental while McCartney sold more. Yet, although John, with sound reason, ridiculed what he called Paul's 'granny music' in the last desperate months of The Beatles, he was to demonstrate an alarming capacity for tweeness throughout the time between the group's disbandment in 1970 and his passing 10 years later.

As well as relevant quotes, anecdotes and episodes from these and earlier – and even posthumously – years from a lively four decades on this planet, *The Gospel According To John Lennon* will incorporate aspects of the late entertainer as a fated youth who was to metamorphose into a quasi-messianic symbol of hipness; whose talents as a vocalist and composer have been acknowledged by every such artist that has mattered, and whose activities and utterances were absorbed deeply and used to form answers by both the common pop consumer and the undergraduate flirting with bohemia before becoming a teacher, proprietor of a multinational corporation or, in the cases of Tony Blair and Bill Clinton, a head of state.

Unlike that contained in a hagiography of some Dark Ages king, we are embarrassed by too much detail. The principal events of almost every day of Lennon's life since 1962 have been chronicled in some publication or other, and even as sources of 'new and rediscovered' details continue to dry up, there are presently nearly 70 books concerning him alone that are readily available in high street book shops. Yet, to the faithful, no sentence is without value, no item too insignificant not to be intriguing.

As the Bible can be used to prove any religious or moral theory, so the millions of words written and spoken about John Lennon can warp his philosophy to any purpose, ranging from elevations to near-sainthood – as exemplified by a Scandinavian fanzine consisting entirely of visual representations of Lennon in the hereafter – to doorstoppers such as Albert Goldman's *The Lives Of John Lennon*, which depicts him as barking mad after a lifetime of unsurpassed human frailty. While his deeds and personality have thus become more nebulous and ambiguous in retrospect, I will be dealing mostly with raw fact within the context of the myriad social, cultural, economic, environmental and other undercurrents and myths that polarise what we can surmise about Lennon's intellectual, domestic, spiritual and other dimensions.

Without treating his most flippant remarks as gospel, this account will embrace personal memories from some of the key dramatis personae, and delvings into press archives, many of them quite obscure, as well as information derived from a re-examination of my own compacted miles of audio tapes and film footage; filing cabinets bulging with God-knows-what; folders vomiting cuttings and complete newspapers that are getting tattier by the day, and other nearly thigh-high clutter that fills the room where I wrote my many tomes concerning John Lennon and The Beatles.

Alan Clayson, June 2005

Life Begins At Forty: Lennon In The Twentieth Century

"I was always psychic, always saw things in a hallucinatory way – and it's scary when you're a child, because there's nobody to relate to. I belonged to an exclusive club. When I looked in the mirror, I used to, literally, trance out into alpha." Thus spake John Lennon, weeks before the 'beautiful sadness' of his death in New York at the trigger-jerk of Mark David Chapman, not so much a fan as a disciple whose adoration had been extinguished. "Are you John Lennon?" asked one of the cops in whose squad car he was hastened to hospital after the shooting. "Yeah," gasped John. Then he died.

As it had been with the early demise of Hollywood heart-throb Rudolph Valentino in 1926, the slaying sparked off suicides. In an attempt to nip these in the bud, Yoko issued a statement via the *New York Daily News*, stressing that "when something like this happens, each one of us must go on".

This was more considered than Paul McCartney's "It's a drag", uttered the following night when accosted by a television camera crew with a stick-mike that was thrust towards him out of the blue. Unlike Paul, George Harrison cancelled the day's recording session, and didn't venture beyond the confines of his country estate in Oxfordshire until the dust had settled.

If as fearful as George and Paul – and, more pointedly,

Yoko – of a copycat killing, Ringo Starr made a grand gesture on his late colleague's behalf by catching an immediate flight to New York to offer condolences, even if he was heard to murmur 'It was her who started all this' as he and fiancée Barbara Bach waited for an audience with the widow in an ante-room at the Lennon home.

A hasty cremation at Hartsdale, a city mortuary, had already been arranged, even as Ringo and Barbara were being shepherded through the tightest security net to a purring Cadillac. Through its one-way windows, they glanced at stark headlines on newspaper stands and electronically transmitted images of Lennon and Ono on TV sets in appliance shops along the stop-start drive from Kennedy airport to the city centre.

Suntanned in the cold, they were self-contained spectators with no stake in the tragedy until, with no parking space in the Dakota forecourt, shock impinged itself on them as they hastened past clutching hands and the pitiless woomph of flashbulbs, in through a side door into the Dakota. As he comprehended the massed and extravagant lamentations behind that corridor of police barricades, Ringo "was not very happy with the vigil. Those people showed very little respect for either John nor Yoko. It was disgusting."

Nevertheless, at Mrs Lennon's request, many sent donations to the Spirit Foundation, a multi-purpose charity organisation set up by her and her late spouse in 1978. Far greater multitudes across the globe observed a 10-minute silence to pray for John's soul at the same time on the Sunday after the shooting.

Most reckoned that John had been killed simply because this Chapman bloke – who'd been sighted sniffing round Todd Rundgren too – was as nutty as a fruitcake, though after trial he would be confined not to a mental institution but New York's Attica Correctional Facility, coincidentally the setting of 'Attica State' from Lennon and Ono's un-remarkable 1972 album, *Sometime In New York City*.

The more credulous, however, paid heed to the theories and a compounding of eschatological analogies that had been flying up and down when flags were still at half-mast and the radio was broadcasting the dead man's music continuously in place of listed programmes. Was it an Art Statement more surreal than anything John and Yoko had done in the dear, dead Swinging Sixties? Had Yoko reneged on an elaborate suicide pact? One particularly powerful rumour was that Ono had eaten Lennon's ashes.

Then there was the notion that it had been a rite whereby some sort of 'kingdom' – the 'Beatle generation', now approaching middle-age – was to be rejuvenated by the sacrifice of its high priest in his prime. It said as much in *The Golden Bough*, one tome of spiritual nature Lennon had devoured in his search for faith. He had also embraced LSD, transcendental meditation and Krishna consciousness, a recipe of mind-bending intoxicants so powerful that the whole experience climaxed with Lennon summoning the other Beatles to a 1968 meeting in order to proclaim himself the Messiah.

Such conduct connected too with that of St Francis of Assisi, who preached naked as an act of holy self-abasement. As if it was a statement St Francis might have made too, Lennon assured *Melody Maker*, "I try to live as Christ did. It's tough, I can tell you."

John, however, was less a divinity than someone who turned his headline-hogging life into an open and often ludi-crous book in which he said things most folk didn't want to hear. He wasn't obliged to do this, of course. Indeed, the repercussions of The Beatles gouged so deep a wound on pop that it wouldn't have mattered if, in the years that followed, their founder member had failed to pursue even a sporadic recording career, let along one that contained odd sparks of the old fire that powered him onwards and upwards when The Beatles were stuck on the Liverpool-Hamburg treadmill.

Even Lennon's latter-day lyrics are still quoted like proverbs, despite the strange goings-on during his four final years spent mainly as a 'househusband' in the Big Apple's smart Dakota Building. Attempting to master his inner chaos, he granted his and his second wife's only child, Sean, far more paternal attention than most can expect from a famous father.

During this period too, he became as unreachable an object of incommunicado myth as Howard Hughes. Rock stars passing through the Big Apple felt compelled to make at least token efforts to pay their respects to the Grand Old Man, and there wasn't a newspaper editor in the world who wouldn't promise a fortune for a Lennon exclusive or an up-to-the-minute photo, especially in the light of tales about his antics behind closed doors.

Sometimes these were so bizarre as to be reminiscent of those he actuated as a troublesome and troubled teenager. His intangible 'something else' had first manifested itself when he was charismatic leader of an entourage united in terrified admiration, as he held forth for hours in a favoured pub or coffee bar, and acted the lunatic around art college and Liverpool's pubs and shopping centres. He appeared able to cajole his disciples into doing almost anything.

In 1966, the media were to sensationalise his off-the-cuff comments about religion in London's *Evening Standard*. When reprinted in the US teenage magazine *Datebook*, his suggestion that The Beatles 'are more popular than Jesus now' and that 'Christianity will go, it will vanish and shrink' were repeated out of context by the general media and interpreted as blasphemy. Let us not forgot that this was a land that was accustomed to pop stars being devoid of independent opinion, where Colonel Parker's manipulation of Elvis Presley set the "sir-and-ma'am" standard of a walking digest of truth, justice and the American way.

The repercussions of this episode fuelled The Beatles' decision to down tools as a working band, and began their journey to a position wherein John Lennon was barely recognisable as the chirpy "yeah-yeah-yeah" Moptop.

Three years later, with hair splayed halfway down his back and bearded to the cheekbones, he'd smoked a Lucky Strike cigarette during a white-costumed wedding, as recorded in The Beatles' last British number one, 'The Ballad Of John And Yoko'. Each chorus began with the exclamation, 'Christ!', which restricted airplay, but it was the 'Bed-Ins' and associated stunts that completed the metamorphosis of 1963's 'nasty bastard' – as one associate described him – to one of the world's most renowned pacifists.

Next up was John's eponymous debut album as a solo artist with its personal exorcisms – notably in 'God'. Further soul-baring surfaced on the *Imagine* follow-up, though its utopian title track would endure as Lennon's most memorable post-Beatles song. Certainly, today's pop pickers have been brought up to regard it as his finest composition, and 'Imagine' continues to be placed at the top of these 'Hundred Greatest Pop Songs'-type polls that rear up periodically in newspapers and on television.

Yet John Lennon hadn't had all that much going for him when he was treading the boards with The Quarry Men skiffle group in 1957. While he could just about find his way around his instrument, he aroused little enthusiasm for either

9

his singing or maiden attempts at songwriting. On the surface, he wasn't that brilliant at anything then. Into the bargain, a combination of a middle-class upbringing centred on the Church and drudgery in a grammar school C-stream had produced an adolescent with a 'bad' attitude, albeit one with so many ideas – and not only musical ones – chasing through his mind that it was all he could do to note them down. Flames of inspiration would kindle when he shuffled from bedroom to doormat for first grab at the *Daily Express*, then a broadsheet that did not label a buyer politically as much as it would later. Others jerked him from a velvet-blue oblivion back in the dungeons where The Beatles slept during their first visit to Germany in 1960.

Even after the group "Made It," tomorrow would seem a year away as, more often than not with Paul McCartney, John would figure out a chord sequence to fragments of melody or rhymes to form a couplet. From a mere title, the ghost of maybe a sketchy chorus would smoulder into form, and a red-eyed objectivity and a private quality control might engross him and Paul until day became night with the pair surrounded by overloaded ash-trays, smeared coffee cups and pages full of scribblings and notations peculiar to themselves.

As he'd never learned to sight-read or write musical script, John was untroubled by the formal do's and don'ts that traditionally affect creative flow. There were only the stylistic cliches and habits ingrained since his teenage self had positioned yet uncalloused fingertips on the taut strings of his first guitar. Grappling with his muse, he drew from virtually every musical and literary idiom he had ever encountered since he was prised into the world at 6.30 p.m. on Wednesday, October 9, 1940 at Liverpool's Oxford Street Maternity Hospital. The BBC Home Service weatherman had forecast a dull but mild night – which it was. Dull but mild it remained for more or less the next fortnight. However, one evening before the baby was brought home, wailing sirens and flares illuminated the sky as the Luftwaffe dropped tonne upon booming tonne of death and destruction in and around the slip-slapping wharfs of dockland where the murky Mersey sweeps into the Irish Sea.

The following morning, brick-dust crunched beneath the hooves of dray horses dragging coal through mean streets to rusty ships, but Julia Lennon's first born was destined for a comfortable middle-class home – with a fitted dining-room carpet, not lino – along Menlove Avenue, one of the main thoroughfares in Woolton, a village-like suburb that aligned itself more with Lancashire than Merseyside.

After his father, Freddie, a seaman of Irish extraction, vanished when John was five, so soon did the concept that there is no God but Mummy, and Daddy is the prophet of Mummy. With Freddie represented – perhaps unfairly – as the villain of the piece, the subsequent complications of his wayward mother's love-life and domestic arrangements made it more convenient for the boy to grow up in 'Mendips', the semi-detached villa of Julia's childless sister Mary Smith – who John would always call by his cradle articulation 'Mimi' – and her ex-serviceman husband, George, once an infinitesimal cog in the global hostilities, but now running his late father's dairy business. George was to die suddenly when his nephew by marriage was 14.

His natural mother Julia – so John was to discover – lived nearby with her second family and, bound by the invisible chains that shackle child to parent, he used her council house as a bolt-hole whenever strait-laced Mimi's rearing methods became too oppressive. The innate confusion of 'Who am I to regard as mother?' affected John's ability to trust adult authority figures whom he mocked and abused as a defence against being rejected by them. Despite the extenuating circumstances of her sudden death in 1958, he felt he'd been cast out by his mother as well as Freddie, having had enough experience of her to know what he was missing – hence the bitterness inherent in outbursts against teachers, friends and his devoted aunt.

Mimi usually blamed doubtful company for John's mischief when, short-trousered and in gaberdine raincoat, he began his formal education in autumn 1945 in the kindergarten at Moss Pit Lane Infant School, a few streets dawdle from Mendips. The following April, John was removed for disruptive behaviour and, chastened by this disgrace, commenced a less wild career at Dovedale Road Primary. For a while, he modelled himself on 'William Brown', Richmal Crompton's outrageous 12-year-old from a well-to-do rural family, whose first exploit, *Just William*, had been published in 1917.

Lennon, however, would go way beyond the rough-and-tumble of acceptable boyhood larks after gaining a place at Quarry Bank, the suburban grammar school that was nicknamed 'the Police State' by the more liberal of local seats of learning for its pretentious affectations and Draconian discipline. An Eton-esque house system was in full force there, as was corporal punishment, administered as often as not with the swish of a bamboo cane on buttocks or outstretched palm.

It wasn't long before John was transformed from a capable if uninvolved pupil to one hanging onto his place at Quarry Bank by the skin of his teeth. By the end of his second year there, he had become a nuisance in class, a known truant, a sharer of smutty stories and an initiate of a caste who'd graduated from the innocence of tooth-rotting boiled sweets to the lung-corroding evil of cigarettes. Indeed, the adult John would tear the cellophane off up to three 20-packs a day.

Leading by example, Lennon had some kind of vice-like grip on his allies in delinquency. "I used to beat them up if they were small enough," John was to admit, not especially ruefully, "but I'd use long words and confuse them if they were bigger. What mattered was that I stayed in charge."

Never standing when he could lean, hands rammed in pockets and chewing gum in a half-sneer, the 'bad' attitude of that Lennon boy – destructive, lazy, narcissistic and, as far as he dared, a bully – was reflected too in extra-curricular activities that had little bearing on what he was supposed to be learning at Quarry Bank. Absorbing a hidden curriculum, he'd developed a messy aptitude as an illustrator and writer of comic verse and stories.

Most relevant to this discussion, however, is John Lennon's acquisition of a guitar, the instrument that Elvis Presley hung around his neck. Lennon didn't only like Presley, he worshipped him from the moment he heard 'Heartbreak Hotel', the Tennessean's debut chart entry, and saw the first photograph of him published in Britain – on January 21, 1956 in *Record Mirror* – as a hybrid of amusement-arcade hoodlum and nancy boy.

Aunt Mimi bought John's acoustic guitar from Frank Hessy's in central Liverpool. This musical equipment store's profit graph for guitar sales had taken a sharp upward turn during the craze for skiffle – seen now as the most homogenously British offshoot of rock'n'roll – that peaked in 1957 when 'King of Skiffle' Lonnie Donegan scored six successive Top 30 hits, including two number ones. Like punk after it, anyone who'd mastered basic techniques could have a go. Most skiffle combos were formed for the benefit of performers rather than audience, but nationwide there were thousands of skifflers thrumming home-made basses and percussion instruments, singing through nostrils just like

Lonnie, and thrashing that E-chord on cheap, finger-lacerating guitars for all they were worth.

John's innate bossiness ensured a walkover in the power struggle for leadership of The Quarry Men, the school outfit created in the image of that fronted by Donegan. Though the style was based on blues, hillbilly and further sub-divisions of North American folk music, the less purist Quarry Men also embraced US classic rock – and it was this element that impressed Paul McCartney when he attended a performance at Woolton summer fete in July 1957. Not long after Paul joined, the younger George Harrison succeeded original lead guitarist Eric Griffiths who, like most of the other personnel, regarded skiffle as a vocational blind alley, a trivial pursuit to be thrust aside on departure to the 'real world' of work, marriage or National Service.

Among a fragmenting Quarry Men's principal assets were John's instinctive if indelicate crowd control, and the vocal interplay between himself and McCartney. Yet the power structure whereby George was to be subordinate to John and Paul for as long as they stayed together was founded on the handshake that had formalised the Lennon-McCartney songwriting partnership – or so you'd read when the myth gripped harder – during John's final year at Quarry Bank.

He left in July 1957 with a reputation as a round peg in a square hole – and a kinder testimonial than he may have expected. This enabled him to enrol at Liverpool's Regional College of Art a few weeks later where, before the year was out, John, Paul, George and a turnover of other musicians were being engaged as a recurring support act at Students Union dances. By then, every other item in their repertoire was a salaam to Elvis Presley, Gene Vincent, Jerry Lee Lewis, Chuck Berry, Little Richard and further rock'n'roll behemoths. The only concession to the oncoming general popularity of traditional jazz was Louis Armstrong's 'When You're Smiling' – albeit with John inserting saucy references to college staff into its lyrics. "Their sound was rubbish," thought Gerry Marsden, another parochial singing guitarist, "but John – and Paul – stood out as talented. Somehow, whatever John did was just different. He seemed to have absorbed all the rock'n'roll influences, and then come out the other side with entirely his own variation on them."

Lennon's preoccupation with the group took its toll on his studies. What did stereoplastic colour, Vorticism and tactile values matter when he and the lads were the support that evening for the Merseysippi Wall City Jazz Band at Gateacre Labour Club?

A lecture-disrupting clown too, academic failure seemed inevitable from the start. In preparation for The Entrance to class on the very first day, he'd risen early to spend an inordinate amount of time combing his hair into a precarious pompadour, glistening with Brylcreem. For quick adjustments, he stuck a comb in the top pocket of a concessionary sports jacket buttoned over the lilac shirt that Mimi detested. Then he walked to the 'bus stop in approved cavalry twills, but when he alighted, he had a slightly pigeon-toed gait, having changed somehow during the jolting journey into drainpipe jeans, so tight that it looked as if his legs had been dipped in ink. Thus attired, he'd stood at the college portals, and narrowed short-sighted eyes. He was too vain to be seen wearing the spectacles he'd needed since Dovedale Primary.

The new undergraduate's self-image was at odds with the only subject he kept quiet about – his privileged upbringing amidst the golf clubs, boating lakes and mock-Tudor colonies of Woolton. An inverted snob, he'd already embraced the machismo values of more proletarian Merseyside males, and generally came on as the Poor Honest Wacker – a working-class hero, in fact, although the only paid work he ever did, apart from as a musician, was as a labourer at a local waterworks, Scaris and Brick, for a month during a summer recess. Nonetheless, by the end of his first term at college, he was speaking in florid Scouse, laced with incessant swearing.

He'd also latched onto the notion that northern women were mere adjuncts to their men. John's overwhelmed girl-friend – and future wife – Cynthia Powell, appeared to toler-ate this role as well as the jealous anxieties that caused him to clench his fists and make exasperating scenes if she so much as said a civil hello to any male not on his mental list of those he considered to have no romantic interest in her.

She came to realise too that when John was in the public eye, he played the fool as if on cue. "He worked so hard at keeping people amused, he was exhausting," said Rod Murray, another student. "One day, I saw him running down the street, holding a steering-wheel – no car, just the wheel. He said he was driving down to town." Lennon's buffoonery would sometimes deteriorate into a nonsensical – and frequently alcohol-fuelled – frenzy, and soon would come the escapades that would get him barred from pubs. Merseyside polymath Adrian Henri once witnessed him lying on the floor of one local tavern, Ye Cracke, pretending to swim. Told by the landlady to stop, John replied that he daren't because he'd be sure to drown.

Back in class, his tutors could not help but imagine that he did very little relevant reading. "You had the feeling that he was living off the top of his head," remarked Philip Hartas, in charge of foundation sculpture. "He was a fellow who'd been born without brakes. His objective seemed to be some-where over there that nobody else could see, but he was going, and in that process, a lot of people got run over. He never did it to me, but he had this very sarcastic way of talking to people."

Impatient of prolonged discussion on Art, it was a veneer of self-confidence rather than any heavily veiled air of learning that swiftly made Lennon a centre of attention. Among those defending him against those at college who wanted him expelled was course tutor Arthur Ballard, who conducted seminars in Ye Cracke. Even 40 years later, this was regarded as, well, unorthodox. In the late Fifties, it verged on lunacy.

While Ballard recognised Lennon's abilities as a cartoonist, Bill Harry, a graphics student, reckoned that "You could see in John's written output the heritage of Lewis Carroll. He also reminded me of Stanley Unwin, his malapropisms, etc., but there was an Englishness about it when everyone else was copying the Americans."

The atmosphere of bohemian Liverpool was sufficiently similar to that of New York's vibrant beatnik district, Greenwich Village, that muckrakers from the *Sunday People* were sent there and to other supposed storm centres of squalor to root out what would be headlined 'THE BEATNIK HORROR!' Lashing those present in Rod Murray's flat with booze, the newshounds assured them that it was to be a feature on the problems of making ends meet on student grants. It certainly was a problem, concurred John Lennon, who didn't actually live there, though he was trying to persuade Aunt Mimi that everyone who was anyone had their own studio apartment near college. Yet, as 'Mendips' – his official address – was within city limits – just – he didn't qualify for living expenses anyway. Nevertheless, with others eager to get their pictures in the paper, he obeyed a directive to dress down and make the place more untidy. You want the readers to think that you're poor, starving students, don't you?

On July 24, 1960, two million read the *Sunday People*'s beatnik article, which was printed alongside a photograph that was the first Britain at large saw of John Lennon. Sporting sunglasses, and with sideburns past his earlobes, he had pride of place, lolling about on the littered floor amongst Murray, Bill Harry and other self-conscious 'beatniks'. He looked as if he probably slept in his vest.

John, see, was suddenly modelling himself on Van Gogh or Modigliani and not Elvis Presley or those who followed in his wake. Much of this was down to the influence of Stuart Sutcliffe, a gifted painter, whose lecture notebooks were as conscientiously full as Lennon's were empty. When written or practical assessment was pending, John would cadge assistance from Stuart – or Cynthia – as openly as he would cadge a Woodbine. Through Stuart too, Lennon shook off enough ingrained indolence to transfer from lettering to painting and actually do a bit of work. He also became less bored in the theoretical side of it to the extent that, now and then, a lecture was not approached as an opportunity for illicit relaxation or exercising his wit at the tutor's expense.

It was certainly through Stuart that what Paul McCartney would describe as the hitherto suppressed 'closet intellectual' surfaced in Lennon. "John debunked a lot of intellectual analysis," said Sutcliffe's younger sister, Pauline, "particularly when people found in his output roots in all sorts of literary and artistic figures that he would claim never to have been familiar with."

In turn, Sutcliffe's wonderment at Lennon extended to observing rehearsals in the College of Art's Life Room whenever George Harrison and Paul McCartney absconded from lessons to meet up with John. Though engagements were still few and far between – and often undertaken for as little as a round of fizzy drinks – The Quarry Men, though not the most exciting act going on Merseyside, were becoming adept at bypassing potentially ugly moments at bookings, often via Lennon's growing ability to 'read' an audience.

The outer reaches of their circuit hadn't extended beyond Liverpool until autumn 1959 when the group – now renamed Johnny & The Moondogs, and consisting of just John, George and Paul – made it through to the final regional heat of Carroll Levis's *Star Search*, the spiritual forerunner of ITV's *Opportunity Knocks*, at the Hippodrome Theatre in Manchester. However, the need to catch the last train back to Liverpool put the tin-lid on any chances of instant stardom here as it left too early for the band to be judged by volume of applause at the contest's finale. Nevertheless, this crestfallen headway mattered more to the group than any progress they were making at college, school or work.

The boys became a common sight, sitting for hours at a kidney-shaped table in the Jacaranda, a coffee bar owned by Allan Williams, who began acting in a quasi-managerial capacity for the group after Stuart Sutcliffe found the wherewithal to make a down-payment on one of these new-fangled electric bass guitars at Hessy's so that he could join John's group. With Lennon, Sutcliffe also originated a more attention-grabbing name, 'The Silver Beatles' – with, added John, ' "Beatles" spelt like in "beat music".'

A more urgent need, of course, was a drummer, something that had been lacking since the dying days of the original Quarry Men. Early in 1960, they found one in Tommy Moore, though it was assumed that, with his heart in jazz, 26-year-old Tommy would suffice only until the arrival of someone more suitable. Drummer or not, at this stage The Silver Beatles were derided as 'posers' by certain members of Cass & The Cassanovas, Rory Storm & The Hurricanes, Derry & The Seniors and other more workmanlike outfits, not least because John and Paul had pretensions to become composers. Surely anyone with any sense realised that neither a teenager in a dance hall nor the director of the BBC Light Programme would be interested in home-made songs.

Nevertheless, The Silver Beatles were developing into a credible attraction in welfare institutes, far-flung suburban dancehalls, and, indeed, any venue that had embraced regular 'beat' sessions. Moreover, Lennon had spat out what remained of his well-spoken Lancashire plum in his singing as well as his speaking, and now had a baritone that was bashed about and lived in – in other words, the voice of a great rock'n'roll vocalist. By European bel canto standards, John Lennon as a young adult 'couldn't sing' – not 'real singing', as sonorous as Elvis when he tried hymns. Unlike Presley, Lennon had lost all vowel purity and nicety of intonation, probably because he had been endeavouring conscientiously to sound like the classic rockers while his voice was either still breaking or just freshly broken. An uncertain church choir soprano had been corrupted for all time by say, the hollered arrogance of Jerry Lee Lewis, neo-hysterical Little Richard, Gene Vincent – 'The Screaming End' – and, to a surprisingly lesser extent, hot-potato-in-the-mouth Presley.

John's singing grew more strangled as he broke sweat and his adolescent spots rose through the lacto-calomine lotion and turned red. He was probably nothing without the public-address system, but when he became intense, every sound he dredged up was like a brush stroke on a painting. Backing off until the microphone was at arm's length, just a sandpapery quaver during a dragged-out note could be as loaded as a roar with him almost swallowing it.

Yet The Silver Beatles were absent from the local fare advertised low on the bill when, on May 3, 1960, Gene Vincent headlined a three-hour extravaganza at Liverpool

Boxing Stadium, promoted by Allan Williams. The celebrated pop svengali Larry Parnes had ensured that Lance Fortune, Julian X and others among the less bright stars in his management stable were also included, though a last minute addition to the show, Gerry Marsden's ensemble, Gerry & The Pacemakers, represented the first division of regional popularity.

In the Jacaranda after the show, Parnes thought aloud about a further, albeit not so ambitious, joint venture with Allan Williams. He wanted, so he explained, an all-purpose backing outfit for use by one of his singers for a string of one-nighters in Scotland. A name he kept mentioning was Billy Fury, a Liverpudlian then on the crest of his first Top 10 breakthrough. Larry would bring Billy along if Allan could hastily assemble some groups for him to audition.

Though John Lennon was present in the Jacaranda too that night, he was unable to summon the courage to approach the Great Man, but two nights later, he asked Williams if The Silver Beatles could audition for the job. Allan assented, but pointed out that they'd be up against Derry & The Seniors, Cass & The Cassanovas, Gerry & The Pacemakers, you name 'em – the very upper crust of Liverpool pop. Yet The Silver Beatles won on the day, insofar as Parnes scribbled on his note-pad, "Silver Beetles [sic] – very good. Keep for future work."

Future work came sooner than expected. Not quite a fortnight after Parnes heard them, John, Paul, George, Stuart and Tommy were off on eight dates in Scotland, backing not Billy Fury, but a lesser Parnes luminary, Johnny Gentle. As each man's small wage dwindled, the spurious thrill of 'going professional' gave way more and more to stoic cynicism, particularly following an engagement notable for Tommy Moore drumming with his head in bandages. He'd been the sole casualty when the van had crumped into a stationary car that afternoon. He had also become a prime target of Lennon's ruthless derision, especially now that young George had started to stick up for himself. Moreover, via shameless manoeuvring, John eased himself between the sheets of the only single bed available in one bed-and-breakfast stop-over, while Tommy and everyone else out of favour spent as comfortable a night as was feasible in sleeping bags on the floor.

Well before they steamed back to Liverpool, a disgruntled Moore – with only two pounds left to show for his pains – had had enough of washing in streams, shaving in public-convenience hand-basins, staring across a wayside cafe's formica table as that loathsome Lennon tunnelled into a greasy but obviously satisfying chips-with-everything fry-up, not to mention the van, that mobile fusion of lunatic asylum and death trap.

A group without a drummer was no use to anyone. Into the bargain, British trad jazz was now midway through a brief golden age. Its bands were more numerous than ever, as were places they could play. In the Cavern, Liverpool's main jazz stronghold, manager Ray Mc Fall would dock the fee of any group that dared to launch into a rock'n'roll number within its hallowed and clammy walls. The Cavern had put up with skiffle in the past, but what it couldn't tolerate was lowbrow rock'n'roll. It was, scowled McFall, detrimental to the club's reputation.

In summer 1960, therefore, all the future seemed to hold for John, Paul, George and Stuart – now trading as just plain 'Beatles' – was the trivial round of recurring local bookings. These included a mercifully brief weekly residency at the Grosvenor Ballroom in a suburb of Wallasey on the opposite bank of the Mersey to Liverpool. Though these were profitable – to promoter Les Dodd anyway – they were a magnet for adolescent disorder and hooliganism. Fists often swung harder than The Beatles, who felt compelled to maintain ghastly grins as their music soundtracked someone getting half-killed in the gloom beyond the footlights. Dodd soon reverted to his old policy of admitting only the over-twenties, and keeping the music to a strict tempo: no jiving, no rock'n'roll and, definitely, no teenagers.

On being told of the loss of the Grosvenor one afternoon in the Jacaranda, Lennon shook a frustrated fist in the direction of London, which was perhaps four hours away on the train, but might as well have been on Alpha Centauri. So The Beatles loitered in central Liverpool's pubs and cafes with other rock'n'rollers in the same boat, small-talking, borrowing equipment, comparing notes, gossiping, betraying secrets. Out would pour lies about how close they were to their first single coming out and how they were a sure-fire certainty to open for Screaming Lord Sutch when his never-ending itinerary next reached the north, carrying on as if these were possibilities long after the trail went cold – if the trail had ever existed in the first place.

It was small wonder that The Beatles were open to an offer of work in Germany. This came about via Bruno Koschmider, owner of the Kaiserkeller, a club in the Hamburg's Grosse Freiheit, one of the most notorious red-light districts in Europe. He needed a comparable draw to Tony Sheridan, a British singing guitarist of unusual flair, who was administering a powerful rock'n'roll elixir at a rival establishment, The Top 10. Bruno's first contact was Allan Williams who sent Derry & The Seniors. Within days, the Kaiserkeller was thriving, and Koschmider's thoughts turned to the Indra, his strip club. With few customers most evenings, it could only be more profitable to put on pop there too.

When another group was requested, Bruno's Man in

Liverpool did not dismiss the idea of sending The Beatles – with the proviso that they enlist a drummer. At the Casbah, a teenage haunt where they'd played as The Quarry Men, they discovered that proprietor Mona Best's handsomely saturnine son Pete was beating the skins with the club's resident quartet, The Blackjacks. With the information that The Blackjacks were about to disband, there was no harm, The Beatles supposed, in asking the fellow if he fancied a trip to Hamburg.

Pete Best would pack his case with his mother's full approval, but 19-year-old Lennon – whose life, incidentally, was nearly half over – had to jump the highest hurdle of parental opposition. Nevertheless, the disapproving Mimi washed her hands of the whole business, although she would not acknowledge – as John did – that his ignominious art college career was over.

On August 17, 1960, John breathed foreign air for the first time when the night ferry docked at the Hook of Holland. Many hours later, he and the others climbed down from Allan Williams' overloaded mini-bus outside the Kaiserkeller, plusher than any palais they'd seen on Merseyside. It was, therefore, a disappointment when Herr Koschmider, taking charge of his human freight, conducted them round the dingy Indra and then to three small and windowless rooms adjoining a toilet in a cinema over the road. This was where The Beatles would sleep. It would have sickened pigs but after a couple of hours convalescent sloth Lennon had recovered enough of his ebullience to joke about Stalag 13, Red Cross parcels and forming an escape committee.

"Raus! Raus! Schnell! Schnell!" he barked when The Beatles rose to give their first ever performance outside the United Kingdom. How could he have imagined that, six years later, they'd be giving a scream-rent concert at the city's Ernst-Merck-Halle – a German equivalent of the London Palladium – to which they'd be driven in state in a fleet of Mercedes with Polizei outriders.

Back in 1960, nearly all newcomers from Britain wished that they were in hell rather than Hamburg at first, but they couldn't wait to get back there when their sojourn was over. There may have been better ways of breaking a group in, but The Beatles weren't to know of any. Being on the road together in Scotland was one thing, but being up each other's armpits in the holes-in-the-wall in which they lived when working for Koschmider was another. All of them – including middle-class Best, Lennon and Sutcliffe – discovered within themselves instincts that they hadn't known existed for dwelling together in their foul quarters, which soon became fouler with the remains of junk food, a perpetual rind of nicotine cloud, empty beer bottles and general sock-smelling malodour.

Musically too, The Beatles came to know each other and a growing following in an almost extra-sensory way. At the Indra, John's runaway tongue unfurled, and the sailors, gangsters, prostitutes, tourists on a night out and teenagers who'd stumbled in from the street laughed with him and even took a chance on the dance floor as they came to recognise the appeal of the newcomers' ragged dissimilarity to the contrived splendour of television pop stars.

A few weeks later, The Beatles were moved uptown to the grander Kaiserkeller where, over six onstage hours a night, six days a week, they were a howling success to a clientele for whom, previously, the personality of the house band had been secondary to boozing, brawling and the pursuit of romance. With John behaving like a composite of every rock'n'roller he'd ever admired, they seized songs by the scruff of the neck and wrung the life out them. The five unkempt Merseysiders had good and bad nights but there were moments when they were truly tearing it up, the most wailing combo on the planet.

As the season progressed, the lads stretched out the 15 or so numbers they'd cobbled together with the newly enlisted Pete until the monotony of duplicating them over and over again caused them to insert even the most obscure material that could be mined from their common unconscious. Few Lennon-McCartney items were unveiled then, but a typical bouncer's memory was of the two composing in the band-room during intervals between sets rather than joining the others at the bar.

That all five Beatles were ex-grammar school, technically of Britain's academic elite, may have been a subliminal lure for Hamburg's 'existentialist' crowd – the 'Exis' – of which Astrid Kirchherr, Jurgen Vollmer and Klaus Voorman were leading lights. In John, they detected a strength of personality lacking in the rest. "Lennon, the obvious leader, was like a typical rocker," estimated Vollmer. "Cool, no gestures except for pushing his body slightly in rhythm to the music: aggressive restraint, a Brando type."

Yet Lennon wasn't all sullen magnetism. He had no qualms about using coarse language in heated moments on the boards, and would attack, say, Presley's 'Hound Dog' with the blood-curdling dementia of one in the throes of a fit. He was also full of 'sieg heils' and 'You zink you play games mit der master race!' and so forth, goosestepping with a Hitler salute and a finger across his upper lip in front of a mob uncomprehending, disbelieving or scandalised into laughter.

An apocryphal fable that did the rounds in Hamburg was that, one evening at the Kaiserkeller, some parochial Al Capone tugged at Lennon's trousers while he was on the boards, and requested Johnny Kidd's 'Shakin' All Over'. John cracked back, "Donner und blitzen! You're the schweinhund that bayoneted my uncle!" There was no answer to that, not in words, and Bruno Koschmider was suddenly an abject, frightened little man, wringing his hands about "all a terrible misunderstanding, Herr Albrecht . . . never forgive myself". In a way, Lennon was in more danger then than he'd be during the "more popular than Jesus" episode in 1966.

His off-duty rampaging gave foundation to further embellished stories that would unfold later too – such as that of the golden rain that squirted from his bladder onto the wimples of three promenading nuns, and the foul-mouthed 'sermons' from the same balcony. Yet, while he was a leader rather than a follower, even his customary Rosencrantz and Guildenstern, George and Paul, cried off at the last fence during an attempt to mug a pie-eyed sailor, who'd just stood them a meal.

The source of many such escapades lay in the gargantuan quantity of amphetamines – 'speed' – as well as alcohol that he poured into himself. It hadn't been immediate, but it was through Preludin and Captigun – brands of appetite suppressants containing speed – that Lennon became more a life-and-soul of the party than he'd ever been as whatever little was left of his Woolton gentility disappeared without trace. He was determined that nothing was going to show him up for the nicely brought-up Mittelstand youth he was. His voice got louder, his witticisms got cruder and his face got redder before he staggered off to puke.

Like many so-called extroverts, John camouflaged an inborn sensitivity by adopting the metaphorical armour of the rough, untamed Scouser. Yet his barbed invective was often laced with brusque affection – as epitomised by a memorable first encounter in Hamburg with Frank Allen, then one of Middlesex's Cliff Bennett & The Rebel Rousers. "Ah yes. It's Frank, isn't it?" acknowledged John after being introduced. "I hear that, next to Cliff, you're the most popular member in the band. I don't know why. Your harmonies are fucking ridiculous."

However, as 1960 drew to a close, it wasn't all smiles with Bruno Koschmider who had grown rather leery of The Beatles. "Ist gut," he'd mutter with a scowl that indicated it was far from 'gut' when one of his finks told him that the group was planning to defect to the Top 10.

Acting swiftly, he gave them a month's notice while withdrawing whatever immunity he'd sorted out with the police concerning the youngest Beatle's nightly violation of a curfew forbidding those under 18 from frequenting night clubs after midnight. Thus George Harrison's deportation was arranged by late November. The others decided to muddle on without him but, within a fortnight, The Beatles were even less of a group after Best and McCartney were ordered out of the Fatherland on a trumped-up charge of arson.

So then there were two, and both were forbidden to seek employment as freshly unearthed paperwork revealed that The Beatles had had no work permits for their three months at the Indra and Kaiserkeller. While Stuart remained in the house of Astrid Kirchherr – now his fiancee – John had little choice but to go home.

On reuniting for the first post-Hamburg date – back at Liverpool's Casbah – a full house remained spellbound until the final chord, and a moment of shell-shocked hush before the clapping reached a bombardment of whistling, cheering, stamping pandemonium. Thereafter The Beatles continued to deliver casually cataclysmic performances that their lengthy stay in Hamburg had wrought. Half the time, you couldn't hear much more than thump-thump-thump because the Germans couldn't have cared less what else the group were doing as long as they kept the noise and the beat going. Yet, in days before onstage monitors and graphic equalisers – when vocal balance was achieved by simply moving back and forth on the microphone – the three-part harmonies of John, Paul and George were hard-won but perfected in readiness for what lay ahead for them, if not for Pete and Stuart. Soon to die, Stuart had, for all practical purposes, left the group by then anyway to resume his career as a painter.

When Paul transferred to bass, The Beatles came to epitomise the two guitars-bass-drums archetype of what would be remembered nationally as 1963's Merseybeat explosion. There'd been little indication of that two years earlier – though, as a testimony to the depth and cohesion of parochial pop, the first edition of *Mersey Beat*, Bill Harry's new fortnightly journal of local pop, had sold out within a day, such was the strength of demand for its venue information, news coverage and irregular features such as Lennon's 'Beatcomber' column, the first published examples of his prose.

Word-of-mouth got round too, and The Beatles' stock-in-trade became regular engagements within easy reach in the beat clubs of Liverpool and its suburbs. Though some found these guitar combos personally objectionable, middle-aged entrepreneurs smelt the money to be made from those foolish enough to pay to suffer this noise. Insides were ripped out of disused warehouses, cellars mucked out and licensed premises extended to make room for a stage and an invariably standing audience.

"I worked out that there were 300 groups in Liverpool of every variety," gasped Bill Harry. "Not just four-man guitars-bass-and-drums. Every youth club, town hall, even ice rinks and swimming pools, had rock'n'roll on. Some outfits were playing seven evenings a week, three or four gigs a night. Incredible!'

Thanks largely to Mrs Best's dogged efforts, a most conspicuous coup for The Beatles was their emergence as fixtures at the Cavern. The club had capitulated almost completely to mainstream pop while The Beatles were in Germany, to where they returned throughout much of 1961's unseasonably cold summer.

The second issue of *Mersey Beat* made much of a Beatles recording date that took place during this return visit. Among their duties on this visit was backing Tony Sheridan, now the city's undisputed rock'n'roll king, and in what was perhaps an ill-advised attempt to capture the *au naturel* power that they and Tony generated onstage, Bert Kaempfert, a freelance producer for Polydor Records, dragged them into a recording studio just hours after the last chord of the night at the Top 10 had faded away. Thus, so he reasoned, their adrenalin could be pumped more profitably onto a spool of tape. So it was that The Beatles accompanied Sheridan on half his debut album, *My Bonnie* – including the title song which, as a spin-off single, was to enter the German hit parade. After fate had taken The Beatles in hand, Kaempfert was to recall that, "It was obvious to me that they were enormously talented, but no one then, including the boys themselves, knew how to use that talent or where it would lead them."

Never mind, even being a backing group on a foreign disc was a yardstick of achievement for The Beatles back home, and in recognition of the fact Lennon would assume Sheridan's lead vocal when 'My Bonnie' was incorporated into the group's act as they resumed a booking schedule in and around Liverpool, describing themselves for a while as

"Polydor Recording Artists." The spectrum of work had broadened – and they'd always have Hamburg – but there was a creeping sense of marking time. They'd taken their impact in Hamburg and Merseyside to its limit, but no one knew how to advance to the step between consolidation of a provincial following and the threshold of the Big Time.

"Which way are we going, boys?" Lennon would chant when spirits were low.

"To the top, Johnny!" was the Pavlov's Dog response.

"What top?"

"To the toppermost of the poppermost!"

On aggregate, an individual Beatle's income was a fraction of that of a dustman, even when – having won the first readers' poll in *Mersey Beat* – they were heading the first division of Merseyside popularity. Unless a bigger stroke than this was pulled, they were in peril of being overtaken by newer acts like The Undertakers, The Merseybeats and Billy Kramer & The Coasters – and some not so new. The Big Three, for example, had risen like a phoenix from the ashes of Cass & The Cassanovas.

Mona Best didn't have the contacts to lift the group off the Liverpool-Hamburg treadmill, but everything changed in autumn 1961 when into their lives came a young man called Brian Epstein. He was the bored and vocationally frustrated sales manager at the city centre branch of NEMS – North End Music Stores – part of his family's chain of shops, specialising in furniture and electrical appliances. On becoming aware of The Beatles through the pages of *Mersey Beat*, Brian attended a Beatles lunch-time bash at the Cavern, and left with the determination to do whatever willingness and energy would do to push them further up the ladder of success, all the way up if the time came. Unlike others of his age – 27 – he didn't show off his ignorance or behave as if all he liked about pop was the money it could generate. Neither was he intending to sell The Beatles like tins of beans – with no money back if they tasted funny.

As Larry Parnes would have advised him, Mr Epstein's first task as manager was to transform the four leather-clad louts – three now sporting German Pilzenkopf 'mushroom head' haircuts – into what a respectable London agent or record mogul in those naive times expected a good pop group to look like. As he'd been a leading light in school plays and had once spent the best part of a year as a student at the Royal Academy of Dramatic Art, Brian was only too glad to impart a few pointers with regard to presentation and professional conduct. Scuttling about like a mother hen, he compelled his new clients to wear the stylish but not too way-out uniform suits plus all the accoutrements. He'd pay for them just as he'd pay off all outstanding hire-purchase debts on their equipment.

Punctuality and playing to a fixed programme were all-important. They weren't to smoke or eat onstage any-more. The Beatles also had to be taught to bow when they'd finished a number, and smile in a gentlemanly way. They had to rest that smile not only on front-row girls but to the general populace. Had they ever come across the term 'back projection'?

He insisted too on no patter that embraced swearing – meaning anything stronger than 'bloody' or 'crap'. John was instructed too not to sing, 'Tonight there'll be no mastur-bating' to rhyme with 'All my life I've been waiting' in Buddy Holly's 'Oh Boy!' Nevertheless, a Professor Higgins job on him proved too Herculean an effort. After he changed the subject when Epstein pondered fleetingly whether the group ought to dispense with stage dialogue altogether, bar 'Thank you very much' and 'Goodnight', there was no choice in the end but to let him cuss, tell off-colour jokes, spit out chewing-gum, give front-row scrubbers the eye and be generally just the kind of exhibitionist yob that Brian had been reared to despise.

Yet presenting his public with a fundamentally changed John Lennon would have been like feeding a pig strawberries. The most marginal of The Beatles' following couldn't have perceived any difference between the old monster and one who'd been painstakingly trained by Brian as they tuned into the epic vulgarity of it all. Nonetheless, some of what his learner-manager had endeavoured to do had rubbed off after a superficial fashion – or perhaps John had become so desperate to Make It that he was prepared to obey Brian to achieve the required result. Not that John ever became a showbiz treasure like Tommy Steele or Cliff Richard – successive English 'answers' to Elvis, who, like him, had now 'gone smooth' – as he could revert to type – or whatever that type had become – whenever he saw fit to.

Any tetchy shows of resistance to the transformation were moderated in any case after Mr Epstein then laid on with a trowel NEMS' position as a major retailer in the north-west in order to cajole Decca recording manager Dick Rowe to summon The Beatles over the edge of the world to London for a recording test on New Year's Day 1962.

They weren't at their best that day as they ran through numbers predetermined by Brian to demonstrate their prowess as 'all-round entertainers' like Steele and Richard. Of the two principal lead singers, McCartney seemed too eager to please while Lennon's attempts at 'I Got A Woman' and 'Money' had about them an unnatural politeness, Overall, Rowe and Mike Smith, his second-in-command, found The Beatles merely competent. Outfits like them could be found in virtually every town in the country.

Decca wasn't the only company to turn The Beatles down. EMI, Pye, Philips, even the lowly Ember also did so on receiving a second-generation copy of the Decca tape. It was all the group had to offer apart from the faded second-hand celebrity of 'My Bonnie' and their rising to the challenge of a ballroom circuit that extended as far as Wiltshire.

Now that the honeymoon was over, Brian was one scapegoat for The Beatles' marking time. Another was the Bests, whose house was, nonetheless, still used as an assembly point. That Mona could no longer regard herself as the patroness of the group was manifested in the way the others started treating Pete, a Tony Curtis among the Pilzenkopfs, whose isolation became more and more noticeable via a gradual exclusion from the group's restricted code and private folk lore. Now and then, he'd find himself straining his ears to catch murmured intrigue when, say, Harrison and McCartney, speaking in low voices, froze him with the malevolence of their glances, or when Lennon and McCartney tinkered secretively on their guitars in a backstage alcove.

While John possessed a picaresque charm, it was hardly Pete's fault that he was the darling of the ladies for his good looks whose unobtrusiveness posed no deliberate threat to the front line. Yet amicability was in short supply generally as the encircling professional and personal gloom worsened. As they hadn't become stars overnight, The Beatles were less a bunch of mates out on what amounted to a subsidised booze-up than one more deadbeat group, lurching from gig to gig.

No one was getting any younger; performing onstage was their only saleable trade, and they were travelling the same long-road-with-no-turning as olde tyme rock'n'rollers like Gene Vincent and Jerry Lee Lewis, with no choice but to go right on doing it, just to break even.

Yet, thanks to Brian dialling his finger to a stub, they were leading what the economist would call a 'full life' after a fashion, with up to three local bookings a day sometimes. A lunchtime session at the Cavern might be followed by an early evening session at the same venue where, before the next act took the stage, The Beatles' van would be halfway down the street on a dash to a technical college hall over the river in Birkenhead. As for Hamburg, they'd be there again from mid-April to late May 1962, wowing 'em at the new Star Club, supporting and proudly socialising with Gene Vincent, Little Richard and other visiting heroes of their schooldays that, unlike the Top 10, the Star Club could afford.

George Harrison hit it off straight away with Billy Preston, Little Richard's 15-year-old organist, but Lennon had made up his mind to exercise an observed disrespect towards Richard. Calling him 'Grandad' and telling him to shut up was the least of it, but John was as diligent as everybody else in making myriad private observations of all performances by the 'Georgia Peach' for incorporation into his own.

A month earlier, as well as the expected Merseyside bookings, Brian Epstein had negotiated both an engagement in Stroud, a market town far to the south, and The Beatles' first BBC radio broadcast, specifically three numbers on *Teenagers' Turn* from Manchester's Playhouse. Even this was no sign that The Beatles were anything more than a classic local group, despite an enthusiastic response – including scattered screams – from the studio audience during the show.

During a stylised mobbing outside, Pete was the recipient of most of the fuss. However, he was to prove the least promising member of The Beatles when George Martin, recording chief of Parlophone, an EMI subsidiary, requested their presence in the company's Abbey Road complex on

Wednesday June 6, 1962. Accustomed to onstage inconsistencies of tempo caused by the mood of the hour, drummers were most prone to behind-the-scenes substitution in the studio. "The reasons were purely financial," elucidated sticksman Clem Cattini, a familiar figure on the capital's recording scene. "You were expected to finish four tracks in three hours. A group might take a week, not because they were inefficient, but because sessions are a different mode of thinking to being on the road. You can't get away with so much."

Having someone like Cattini ghost his drumming would, therefore, have been no slight on Pete Best, but the mere suggestion of it was sufficient to confound the doubts, justified or not, that the other Beatles had about him. It would precipitate his heartless sacking a few weeks after George Martin had decided to contract the group for an initial two singles with an option on further releases if these gave cause for hope. When they returned to tape the first of these in September, Pete had been replaced by Ringo Starr, once of Rory Storm's Hurricanes.

The new recruit wasn't the most versatile drummer in Liverpool, but he posed no limelight-grabbing challenge to John, Paul and George. Ringo was no heartthrob but he was bright enough not to ask too many questions and, despite a hangdog appearance, was blessed with a ready wit as guileless as Lennon's was cruel. "Ringo was a star in his own right in Liverpool," asserted John. "Whatever the spark is in Ringo, we all know it, but we can't put our finger on it. Whether it's acting, singing or drumming, I don't know. There's something in him that's projectable."

With a session hireling Andy White on stand-by, Ringo was the least significant participant when The Beatles recorded 'Love Me Do', the maiden A-side. EMI's executive body

were to be in two minds about it during their weekly conference where, before committing themselves, the more obse-
quious underlings tried to gauge the opinion of each label's
artists-and-repertoire head. Therefore, after the usual 'I don't
know. What do you think?' discussion, it was decided that
'Love Me Do', the merest tip of what would prove to be a
gigantic commercial iceberg for the company, would be
released in the first week of October.

John's euphoria at this latest development was undercut by
a grave personal complication. Pregnancy wasn't what happened to nice girls like Cynthia, but one afternoon in the
summer she'd announced that her period was a week
overdue and she'd been sick in the morning, though that
might have been the result of stomach-knotting worry. That
her waist measured one inch bigger may have been nothing
either, but her wrists, armpits and ankles felt funny.

She was seeing prams and pregnant women everywhere,
in the streets, in public parks and on television. In an episode
of *Dr Kildare* on ITV, there'd been an unmarried mother.
Her boyfriend smiled like John. The screen couple had
separated and the baby was adopted – but perhaps there'd be
a delightful romantic scene with John proposing on one
knee, and promising to love Cynthia forever. Gruff pragmatism ruled, however, and she may have been left with the
impression that, if the words to some of The Beatles'
numbers – about dream lovers and mister moonlight – were
anything to go by, she and John were being conned out of
something.

John's wooing of Cynthia had been fraught much of the
time, but that was when they'd been closest because, as far as
John – torn between resentment and panic – was concerned,
the minute they left the registry office on August 23, 1962,
they were already over somehow. The heart, the core of

what they had been, was wrapped up by the time they arrived at the reception – at which Aunt Mimi was pointedly absent – in an unlicensed restaurant, where the toast was drunk with tumblers of water. That was with the benefit of hindsight but, while marriage wouldn't blinker his roving eye, Cynthia at least felt hopeful during that hiatus between the wedding celebrations – interrupted by a Beatles' engagement in Chester – and the issue of 'Love Me Do'.

Airplay for the single began humbly with a solitary spin crackling from Radio Luxembourg between the epilogue that concluded the evening's viewing on BBC television and the pre-dawn shipping forecast that was underway on the Home Service. The Light Programme picked up on 'Love Me Do' too, and it slipped into the *New Musical Express* list at 21 on December 8, hovering on the edge of the Top 20 until just after Christmas. At number one was Frank Ifield, the latest pretender to Cliff Richard's crown, with a revival of a 1949 country & western million-seller, 'Lovesick Blues'. He'd headlined over The Beatles earlier that month on a mismatched bill at Peterborough's Embassy Cinema.

The local paper reported that they'd 'made far too much noise', adding insult to injury as 'Love Me Do' continued to lose its tenuous grasp on the British charts. If The Beatles had any of the prima donna attitudes that often came with even qualified fame, a couple of weeks back at the Star Club took them down a peg or two. There, they were considered to be no more deserving of red carpet treatment than Cliff Bennett & The Rebel Rousers, Kingsize Taylor & The Dominoes and The Carl Fenn Trio, likewise supporting Johnny & The Hurricanes, a saxophone-dominated combo from Ohio, nearly all of whose hits – and there hadn't been any recently – were rocked-up treatments of old chestnuts.

The Beatles might have been on the verge of becoming

bigger than Hitler, but it was the here-and-now that mattered. The customers were getting restless. The Nightsounds had just started their set at the Top 10, and the outer fringes of the Star Club audience were beginning to drift away because The Beatles weren't under the spotlight yet. Their new drummer had gone missing, but he excused himself with a joke when fearsome Horst Fascher, the club's chief bouncer, came upon him back at the group's lodgings: "So I told him that if he wasn't onstage on time, I would kick him up the arse."

Horst agreed that The Beatles had done well for first timers in the British charts, but who would assume that they were anything other than a classic local group who'd caught the lightning once and would probably be back on the trivial round of Hamburg and Merseyside bookings by this time next year, even as Brian Epstein negotiated their maiden national tour? They would be low on the bill to Helen Shapiro, the kingdom's most popular female singer, according to the most recent *NME* popularity poll.

However, the distant rip-tide of Merseybeat that was to overwhelm Helen, Johnny & The Hurricanes and Frank Ifield crept closer as the New Year got underway. Ifield would be performing in venues where current chart standing had no meaning within 18 months of *Mersey Beat*'s announcement in January 1963 of the impending release of a second Beatles single, 'Please Please Me'. Hinged loosely on a Bing Crosby ballad from the Thirties – which Frank Ifield had sung at Peterborough – it was written mostly by John, and conceived initially in the style of Roy Orbison, the US singer-songwriter still typecast as a merchant of melancholy.

Similarly, 'Love Me Do', had been as dirge-like in embryo, presented as, recalled Lennon, "a slower number like Billy Fury's 'Halfway To Paradise', but George Martin suggested we do it faster. I'm glad we did." He confessed later, "We all owe a great deal of our success to George, especially for his patient guidance of our enthusiasm in the right direction."

From the onset, Martin had involved the group in the technical side of studio methodology. He'd also been pre-pared to accommodate the most radical suggestions; initially, The Beatles' preference for another Lennon-McCartney original 'Please Please Me' as a follow-up to 'Love Me Do, instead of the perky and 'professional' 'How Do You Do It' that Martin considered ideal for them.

At this early stage Martin discovered that John Lennon, immodest in other matters, was genuinely unconceited about his singing to the point of insisting, "I can't say I ever liked hearing myself." It made him wary of compliments about such dissimilar items on The Beatles' first LP as the downbeat and carefully handled 'Anna' to 'Twist and Shout' on which he almost ruptured his throat with a surfeit of passion.

"I could never understand his attitude," sighed Martin, "as it was one of the best voices I've heard. He was a great admirer of Elvis Presley's early records, particularly the 'Heartbreak Hotel' kind of sound, and he was always saying to me, 'Do something with my voice. Put something on it. Smother it with tomato ketchup. Make it different.' He was obsessed with tape delay – a sort of very near-echo. I used to do other things to him, and as long as it wasn't his natural voice coming through, he was reasonably happy – but he'd always want his vocals to get special treatment. However, I wanted to hear it in its own natural quality."

The timid songbird and his new bride were living briefly with Aunt Mimi in Woolton when 'Please Please Me' was released. Children would swoop from nowhere to see John Lennon, Woolton pop star, answer the door or be collected in the van for transportation to a dancehall maybe two counties away. Wherever "the newest British group to challenge The Shadows" – as they were described in *NME* – went nowadays, it always seemed to be one week after Cliff Bennett & The Rebel Rousers and one week ahead of Johnny Kidd & The Pirates in Chatham's Invicta, Manchester's Three Coins, the El Rio in Macclesfield and like venues played by every group that had broken free of its local orbit and who expected its run of luck to peter out at any minute.

Back on Merseyside, heads turned when Ringo's old Ford Zodiac stopped at a zebra crossing, but no Beatle yet attracted the beginnings of a crowd. Moreover, after 'Please Please Me' almost-but-not-quite topped the charts, Decca and other EMI rivals liked to fool themselves that they smelt a perishable commodity. The north-west was hardly the epicentre of pop, was it?

Nevertheless, "Who's this Liverpool combo everyone's talking about?" was a question asked with increasing frequency by elderly executives in London's music industry while office juniors discussed whether The Beatles had got into a rut, what with their next A-side, 'From Me To You', having the same overall sound as 'Love Me Do'. Next, talent scouts from the capital came sniffing round the north-west just in case all this talk about a 'Liverpool Sound' or 'Mersey Beat' carried any weight, especially as other Epstein clients – Billy J. Kramer, The Fourmost and Cilla Black – had been tossed spare Lennon-McCartney songs almost as a licence to print money. John and Paul's respective bank balances had been swelled further by the first shoal of unsolicited cover versions. Their music was also to be used for a West End 'beat-ballet' entitled *Mods and Rockers*.

Having let The Beatles escape from their then unconcerned

clutches in 1962, Decca adopted a scattershot approach by flinging numerous discs by beat groups from Liverpool and beyond at the public, albeit by being, let's say, 'excessively thrifty' over the publicity needs of all but the most consistent best-sellers – as The Rolling Stones would prove to be. These were not, however, to include Pete Best, who was now in Lee Curtis & The All-Stars, a dependable draw both in Liverpool and Hamburg.

By autumn 1963, Pete's former bandmates had been superimposed upon the grid of a Fleet Street that had been relentlessly overrun with 'heavy' news of the Profumo Scandal, the nuclear test ban treaty, the Great Train Robbery, racial unrest in Alabama and, to cap it all, the West Indies beating England at cricket. Between radio reports of England's shame and east-west-black-white tension came the sinless strains of 'She Loves You', the Beatles fourth single and a bone-fide smash. While they gestured with cigarettes during TV interviews and let loose the odd mild expletive, "They were regarded as clean-living lads during the time they were getting established," confirmed Harold Wilson, then leader of Her Majesty's Opposition, "whatever may have gone on later" – or before.

Innocent scamps, The Beatles' much-copied mid-air leap on their *Twist And Shout* EP sleeve was the epitome of anti-dotal Merseybeat that shook theatres with healthy, good-humoured screams. There were also the asinine poems written and sent by subscribers to glossy monthly magazines dedicated solely to both The Beatles and, for four editions, Gerry & The Pacemakers – then tussling with each other for chart supremacy. A Pacemakers show in Bristol was halted by the authorities after repeated warnings about rushing the stage, and queues formed outside a Lincoln box-office a week before Beatles tickets went on sale.

Scouse was now the most romantic dialect in the country, and the bigger chain stores were stocking Beatle wallpaper, 'Fab Four' powder compacts and 22-carat 'Beetle' [sic] bracelets. Woolworth's had Moptop wigs as another department store had guitar-shaped cakes – "The cake for SWINGING parties". The jacket of The Beatles' collarless Cardin stage suits was "the Liverpool Look for you to knit for the man in your life" as a cardigan, its pattern obtainable via an order form in *Fabulous* magazine. Learning that the manufacturers of NEMS-sanctioned Beatle boots could barely cope with demand, an enterprising Sussex company marketed "Ringo the new Beat Boot" which also boasted elastic gusset sides and rounded toes.

By the time The Beatles appeared on the Royal Variety Show on November 4 – where Lennon's larger-than-life bluntness raised a laugh with his 'rattle yer jewellery' announcement – they were a phenomenon, far and away the biggest thing ever to hit British pop. Soon the first biography of The Beatles was in preparation, and the year ended with seven Beatles discs in the singles chart – including three EPs – extended play – and the top two positions on the album list.

The following year, the Olympic torch of UK pop was being carried to nooks and crannies across the Channel too. All over western Europe, North America's domination of post-war pop was over for the time being now that the British beat boom, spearheaded by John, Paul, George and Ringo, had set new commercial and artistic goals for teenage groups engaged in garage rehearsals, all of them daring to dream of Beatle-sized renown.

"Kids everywhere go for the same stuff," was John's forthright explanation why, in 1964, they subjugated the rest of the world in a large scale re-run of the hysteria they'd long known at home. Now they faced even more presentations to civic heads, louder screams every stop of the way and longer queues of handicapped unfortunates wheeled down back-stage corridors for the group's curative blessing.

Beatles singles – even a reissue of the one with Tony Sheridan – were swamping foreign Top 10s five or six at a time. The Indonesian Minister of Culture outlawed Beatle hairdos, and *A Hard Day's Night*, the group's first movie, came to Warsaw. Back home, Ringo Starr had been pro-posed as president of several higher education establishments, and a *Daily Express* cartoon had Harold Wilson and Prime Minister Sir Alec Douglas-Home soliciting The Beatles for their votes in the post-Profumo general election, thus lend-ing credence to the homily, "I care not who makes a nation's laws as long as I can write its songs." The quartet had also been earmarked for a cameo appearance in the ITV soap-opera, *Coronation Street*, though they declared themselves too busy for this. More than just another pop group as transient and gimmicky as any other, they were now part of the national furniture.

"Our appeal," declared Ringo, "is that we're ordinary lads" – which, as it had in Britain, won over a United States depressed with its own traumas: the Kennedy assassination, vehement opposition to the Civil Rights Amendment, and the first boy-soldiers blown to bits in Indochina. Into the bargain, its Top 20 was sodden with unmemorable instru-mentals, drivelling ballads and wholesome anthems like The Beach Boys' 'Be True To Your School'. To the chagrin of The Beach Boys, The Four Seasons, The Lettermen and others on Capitol, The Beatles US label, the Fab Four – already at number one with 'I Want To Hold Your Hand' – were launched with one of the most far-reaching publicity blitzes hitherto known in the record industry. North America was, therefore, theirs for the taking when they arrived in

February 1964 for appearances on *The Ed Sullivan Show* – America's *Sunday Night At The London Palladium*.

Even after The Beatles flew back to London, 'I Want To Hold Your Hand' remained at the top – while hurtling upwards in its wake were all their singles that, the previous year, had been aired to negligible listener reaction in America. As is their wont, the North Americans exhibited an enthusiasm for the group that left reserved British Beatlemaniacs swallowing dust. Our colonial cousins were devouring the grass on which the group had trodden and retrieved jelly-beans that had rained onto stages where the quartet had played. Girls would faint on fingering the fully autographed Rickenbacker guitar, owned by some pensioner in a moptop wig, the self-styled 'Oldest Beatles Fan'. The whingeing of their children would cause well-off parents to interrupt European holidays with a trip to Liverpool where back-copies of *Mersey Beat* would fetch hugely inflated prices, and the chair on which John was said to have sat in the Cavern kissed like the Blarney Stone.

During what has passed into legend as 'the British Invasion', most other major UK outfits – and some minor ones – made headway in the US too. Even poor old Pete Best milked his affinity via a six-month run of sell-out dates with his Pete Best Combo. Fascination with all things British peaked most conspicuously one week in 1964 when two-thirds of the US Hot 100 singles chart was British in origin, and The Beatles occupied nine positions in the Canadian Top 10.

The only direction should have been down, but Beatles discs continued to sell by the mega-tonne, and their second film, *Help!*, broke box-office records, even in the teeth of vitriolic reviews stating that they'd been overshadowed by a distinguished supporting cast that included Eleanor Bron, Roy Kinnear, Leo McKern and Victor Spinetti. The group were determined that the next film, if there was one, wouldn't portray them as happy-go-lucky funsters.

They were not, however, in complete agreement about their investiture by the Queen – on Prime Minister Wilson's vote-catching advice – as Members of the British Empire. Paul cut short his holiday to attend the associated press conference, while John sauntered in 20 minutes late after Brian Epstein had had to send a car to fetch him. To Lennon, the acceptance of it was as absurd as a demand in one of Screaming Lord Sutch's political manifestos that they should be knighted. Meanwhile, McCartney was delighted with his MBE. Not knowing what to think, George and Ringo smiled and waved as The Beatles were driven through cheering crowds to Buckingham Palace on October 16, 1965.

Overseas, The Beatles continued to flourish too. Yet there was a perceptible falling-off of attendances, sometimes as low as half capacity, by 1966. Though they'd pruned down their concert schedule to avoid over-exposure, they were becoming as common a forthcoming attraction in the USA as they'd been in Liverpool, circa 1962. Like London buses, if you missed a Beatles show, there'd be another one coming along soon if you waited. In Germany, another important sales territory, Dave Dee, Dozy, Beaky, Mick & Tich were about to beat The Beatles by over three thousand votes to win pop periodical *Bravo*'s Golden Otto award – the equivalent of being Top Vocal Group in *NME*'s annual poll.

The momentum had slackened, but the screams hadn't, and any subtleties crammed into The Beatles' 30 minutes of stale, unheard music, night after artless night, were lost on audiences that had bought tickets for not so much a musical recital as a tribal gathering. Besides, tracks from the latest album, *Rubber Soul*, couldn't be reproduced with the conventional beat group line-up – as instanced by 'Norwegian

Wood', John's smokescreening of an extra-marital affair, which featured an Indian sitar.

No home venues could yet compare with foreign sports stadia and exposition centres that could rake in the most loot with the least effort by accommodating thousands in one go. Brian Epstein had cut down on press conferences too, not least because the group – and Lennon in particular – were fed up with the shallowness of the questions. "Epstein always tried to waffle on at us about saying nothing about Vietnam," John would confide later to a journalist's cassette recorder, "so there came a time when George and I said, 'Listen, when they ask us next time, we're going to say we don't like the war, and we think they should get out.'"

Brian cringed as zany merriment about mini-skirts swung in seconds to two-line debates about inflammable issues. Recently, he'd had to quiet friction over the front cover of a US album *Yesterday... And Today* that – with Lennon as chief advocate – had depicted The Beatles as white-smocked butchers gleefully going about their grisly business. It hadn't mattered that the heads and limbs of dolls were among the bloody wares when this picture appeared in Britain to advertise their new single 'Paperback Writer'. Such a scene was comic opera in a realm that housed Madame Tussaud's Chamber Of Horrors and Screaming Lord Sutch. Nevertheless, with boy soldiers being blown to bits in Indochina, the 'butcher sleeve' was hastily withdrawn from circulation in sensitive North America.

"All this means," beamed diplomatic Paul, "is that we're being a bit more careful about the sort of picture we do." John, the instant pundit, however, had no time for tact. "Anyway, it's as valid as Vietnam," he quipped unfunnily.

John had also taken to bawling purgative obscenities in the teeth of the screams. He had become, to Dezo Hoffman, one of the group's principal photographers, "like a dog with rabies. You never knew when he would jump and bite." You could understand his attitude. What had been the point of travelling so far and seeing only glimpses of a world beyond a sea of faces and camera lenses?

The Beatles' cocooned travelling life was becoming increasingly dangerous as well as uncomfortable. Matters came to a head during an exceptionally stressful world tour in 1966. One of its rare oases of calm had been the Hamburg stop on June 26 where they had doled out bite-sized chunks of unspoilt-by-fame attention to each of the old pals allowed backstage after the show at the capacious Ernst-Merke-Halle, an area as protected as Fort Knox.

Yet for all The Beatles' affability, there was a lull when Lee Curtis, Bert Kaempfert and the rest fell silent and stared for a long moment, wondering if they were real. After that, the atmosphere loosened up between them before Paul and John risked a wander round some of the old haunts still standing down the Reeperbahn. Then it was back to the party.

In the final weeks of their most public journey, The Beatles made the best of the pleasanter lulls in the itinerary. There was little else to enjoy. The four performed for three evenings in the Nippon Budokan Hall in Tokyo with the disquieting knowledge that, outside, there were frenzied demonstrations of protest about pop singing ketos polluting this temple of martial arts.

This was nothing to the naked malevolence at Manila International Airport where, in official retaliation for unwittingly snubbing the Phillipine president's wife, Imelda Marcos, The Beatles entourage underwent an ordeal of red-tape in the customs area after "the roughest reception we've ever had," recalled Ringo Starr, "They really had it in for us." John was bemused that the airport officials insisted on treating them like "ordinary passengers". "Do you kick ordinary passengers?" he asked. Never had arguments – particularly from John and George – about the discontinuation of touring made sounder sense.

Another battering, this time psychological rather than physical, awaited them in North America where sections of the media had sensationalised a London *Evening Standard* interview, in which John, if anything, appeared to bemoan the increasing godlessness of the times. He was trotted out to make a statement that most took as an apology for his 'blasphemy' hours before opening night in Chicago. The previous week, in the Deep South – the heart of the Bible Belt – thousands of Beatle discs were ceremonially pulverised in a tree-grinding machine to the running commentary of a local disc-jockey. "They have to buy them first," noted George. Other mass protests were just as demonstrative. The group's new long-player, *Revolver*, was removed from 22 southern radio playlists; box-offices were picketed by Ku Klux Klansmen, and hellfire sermons preached of the damnation that would befall any communicants who attended any forthcoming Beatles spectaculars.

Radio blacklisting and hostile audiences were trifling compared to the possible in-concert slaughter of Lennon by divine wrath – or someone acting on the Almighty's behalf – even if hard-nosed US promoters considered this insufficient reason for cancellations, despite Brian Epstein proffering millions if only they'd call off the entire tour. Yet, engagements in the north passed without incident, and below the Mason-Dixon line, the anti-Beatles ferment was counterbalanced by 'I Love John' lapel badges outselling all associated merchandise. A promise was made to Epstein from a pay phone, nonetheless, that one or more of The Beatles would die before the footlights at the Mid-South Coliseum in

Memphis. Though a firework that exploded onstage gave all four a horrified start, the show was delivered, as was the final show of their collective career at San Francisco's Candlestick Park on August 29, 1966 in front of a crowd of 25,000.

The professional bond between members of the group loosened after the abandonment of touring. George went off on a spiritual safari to India, Paul wrote the soundtrack to a film, and Ringo was the titular head of his own building firm. John had entered a separate orbit long before, and would be well into a career as a non-Beatle long before the quartet dissembled in 1970.

As token Beatle, it was he who'd been invited to take part in BBC television's *Juke Box Jury* months prior to when the whole quartet comprised the panel in a special edition at the Liverpool Empire. While mere sideshows to his pivotal role in The Beatles, among solo projects that followed were two slim but best-selling volumes of verse, stories and cartoons, and a bit-part in *How I Won The War*, a movie put on general release in 1967

More insidiously, on their records, even non-fans could differentiate between Lennon, McCartney and, nowadays, Harrison tracks. On tour around the world, Paul and John couldn't help but get together to compose, but now John, a family man on a stockbroker estate in Surrey, and Paul, a London-based bachelor, tended to present each other with songs in more advanced states of completion than before.

Yet, if not as inseparable as they once were, The Beatles still kept pace with each other's caprices. Following George, they were, for instance, all sporting moustaches as 1967 got underway. They were also inclined to be photographed at the same premieres, cover the same exhibitions and sample the same stimulants.

By now The Beatles were much changed from the beat

merchants of 1962, not least in their experiences with drugs. Whereas once this had simply been a bit of speed to wire them up for the show and a marijuana joint to unwind tense coils afterwards, all four, especially Lennon, were on nodding terms with lysergic acid diethylamide – LSD. It had been part of the 'anything goes' – some would say nihilistic – spirit of swinging London for many months before John and George were 'spiked' by their dentist. The 'psychedelic' mental distortions were to transport John to untold heights of creativity – and further from 'Twist And Shout' than any Cavern dweller could have imagined.

One result of their LSD intake was that The Beatles were more open to the music of other cultures – what would be termed 'world music' – particularly from India, in the watershed year of 1967 when pop, passing hastily through its 'classical' period, was elevated from ephemera to Holy Writ. Naturally, The Beatles were to the fore in this, notably when, after declaring his independence of EMI in 1965, George Martin reached his apotheosis as a console boffin during the making of The Beatles' eighth album, *Sgt. Pepper's Lonely Hearts Club Band*. Like Bill Haley's 'Rock Around The Clock', *Sgt. Pepper* was judged to be some sort of milestone of pop. "It was a milestone and a millstone in music history," demurred George Harrison. "There are some good songs on it but it's not our best album."

Nevertheless, many – especially in the States – listened to this, The Beatles' latest gramophone record, in the dark, at the wrong speeds, backwards and even normally. Every inch of the cover and label was scrutinised for concealed communiques. By 1969, for instance, clues traceable to *Sgt. Pepper* would support a widespread rumour that Paul McCartney had been killed in a road accident, and replaced by a doppelganger.

With McCartney and George Martin as prime movers, the album was conceived as a continuous work with no spaces between songs – but though it did contain various cross-fades and links, only at the start and towards the end were you reminded of what was supposed to be *Sgt. Pepper*'s show. "It was as if we did a few tracks," explained Ringo Starr, "and suddenly there was a fire and everyone ran out of the building but we carried on playing." Technically, it improved on 1966's *Revolver*, creating, averred Harrison, "new meanings on old equipment" as close-miked vocals floated over layers of treated sound.

Soon, every other group that carried any weight was demanding the same but not every other group had a multi-million selling LP that vied with its nearest 45 – 'All You Need Is Love' – in topping the Australian singles chart. Fittingly, *Sgt. Pepper*'s 'A Day In The Life' epilogue was also the valedictory spin on Britain's pirate Radio London when it went off the air in August 1967. This was but one incident that would tie the album forever to the past psychedelic times that it had unquestionably inspired. Listening to it decades later, a middle-aged hippy could almost smell the joss-sticks and see its fabled montage sleeve being used as a handy working surface for rolling a joint.

Yet, for the man-in-the-street, 1967's Summer of Love climaxed not with the release of *Sgt. Pepper* on the first of June, but on the 25th when The Beatles convened before the BBC's outside broadcast cameras in Abbey Road's cavernous Studio One to perform 'All You Need Is Love' as Britain's contribution to *Our World*, a satellite-linked transmission with a global viewing figure of 400 million. Cross-legged at the group's feet for the omnes fortissimo chorus of this flower-power anthem was a turn-out of selected relations, famous friends – among them Mick Jagger, Keith Moon and

Eric Clapton – and, of course, Brian Epstein.

Brian had been on stand-by for most of the period since Candlestick Park, but still he waited, poised to serve his boys whenever they wanted him again. Nonetheless, his stake in Beatles affairs was becoming more and more detached as the expiry date of his contract with them crept closer – as did his association with them in more absolute terms.

During the last month of Brian's life, another saviour had materialised as he himself had at the Cavern in what seemed like centuries ago. In robes, silvery beard and dark skin, his Divine Grace, the Maharishi Mahesh Yogi seemed at first glance as different from Mr Epstein as he could be. He was, he replied, a dealer "in wisdom, not money" when taxed about how his International Meditation Society was financed.

The Beatles were serious enough about meditation to undergo the Society's initiation course, conducted by his Divine Grace at a university faculty in Bangor, Wales, during the Bank Holiday weekend of August 1967. Brian had half-promised that he'd join the boys there. However, his lonely life ended abruptly on the Saturday night in London through what a coroner would conclude later as an "incautious self-overdoses" of prescription tablets.

As twilight thickened the next day, The Beatles brushed past a hovering media as they walked from the university building for the journey home. For all the dicta they'd just absorbed that trivialised death, they were visibly shaken. "I knew we were in trouble then," John was to state with retrospective honesty. "I didn't really have any misconceptions about our ability to do anything other than play music, and I was scared."

Could Brian manage The Beatles from the grave? Time after time he'd turn in it as they became like kites in a storm in an industry noted for its time-serving incompetence, its fake sincerity and its backstabbing. No more qualified to handle their own business affairs than Brian had been to play lead guitar, to John, George, Ringo and Paul, experience meant recognising mistakes before they occurred again.

Once, a heading emblem on a NEMS press release had been a caricatured Epstein in a mortar board in the midst of his clients with their impish schoolboy grins. Now that Sir had left the classroom, the children started doing whatever they liked. With adolescence extended by adulation, most of their ideas were more intriguing conceptually than in ill-conceived practice. In the end, their idyll was threatened not by any external danger, but by their own inner natures and desires, when it dawned on them that not everything they did was great. Long before their partnership was officially dissolved, each Beatle – however reluctantly or unknowingly – was well into his solo career.

Shortly after Brian's funeral, 1967's flowers wilted, and vehement critical reaction chased The Beatles' self-produced *Magical Mystery Tou*r, an interesting-but-boring television spectacular that was tempered by its music – which filled a double-EP that grappled for UK chart supremacy with a new single, 'Hello Goodbye'.

Next up was *Yellow Submarine*, a cartoon epic which, without making The Beatles too cuddly, portrayed them as Sergeant Pepper's bandsmen in surreal encounters during a 'Mod Odyssey' from Liverpool to Pepperland.

A real life journey from England to the forested foothills of the Himalayas took place in February 1968 when The Beatles joined other seekers of nirvana at the Maharishi's yoga-ashram – theological college. Ringo and Paul, however, went home early, and, when John chose to believe tittle-tattle about his Divine Grace's all-too-human attitude towards a female student, he announced his immediate departure, to the dismay of his wife, Cynthia, for whom the trip had seemed an opportunity to save their marriage.

When George returned to England too, a rock'n'roll revival was in the air, and The Beatles moved in on it with their next chart-topper, 'Lady Madonna', reminiscent of Fats Domino. For correlated interviews, Paul, George, Ringo and John were their usual plain-speaking selves cracking back at critics with faultless logic and calm sense laced with quirky wit.

The Beatles' next hit, 'Hey Jude', was to be released via EMI on the group's own record company Apple, a division of Apple Corps, launched in spring 1968. It was an enterprise intended to cater for maverick artistic and scientific ventures – what Lennon called 'controlled weirdness'. According to clever newspaper advertisements, a kindly welcome awaited not just those who'd nurtured a connection with the group's inner circle but any old riff-raff who wished to solicit Apple's finance for pet projects. Impetuous cash was flung at two unprofitable shops, and a troupe of grasping Dutch designers trading misleadingly as 'The Fool', film-makers who wouldn't make films and poets who didn't write poems.

By way of a more specific example, John put a certain Alexis Mardas in charge of Apple Electronics, a post that rapidly became a sinecure as, one after another, Alex's wondrous patents progressed no further than him talking about them. Another plan formulated by Lennon was for ex-Quarry Man Ivan Vaughan – now a Cambridge graduate – to set up a school for The Beatles' children and those of their friends. Various properties were inspected and the skeleton of a steering committee established before Apple's accounting division argued that it wasn't a viable proposition.

In his memoir, *As Time Goes By*, Derek Taylor, who organised Apple's press office, likened his two years there as being "in a bizarre royal court in a strange fairy tale". His urbane, sympathetic manner won many vital contacts for Apple, but John Lennon's was, ostensibly, the loudest voice of reason amid the madness. The music papers had been full of how 'mellow' he was in his late twenties too. "It's a groove growing older," he'd told them in December 1967, giving the outward impression of someone completely in command of his faculties, an affluent and happily married family man in perfect health, smiling and laughing, with no worries.

Within months, however, all that had changed forever. By the end of 1968, Lennon was regarded by Average Joe as being as mad as a hatter. In restaurants that fame hadn't prevented him from frequenting, strangers on other tables would speak in low voices and glance towards him. Some insisted they could sense an aura of insanity effusing from him as others might the 'evil' from child murderer Myra Hindley's eyes. Was he really off his head? Had he – like Friedrich Nietzche, philosopher of irrationalism – lost his mind during the interminable contemplation of his own genius and glory?

He had seemed to teeter on the edge of madness before – like when he first took acid – but he seemed lucid enough in interviews and, in all respects, he appeared sane to Cynthia.

Neither of them were infatuated teenagers any more, holding hands while roaming around Liverpool. Before they even tied the knot, all such pretty fondness had long gone. Pregnancy had obliged him to wed her in the teeth of unfocussed inner objections – though, had he been reading Nietszche in 1962, Lennon may have stumbled upon and agreed with the German philosopher's personal credo: that marriage and family are incompatible with a life of constant creativity. In other words, domesticity is the enemy of Art.

For him and Cynthia, therefore, there had never been much hope. He could have, but didn't make anything approaching enough of their relationship.

That isn't to say he didn't care about the mother of his child – for all the confusion there still was between Lennon the husband-and-father and Lennon the 'available' pop star. Neither was he immune to twinges of conscience as the enormity of what he was about to do sank in – but by 1968, he had no apparent option but to burn his boats as far as he was able, and either instigate a new beginning or anticipate a fall from grace by destroying himself. In the death, he did both.

To a newsperson's tape recorder again, he had declared his love for Yoko Ono, who had captured his heart during a period when, according to Barry Miles, Paul Mc Cartney's biographer, a vulnerable John was in the throes of a nervous breakdown, informing Miles later that "I was still in a real big depression in *Pepper*. I was going through murder."

Yoko – who'd said she was "very fond" of John – was a most unlikely Morgan le Fay-esque figure – but then so was Mrs Simpson for whom Edward VIII had given up the throne. A small, bossy Japanese-American who would conjecture that "You don't need talent to be an artist," Yoko Ono was to Art what the sadly missed Screaming Lord Sutch was to British politics. As some mug with a pocketful of money, John had been introduced to Yoko in 1966 during the London preview of her 'Unfinished Paintings and Objects' exhibition. Charmed by the all-white chess set, the apple with the £200 price tag and other puzzling displays, he funded Yoko's next event, taking a benevolent interest in her activities, past and present.

Yoko had also tried to make it as a pop singer, but had found a niche in the distant reaches of avant-garde jazz. In the company of respected figures like Ornette Coleman, she used her voice like a front-line horn, interjecting screeches, wails and nanny-goat jabber into the proceedings – as she did at a Cambridge arts performance in 1969 with Lennon squatting at her feet, back to the audience, holding an electric guitar against a speaker to create ear-splitting feedback.

Her association with John Lennon and The Beatles, however, will always remain central to any consideration of Yoko Ono as a figure in time's fabric. To the man-in-the-street, she appeared as if from nowhere not long after Epstein's demise, when quizzical eyebrows were being raised at The Beatles increasingly more wayward activities together – and apart for, just as US go-getter Allen Klein was to replace Brian Epstein as Lennon's man-of-affairs in 1969, so Yoko Ono had already superceded Paul McCartney as his artistic collaborator as she had Cynthia in his bed. Through her catalytic influence, the planet was confronted with a John Lennon it had never known before, one for whom The Beatles would soon no longer count.

Yet Yoko had amassed a qualified fame – or infamy – long before she captured Lennon's heart. In remote regions of the world of Art – and music – she had been known as a performance artist of extreme strategy since the late Fifties. While this may have pointed the way to more highly regarded achievement, much of Ono's legitimacy as an artist would be destroyed by her affinity to The Beatles – though, conversely, it was through this uneasy liaison that her thoughts and activities – many of which seemed to the uninitiated to be as devoid of ante-start agonies as an Ernie Wise play – reached a far, far wider public than they might have warranted in a less abnormal course of events.

Like most of their fans, the group's authorised biographer, Hunter Davies, blamed – and continues to blame – 'the

arrival in John's life of Yoko Ono' for The Beatles' disbandment. Furthermore, after nature had taken its course one
1968 night when Cynthia was away from the family home –
still in the stockbroker belt of Weybridge, Surrey – a female
writer to *Beatles Monthly* expressed the widespread view that
Cynthia and John's subsequent divorce eroded The Beatles'
magic even more than the absence of the anticipated Yuletide single had in 1966.

For such a person, John could come up with the witty
'Lennon-seque' asides and sing 'Twist And Shout' for the
next thousand years and yet never wipe out the memory of
his flaccid penis on the sleeve of John's first non-Beatle
long-player. The unmelodious avant-gardenings of his and
Yoko's *Unfinished Music No. 1: Two Virgins* might have been
anticipated, even tolerated, but not its cover photographs of
the pair doe-eyed – and naked, front and back. It was, they
explained, an Art Statement. Joe Average was, however, in
too much of a nonplus to give an Art Reply to this and two
more funny-peculiar albums whereby John pledged himself
to Yoko more symbolically than a mere engagement ring
ever could.

Issued on Zapple, Apple's short-lived subsidiary record
label, *Life With The Lions* was concerned principally with
Ono's miscarriage. Most self-centred of all was 1969's
Wedding Album; one side of which was the two's repeated
utterances of each other's name suspended over pounding
heartbeats.

Yet the white-costumed wedding ceremony in Gibraltar
on March 20 had been a relatively quiet matter. It was,
however, to be mentioned in the million-selling 'The Ballad
Of John And Yoko' in a narrative that confirmed the
Lennons' status as a Scandalous Couple on a par with Serge
Gainsbourg and Jane Birkin after they'd simulated sexual

congress on that summer's BBC-banned UK chart-topper, 'Je T'Aime...Moi Non Plus'.

Ono and Lennon's canoodling, however, went beyond the bounds of mere bad taste via such bewildering escapades as press conferences from inside kingsize white sacks; sending acorns to world leaders, the *Self Portrait* film short starring Lennon's infamous willy, and his scrawly lithographs of he and Yoko having sex. Taped at their Toronto 'Bed-In' for world peace was the 'Give Peace A Chance' anthem which, attributed to the ad hoc 'Plastic Ono Band', was John's first smash without Paul, George and Ringo.

With hastily rehearsed accompanists (that included guitarist Eric Clapton), the Lennons next performed at around midnight on Saturday 13 September 1969 at an open-air pop festival in Canada that already had a majority of olde-tyme rock'n'rollers – Bo Diddley, Gene Vincent, Little Richard, Fats Domino and Chuck Berry – on the bill. Issued as Live Peace In Toronto 1969, The Plastic Ono Band's ragged set consisted mainly of Fifties classic rock, Yoko's screech-singing and a nascent arrangement of 'Cold Turkey', a forthcoming new single. Regardless of its content, however, it was sufficient for the 20,000-odd onlookers that it had happened at all. If not on the scale of Moses re-appearing with the Ten Commandments from the clouded summit of Mount Sinai, it was the proverbial 'something to tell your grandchildren about': John Lennon's first major concert – the first by any Beatle – since the showdown at Candlestick Park.

That he was on a firm footing to commence a career without Paul, George and Ringo was emphasised further that same year when he topped a *New Musical Express* poll in which other famous vocalists had each been asked to nominate their own three favourites. He was, debatably, as adept as he'd ever get by the late Sixties – as illustrated by the coda of 1968's 'Happiness Is A Warm Gun' when he swerved cleanly into falsetto, having already built from muttered trepidation to strident intensity earlier in the song, tackling its surreal lyrics without affectation.

With vocal vehemence taking precedent throughout over nicety of intonation, the studio version of 'Cold Turkey' was issued, so Lennon put it, 'as an escape valve from the Beatles'. Its B-side was Yoko's 'Don't Worry Kyoko (Mummy's Only Looking For Her Hand In The Snow)' – which could have been about anything – or nothing. However, a Beatle-ologist might conjecture that it was an exaggerated commemoration of John missing a bend and rolling over a hired Austin Maxi somewhere in the Scottish highlands. Only one passenger – Julian, the only issue of his late marriage to Cynthia – escaped uninjured; John, Yoko and her daughter, Kyoko, needed stitches.

Lennon found 'Don't Worry Kyoko' as potent as his adolescent self had Little Richard's 'Tutti Frutti'. Work-outs of 'Don't Worry Kyoko' and 'Cold Turkey' filled his last stage appearance in Britain – with a 'Plastic Ono Supergroup' at a charity knees-up at London's Lyceum ballroom in December 1969. However, when 'Don't Worry Kyoko' plunged into its twentieth cacaphonous, headache-inducing minute, he and the other musicians – including George Harrison and Keith Moon – exchanged nervous glances.

'Cold Turkey – like 1970's echo-laden 'Instant Karma' – was issued, so Lennon put it, 'as an escape valve from the Beatles' from whom he'd cast his net furthest. In its death throes, the group had been wringing its corporate hands in the Apple offices along London's Savile Row, where it was a boom time for the more unscrupulous members of staff now that they'd assimilated the heedlessness of their paymasters' expenditure. A dam burst for a river of wastefulness to carry off gluttonous restaurant lunches, bottle after bottle of liquor, illicit trunk calls to other continents and wanton purchases of trendy whimsies swiftly to lie forgotten in a desk drawer. With a stroke of a pen, a bold executive could award himself a Rolls-Royce, a house extension, even a whole house. His secretary would conceal his thefts to better hide her own.

Eventually, The Beatles called in Allen Klein, championed by Lennon as the biggest ape in the US music business jungle, to help sort out the mess. However, 12 days before John's nuptials, Paul had wed Linda Eastman, from a family of New York showbusiness attorneys. His acceptance of Linda's father as Epstein's successor rather than Klein had widened the chasm between McCartney and the other Beatles as they muddled through what became known as 'The White Album' – after its plain cover. Studio engineers grew accustomed to two or even three of the principals being absent from any given session. Paradoxically, more catalytic familiars and guest players than ever were invited to add icing to the cake – as instanced by Eric Clapton's guitar lacquering 'While My Guitar Gently Weeps' – on which Lennon was unheard – and Yoko's voice loud and clear on 'The Continuing Story Of Bungalow Bill' and 'Revolution 9'.

She was also present, though not an audible participant, on *Let It Be*. The intention was to get back to a Merseybeat womb by not inflating songs with gratuitous frills. Other than guitars, bass and drums, there were to be only keyboards where necessary. These were fingered by Paul – and Billy Preston, whose jovial personality and energetic instrumental dexterity had first impressed The Beatles at the Star Club back in 1962.

However, *Let It Be* only hastened The Beatles' sour freedom from each other. The sessions were filmed for eventual cinema release, during which at Twickenham studios, George Harrison upped and quit, albeit temporarily. Later, George Martin shrugged off the project, and Phil Spector, an American producer past his best, was drafted in to edit, spruce up and mix the tapes. To Paul's chagrin, he also, in the pungent words of engineer Glyn Johns, 'over-dubbed a lot of crap all over it, strings and choirs and yuck,' that contradicted the original roots-affirming endeavour.

Yet, even when McCartney was on the verge of setting irreversible legal wheels in motion for the dissolution of The Beatles by 1971, the atmosphere during the making of the next album was more co-operative, even amicable, than it had been during *Let It Be*. The sub-text was that the four protagonists had agreed – at least tacitly – that *Abbey Road* was to be the finale, and they might as well go out under a flag of truce.

Fanning dull embers, Harrison spoke to the press of a follow-up, and the illusion of reconciliation that was *Abbey Road* tricked the general public into believing that The Beatles would continue, one way or another. Indeed, until well into the Seventies, not a week would pass without some twit or other asking John, Paul, George or Ringo when the group was going to reform. It was seen as almost inevitable by even the most disaffected outsider, let alone the diehard fan for who the concept of collecting every-record-The-Beatles-ever-made was not yet economically unsound. Thus an ex-Beatle was assured of at least a minor hit, even with sub-standard product of which there was going to be plenty – for, after shilly-shallying between ineffectual endeavours to get back to their Hamburg-forged genesis and the colour-supplement art of *Abbey Road* – neither Lennon, McCartney, Harrison or Starr would be able to adjust to the next decade.

All four were above the tour-album-tour sandwiches

incumbent upon poorer chart contenders, and each could wait until he felt like going on the road again or making a new record. However, an unkempt-looking Lennon still took the trouble to plug 'Instant Karma' – a 1970 single recorded and mastered within a day of its composition – twice on *Top Of The Pops*, with Yoko next to him on a stool, either blindfolded and holding up scrawled signs with BREATHE, SMILE, PEACE and further cryptadia on them; knitting a jumper, or mouthing silently into a microphone.

Lennon's eponymous album debut as an ex-Beatle, almost a year after the group's final January 1970 recording date – at which he was not present – was, like its vinyl companion, *Yoko Ono: Plastic Ono Band*, the cathartic result of Primal Scream therapy under North American psychologist Dr Arthur Janov. This was evidenced in the album's personal exorcisms (e.g. 'Mother,' 'Isolation') as well as stark rejections of former heroes and ideals. Lennon's projection of himself as a 'working class hero' in an acoustic ballad of the same name that railed against the mysterious 'they', got itself banned for its use of the f-word, even if Lennon was no more the Salt of the Earth than Mick Jagger, also a scion of privet-hedged suburbia. In affected raw Cockney instead of thickened Scouse, Jagger came on even more falsely as a workin' class 'ero.

Ripe language and soul-baring were apparent in contemporary newspaper interviews too – as was the almost audible snigger whenever Lennon sniped at McCartney. His old comrade was pilloried further in 'How Do You Sleep' from 1971's *Imagine*, though the two remained on speaking terms, with John ringing Paul when the track was on the verge of release. By contrast, *Imagine* also contained paeans of uxorious bent such as 'Oh Yoko', 'Oh My Love' and the apologetic 'Jealous Guy'. 'How Do You Sleep' had George Harrison in support on slide guitar – and the month before the release of *Imagine* in September 1971, Harrison had invited Lennon to participate in his Bangladesh charity concerts in New York, on the understanding there'd be no place onstage for Yoko too. 'Don't Worry Kyoko' at the Lyceum was too vivid a memory. However, as the evil hour when her husband was actually going to perform without her crept closer, Ono's rage exploded in a tantrum of such violence that, crushing his spectacles in his fist, John had slammed out of their hotel for the next flight back to England.

Harrison's giant step for Bangladesh took place regardless, and in one throw, he outshone all the Lennons' more mystifying tactics to right mankind' wrongs. Perhaps in a spirit of one-up-manship, John briefly spoke of a Wembley charity show featuring his and Yoko's sort of people. This was jettisoned when Lennon left his country of birth forever on August 31, 1971.

Lennon's attempts to settle in the U.S. were hindered by an earlier conviction in Britain for marijuana possession. This meant that he had to keep reapplying for an extension of his visa to stay there. Purportedly, ceaseless official harassment may have also been provoked by anti-government sentiments expressed on the 1971 single, 'Power To The People,' and on his and Ono's slogan-ridden *Sometime In New York City* double-album on which they were backed by local combo Elephant's Memory.

This joint venture also embraced excerpts from both the Lyceum extravaganza and a jam session with Frank Zappa's Mothers of Invention. Nevertheless, other than a few inspired moments, the kindest critics agreed that *Sometime In New York City* was documentary rather than recreational. The music was strong enough, but lyrically, it raised the question:

what becomes of topical ditties when they are no longer topical or the topic is tedious anyway? That's how it was with John and Yoko's statements about the National Guard shooting rioting convicts in an upstate 'correctional facility' ('Attica State'); some bloke receiving a 10-year gaol sentence for possession of an inappreciable quantity of dope ('John Sinclair') and further current – and, generally, very North American – events and cause celebres.

Lennon was the central figure of one such cause celebre when he and Yoko did an acoustic turn at a concert cum political rally in Ann Arbor, Michigan on 10 December 1971 on behalf of marijuana miscreant Sinclair, who was freed three days later. The following August, the Lennons hosted a bigger spectacular, One To One, at Madison Square Garden for a retarded children's charity.

Yet for all this latest display of artistic and romantic unity, there was trouble in paradise, and Lennon left Ono in 1973 for a 15 month 'lost weekend' in California where he lived with May Pang, their Chinese PA. He also fell in with Harry Nilsson, Keith Moon and other hard drinkers. With their own marriages floating into choppy seas too, Ringo Starr and Malcolm 'Mal' Evans, formerly one of The Beatles' two main road managers, also flopped onto the next stool for three-in-the-morning bar-hopping and late afternoon mutual grogginess by the swimming pool at a rented ocean-side chalet in Santa Monica.

If futile, the gang's attempts at staying the phantoms of early middle-age were mostly harmless. Among these was John's excessively worshipful and inebriated encounter with Jerry Lee Lewis, and Ringo securing Cherry Vanilla, a singing thespian much given to exposing her bust, to recite a Shakespeare soliloquy during John's 34th birthday celebrations. More widely reported was the incident when Lennon

– with a sanitary towel fixed to his forehead – was ejected from a night club where he and Nilsson had been heckling The Smothers Brothers comedy duo.

John managed to keep a civil tongue in his head when he and Paul got together for a chat in Los Angeles in the light of appeals from the United Nations on behalf of the Vietnamese boat people, and from someone with more money than sense offering $50 million for just one more Beatles performance, even if there was a danger that what he'd hear might not be magic, just music.

As things turned out, a 1973 Ringo Starr album would be the closest the living members of the group would ever come to a reunion on disc, embracing as it did compositions – and participation – by all four – though never on the same track. Nevertheless, that Ringo, John, Paul and George were, theoretically, together on the same piece of plastic was sufficient to feed hope that soon everything would be OK again, and that The Beatles would reform officially to tour and record the chart-toppers that John and Paul – all friends again – would be churning out once more – just as they had before John went peculiar in 1968.

Time hadn't healed, but there lingered memories of the early career struggles and their unbelievable consequence. In a dark hour professionally, Paul let slip that he wouldn't mind working with John again on a casual basis, while Lennon was now saying how wrong it had been for the group to have sundered so decisively. However, for all the 'hail-fellow-well-met' cameraderie, that all four were losing their grip one way or another wasn't the firmest foundation for a second coming. Pressed on the subject, Gary Glitter hit the nail on the head: 'They'll have to come back as a bigger creative force than before, which will be very difficult indeed.' As difficult too had been Muhammed Ali regaining his world heavyweight title in 1974. Possibly, The Beatles might have regained theirs, even though the world had become wiser to their individual weaknesses.

As the weeks since the reunion was first suggested began to turn into months, a musical, *Beatlemania*, shattered box-office records in London's West End and Beatles conventions became annual fixtures in cities across the globe, complete with guest speakers – such as Pete Best – archive film, weird-and-wonderful exhibitions and groups copying the founders of the feast, note-for-note, word-for-word, mannerism-for-mannerism.

Because EMI still owned the genuine article's master tapes, it was able to run riot with million-selling double-album retrospectives like the all up-tempo *Rock 'N' Roll Music* which, in the States, spawned a smash 45 in the *Revolver* track, 'Got To Get You Into My Life.' Meanwhile, Britain experienced the chart-swamping aftermath of 20 Beatles singles being re-promoted on the same spring day in 1976. Perusing the UK Top 40, a correspondent from *Time* magazine enquired rhetorically, "Has a successor to the Beatles finally been found? Not at all – it is the Beatles themselves." Just prior to The Sex Pistols shaping up as if they might, Ringo pleaded doubtfully for "a band that gets up there and wipes us out."

A perennial alternative, of course, was for The Beatles themselves to deliver the coup de grace. However, their continued vacillation over the matter – if it had ever been taken seriously – indicated neither destitution nor any real enthusiasm, and John returned to the glassy-eyed musings and vocational turbulence that slopped over onto albums like Nilsson's Lennon-produced *Pussycats*. Reflecting his marital (and business) ructions, John's own *Mind Games* was so-so, but *Walls And Bridges*, if rehashing some old ideas, still effused potent singles in the ethereal 'No. 9 Dream' – which, as usual, climbed far higher in the US Hot 100 than anywhere else – and, also in 1974, the US chart-topping 'Whatever Gets You Thru The Night'. Lennon also wrote the title song to Ringo's *Goodnight Vienna*.

In publicity photographs taken at the time, John didn't look much different from the way he did in 'The Beatnik Horror'. As regressive in its way was 1975's non-original *Rock 'N' Roll*; its content telegraphed on the sleeve by a photograph of 1961 vintage, and the artist's own printed sentiment: 'You should have been there'. Its spin-off 45, Ben E. King's 'Stand By Me' was the subject of an in situ promotional film for the UK TV rock showcase *The Old Grey Whistle Test*, centred on Lennon at the microphone in New York's Record Plant, giving British viewers both an exaggerated broad wink directly at the camera and a curiously stentorian vocal. Neither were very appealing.

Having gone full circle with this retrospective of favourites from the Hamburg era; a 'best of' compilation entitled *Shaved Fish*, and the en bloc re-issues of The Beatles 45s, Lennon chose to take a year off to take professional and personal stock. While growing to manhood in the hothouse of the beat boom and its endless aftermath, he'd been treated like a food pigeonhole in a self-service cafeteria. No more could it be taken for granted that John Lennon existed only to vend entertainment with a side-serving of cheap insight. He'd let go, stop trying to prove himself. All the intolerable adulation his life contained, the hit records, the money down the drain could be transformed to matters of minor importance.

Reunited with Yoko, John was finally granted U.S. residential status. He and his wife's happiness was completed by the arrival of their son, Sean, on John's 35th birthday, which was judged to be an appropriate moment to enter a period of artistic lassitude, spent mostly in the exclusive Dakota apartment block. He wasn't unduly worried. What was the use in any case of continuing to mine the same worn-out creative seams over and over again from new angles in wrong-headed expectation of finding gold? Not a melody or lyric would be heard commercially from Lennon for not one but four years after 'Cookin' (In The Kitchen Of Love)', an apt donation to a Ringo Starr album in 1976. What right had anyone to expect more? He said as much in a reluctantly granted press conference in Japan a year later.

A centre-page spread in the *NME* would plead for, if not a full-time return, then Lennon's blessing on the burgeoning punk movement, but elicited no response. Once you'd seen too much of him, but now John Lennon was sighted less frequently than the Loch Ness monster.

Yet belying the growing legend of John as pop's foremost hermit, a chance encounter with him on holiday in Bermuda caused one journalist to report that John's songwriting well was not as arid as many imagined. This was confirmed in August 1980, when he and Ono recorded material sufficient to fill two albums. There were even enough numbers left for Lennon to give 'Life Begins At Forty' and three more to Ringo when, that November, the two ex-Beatles spoke for the last time.

The first comeback album, *Double Fantasy* – which could almost be filed under 'Easy Listening' – was issued that autumn when, from Rip Van Winkle-esque vocational slumber, a fit-looking 40-year-old was suddenly available for interviews again with the unblinking self-assurance of old.

What's more, some of his new songs were more than halfway bearable. 'Watching The Wheels', 'Nobody Told Me' – which borrowed the tune of 'Mama Said', a Shirelles'

B-side – and the remaindered 'Help Me To Help Myself' were riven with an amused, grace-saving cynicism, while the first single extracted from *Double Fantasy*, '(Just Like) Starting Over,' hinted musically at his Merseybeat genesis. Overall, however, both *Double Fantasy* and the posthumous *Milk And Honey* follow-up were smug, slight statements from a refined and disgustingly rich couple long detached from the everyday. "John and I were so exclusive to each other," commented Yoko, "that we didn't really have many friends."

Long ago, their stunts had been wilder than those of any punk rocker, but with the dawn of the Eighties, the Lennons had been derided by punks and hippies alike as indolent 'breadheads' and wholesomely North Americanised mainstays of 'contemporary' rock's ruling class. Nevertheless, Lennon conjectured that no time was better for a re-emergence as a concert attraction, and a spokesman assured the media that "next spring, John and Yoko will be touring Japan, the USA and Europe". Thus, the public awaited a carnival of comparable magnitude as a Fab Four tour, albeit with no screaming and, as Brian Epstein had hoped for after Candlestick Park, "not in the context of the previous terms".

During a media scramble back in 1964 at the height of the frenzy, John had answered a question about retirement with a rhetorical "Who'd want to be an 80-year-old Beatle?" Well, he was halfway there now.

Two months after Yoko had splashed out on a skywritten 'Happy Birthday John & Sean' across New York's rind of smog, the tragedy of Lennon's subsequent slaying on the pavement outside the Dakota late one evening in December 1980 precipitated an element of ghoulish Beatlemania that implied portent in tracks such as 'Beautiful Boy' which advised five-year-old Sean Lennon of 'what happens to you when you're busy making other plans'.

Needless to say, the fall of *Double Fantasy* and '(Just Like) Starting Over' from their respective listings was reversed, and John would score a hat-trick of British Number Ones within a month of the cremation, an achievement that matched that of the Beatles in the dear, departed Swinging Sixties. Out of sympathy too, as that ghastly Christmas petered out, Yoko engineered her only Top 40 entry without her husband – with 'Walking On Thin Ice', sub-titled 'For John'. It was also to be nominated for a Grammy award, thus lending credence to the cruel old joke: death is a good career move. Finally, for the first time since *Two Virgins*, Lennon's backside made the cover of *Rolling Stone*.

You didn't want to laugh either when a *New Musical Express* reader's letter back in the aftershock had proclaimed 'The leader of the band's arrived!' This was based on the presumption that John was being conducted to the table head in some pop Valhalla. A spiritualist au fait with Lennon's afterlife adventures knew of his affair with a long-departed Hollywood actress – intelligence that did not inflame Yoko as much as the bursting of a commercial dam of such force that John Lennon's name would continue to sell almost anything.

A particular wellspring of much anguish resulted from publishers liaising with biographers while the corpse was still warm. One team of writers had a life of Lennon – entitled *Strawberry Fields Forever* – in the shops inside a fortnight, and Mark David Chapman let it be known that he wanted to write his own version of events, but would refrain if Yoko didn't wish it. That must have been as great a comfort to her as the knowledge that Chapman had been separated from other Attica State prisoners for the sake of his own safety, particularly when he seemed to be becoming something of a celebrity as the focal point of a video documentary and numerous magazine features.

Chapman's perspective hasn't yet been read by a general public, but the memoirs of Lennon associates like May Pang reached the shops before Albert Goldman weighed in with his doorstopper which, while portraying Lennon as sectionable a lunatic as Chapman, portrayed Ono as a cross between pop's Wallis Simpson – and Beryl Formby, who watched her henpecked husband, George, the Lancashire music-hall entertainer, like a hawk, and ruled him with an "iron petticoat". In parenthesis, at the time of his own death in 1994, Goldman was, purportedly, in the throes of a biography of Yoko Ono with the ominous title, *Black Widow*.

The surviving Beatles were united with Yoko in condemning this ignoble account by Goldman who, having dished the dirt already on Elvis Presley, was as twisted in his way as Chapman, but morbid inquisitiveness ensured, nevertheless, a mammoth return for his *Lives Of John Lennon*. This, in spite of a prototypical protest from George Harrison that its purchasers "don't realise it's the same old clap-trap, and that the Goldman's of this world can make a hell of a living, a lot of money, for slagging off someone who's dead."

Harrison's 'All Those Years Ago' was the best known of tribute discs to Lennon. Regardless of its sing-along mediocrity, one incentive for buyers was the superimposed presence of Paul and Ringo. During Lennon's 'lost weekend', Harrison had suggested the two of them ratify an old rumour by forming a group with Starr and Klaus Voorman, now an accomplished bass player, but John – still peeved perhaps by the Bangla Desh business – had shrugged off this idea as a social faux pas.

How different could John Lennon's life have been? What follows is probably a silly hypothetical exercise, but let us turn to a parallel dimension for a few minutes. In it, John quits The Beatles, an obscure Sixties beat group, in 1963 for a hand-to-mouth existence as a jobbing commercial artist in Liverpool. For a while, he's on the periphery of the 'Liverpool Scene' before a supplicatory chat with Arthur Ballard gets him a post as technician in Ballard's department at the college. As his marriage to Cynthia deteriorates, John becomes a fixture in Ye Cracke, the student pub, where he often rambles on with rueful and misplaced pride about The Beatles' meagre achievements. On one maudlin evening, he brings in his photo album – "us with Tony Sheridan", "me, Paul and George with Ringo Starr in the Top 10. Ringo was in Georgie Fame's Blue Flames later on, you know . . ." Most regulars find both John's reminiscences and the pictures mind-stultifyingly boring, but he cares as little about their opinions as a chimpanzee in the zoo does about those of people peering through the bars.

For beer money and a laugh, Lennon reforms the group for bookings in local watering holes. They become as peculiar to Liverpool alone as Mickey Finn, a comedian unknown nationally but guaranteed work for as long as he can stand on Merseyside. A typical engagement is providing music after Finn's entertainment at a dinner-and-dance at Lathom Hall on December 9, 1980 when The Beatles leave a dancing audience wanting more. The group's personnel on that night-of-nights consists of Pete Best, deputy manager at Garston Job Centre on drums; George Harrison, a Southport curate, on guitar; Paul McCartney, a Radio Merseyside presenter and amateur songwriter, on bass – and Lennon, his singing voice darker and attractively shorn of Sixties ingenuity, now a slightly batty art lecturer who'd wed a Japanese performance artist he'd seen at a 1967 'happening' at the college.

Unreal life isn't like that – at least, it wasn't for John. Like it was with Kennedy and, in 1977, Elvis Presley, everyone remembers the moment they heard of his passing. "John who?" Pete Best spluttered from his shaving mirror when his missus shouted the news upstairs that strange morning on Merseyside. Before the day was out, it became clear that John Lennon wasn't going to recover from being dead. Before they'd even wiped away the tears, record moguls pondered what tracks by Lennon or associated with him they were entitled to rush-release or re-promote.

Under the editorial lash, pressured denizens of the media cobbled together hasty obituaries and special supplements for the Sunday editions. One of the more memorable comments any of them reported was by the then-recently-retired Arthur Ballard: "I think his death is more significant than that of a leading politician. Like Michaelangelo has never been forgotten, neither will John Lennon be."

Aspects Of Lennon

LOVE . . .

THREE'S A CROWD

The young George Harrison's hero-worship impinged upon John's amour with Cynthia Powell, a fellow art student. Because John liked her, so did George – although, as he confided to John, man to man, "She's got teeth like a horse."

With the insensitivity of puberty, George would wait outside the college for the couple to emerge after lectures. Initially, he'd follow at a distance as the couple quickened their pace, intending to get up to he knew not what during, say, an intended tryst in a mutual friend's bedroom in Gambier Terrace, just round the corner from the college.

When George caught up to them, neither had the heart to tell him to get lost. Growing bolder, he'd greet the couple with a trademark piercing whistle and once more, with their hearts in their boots, they'd be stuck with George for the afternoon.

Cynthia's patience broke finally when she was hospitalised with an ill-humoured appendix. Anticipating an hour of sweet nothings during John's first ward visit, she burst into tears when he approached the bed with his admirer in tow. This time, George was told to go away.

WEDDING #2

When Yoko Ono became the second Mrs John Lennon on March 20, 1969 at the British Consulate building on Gibraltar, Beatle assistant Peter Brown gave the bride away. 'Intellectually, we didn't believe in getting married', commented the groom, 'but one doesn't love someone just intellectually'. Within the hour, the happy couple were on a flight to Paris.

THE BEATLES' SHADOW

2001 saw the publication of *The Beatles Shadow: Stuart Sutcliffe & His Lonely Hearts Band*, his younger sister Pauline's subjective re-write of the tie-in to the 1994 *Backbeat* biopic. The lady now claimed that her brother and John Lennon had oral sex on a bunkbed during The Beatles' first trip to Germany, but if it happened, she didn't witness it. Indeed, her dubious source for this story was Geoffrey Giuliano's *Lennon In America* – and Giuliano was guessing too.

IDA HOLLY

Lennon's first illicit affair following his espousal to Cynthia Powell was early in 1963 with a 17-year-old Liverpool brunette, Ida Holly. He did not tell her he was married, but, by circuitous enquiry, her father found out and was on the point of informing the press when the liaison ended.

RONNIE SPECTOR

Both John Lennon and, apparently, Keith Richards of The Rolling Stones developed a crush on Veronica 'Ronnie' Bennett of US vocal group The Ronettes, when they co-headlined a British tour with the Stones in January 1964.

She found Richards "not so much shy as quiet. I could make him laugh, but most of the time, nothing was funny to him." Lennon, however, wasn't one for silent worship. At a

London party in The Ronettes' honour, he forewent even perfunctory chivalry by seizing Ronnie by the arm, and steering her upstairs, but, in the romantic seclusion of an empty bedroom, this went no further than a two-minute snog during a wistful embrace in a window seat that looked out over the city's starry panorama.

Still a virgin and faithful to her paramour, producer Phil Spector, Ronnie resisted Lennon's attempts to manoeuvre her onto the bed. John, however, wasn't upset. Indeed, he brushed off her rejection with a resigned, almost amused disappointment. Now Ronnie's husband Spector was drafted in to edit, spruce up and mix *Let It Be*, 1970's 'new phase Beatles album'. Ronnie also recorded a one-off single on Apple Records in 1971.

Three years later in New York, a now-divorced Ronnie met Lennon's then-girlfriend, May Pang, who invited her back to their apartment to renew her acquaintance with John. The meeting was cordial and memorable chiefly for John lamenting Phil Spector's spent 'genius'.

The next time Ronnie met John – by chance outside the Dakota two years later – a brief conversation ended with 'househusband' Lennon vanishing into the building to attend to his infant son Sean's last meal.

STUART AND JOHN

During the turbulent adolescence that prefaced a turbulent manhood, hardly anyone knew Lennon as intimately as Stuart Sutcliffe. If they weren't exactly David and Jonathan, June Furlong, one of the life models at Liverpool's Regional College of Art, had "never seen two teenagers as close as those two". Moreover, although all The Beatles were the most heterosexual of males, the vice-like grip Stuart appeared to have on John – and vice-versa – provoked in George and, especially, Paul an apprehension akin to that of a child viewing another sibling as a barrier to prolonged attention from an admired elder brother. For a similar reason, Lennon was to be dismayed initially when Sutcliffe and Astrid Kirchherr became an 'item' – though, alternatively, this may have been simple jealousy because he fancied her himself.

The general underminings and sly machinations that make pop groups what they are also caused Stuart to shilly-shally about whether to quit the group and resume his career as a painter. Either way, it did not bode well for The Beatles – especially after John issued the naked threat: if he goes, I go. No one knew whether to take it seriously.

In the end, John remained a Beatle while Stuart jumped before he was pushed. Casting The Beatles aside as adolescent foolishness, he'd since got his hair cut "almost respectable," he told his sister, "I think I must be growing up." The emotional and physical cost of being a Beatle and then making up for lost time as a painter, however, incited fears for his health as dizzy spells, convulsions, chronic indigestion and other maladies he'd been suffering for some time became more persistent.

On Tuesday, April 10, 1962, death took Stuart Sutcliffe without effort on the stroke of 4.45 p.m. In the ambulance, Astrid's face was his last vision before he passed away. John learned of Stuart's death directly from Astrid when he arrived in Hamburg the next day before The Beatles' opened at the Star-Club, soon to be the most famous landmark in the Grosse Freiheit. The terrible news struck home, and Lennon struggled not to lose his cool. He strained his wits for some hilariously appalling remark to show how unaffected he was. He ought to combust with laughter or at least shrug his shoulders indifferently, not turn an eyelash. At the end of that briefest of pauses, he could manage neither of these pretences. At a loss for words for once, he buried himself in Astrid's embrace.

The next day, however, he stood apart from the bear-hugging outbursts when he, Astrid, Paul and Pete greeted Millie, Stuart's mother at Hamburg-Fuhlsbuttel airport. He seemed too calm to her – like a detached spectator with no interest or stake in the tragedy. Since yesterday, he'd made up his mind to be the hard man again: too tough to cry.

Within hours, The Beatles were pitching into their first number at the Star-Club with all their customary verve. However, when all the stupid songs about fast cars and girls were over, John could no longer contain it. During the expected after-hours carousing, he fell silent as shards of disjointed memories pierced an already over-stimulated mind. What amounted to an unspoken wake for Stuart ended with a now-forgotten altercation with persons unknown that reverberated around some six-in-the-morning bar.

POLYTHENE PAM

Remaindered from the White Album, 'Polythene Pan' was resurrected as one of the songs in *Abbey Road*'s closing medley. It was, smirked composer Lennon, "me remembering a little event with a woman in Jersey: perverted sex in a polythene bag."

'Polythene Pam' was also the nickname of a Liverpool barmaid with whom John used to flirt. She wondered if the number concerned her, but with the qualification, "If you listen to the lyrics, it's not the kind of song you'd want dedicated to you."

HELEN SHAPIRO

On their first British tour, The Beatles were flattered if at first not quite comfortable when Helen Shapiro chose to travel with the supporting bill in the coach, rather than be chauffeured like the headlining star she was. Part of her motivation for doing so was that she had developed a crush on John Lennon: "I really fell for him, but, alas, as I was 15 at the time, and he was 21, John always treated me like a kid sister. It was only later that I found out that he was married."

BLESS YOU

John suspected that Mick Jagger had reworked 'Bless You', a celebration of Yoko, on 1974's *Walls And Bridges*, 'and turned it into 'Miss You'. The engineer kept wanting me to speed that up. He said, "This is a hit if you'd just do it fast." He was right – because as 'Miss You', it turned into a hit.' Lennon himself had lifted the 'Bless You' title from either a 1961 smash by Tony Orlando or, earlier still, a 78 rpm side by The Ink Spots.

Expressing a gloomier but related sentiment 'Miss You' was a 1978 million-seller for the Rolling Stones. When it blasted from Lennon's radio, John upped the volume, remarking that Mick had got a great song from his recent divorce. The former Mrs Jagger may have agreed, but although he was reluctant to discuss its lyrical motive, Mick explained that 'It's not really about a girl. To me, the feeling of longing is what the song is about.'

PADDY, KLAUS AND GIBSON

With the sundering of Faron's Flamingos, Liverpool singing guitarist Paddy Chambers served The Big Three until summer 1964 when he passed through the ranks of Kingsize Taylor and the Dominoes, prior to a sojourn in Hamburg where he ventured into jazz-rock in The Eyes with a line-up that included drummer Gibson Kemp (Ringo's successor in Rory Storm and the Hurricanes) and Klaus Voorman, a friend of The Beatles from Hamburg, on bass. With Chambers, these two were to try their luck in London as 'Paddy, Klaus and Gibson'.

Among initial assignments was accompanying Tony Sheridan on the BBC Light Programme's *Saturday Club*, and a residency at the Pickwick, a night spot frequented by London's pop 'in-crowd'. At the urging of John Lennon, Brian Epstein – enthralled particularly by the handsome Chambers – became the trio's manager in June 1965, but was unable to engineer Beatle-sized success for Paddy, Klaus and Gibson. "I don't think he had a clue," sighed Chambers, "but it was obvious that, having failed to get anywhere with Lennon, he was getting emotionally very hung up on me. I actually ended up in bed with him one day, but after five minutes, I got up and walked out."

BAD VIBES

"I don't think you could have broken up four very strong people like that," theorised Yoko Ono in 1980. "There must have been something that happened within them – not an outside force at all."

Just after the Beatles' break-up, Ringo Starr had conjectured that John and Yoko's amour had not taken priority over group commitments. "Ringo was a little confused," deduced Klaus Voorman, nonetheless, "because John's closeness to Yoko was sad to him. John and Yoko were one person, which was difficult for him to accept."

George Harrison did try to come around, initially. He and John Lennon were the only Beatles heard on Lennon's 'What's The New Mary Jane', intended for but left off the White Album. Though it had lyrics and a tune, it was closer in concept to 'Revolution 9' than 'Birthday' – on which Yoko Ono and George's wife Pattie had provided backing vocals. But his support for John and Yoko's union wasn't destined to last and one day at Apple, he could no longer contain his resentment. He burst into the couple's office and came straight to the point. Naming Bob Dylan among those with a low opinion of uncool Yoko, Harrison went on to complain about the present 'bad vibes' within The Beatles' empire that were co-related with her coming. "We both sat through it," shrugged John. "I don't know why, but I was always hoping they would come around."

SPOTLIGHT ON JOHNNY

"She thinks I'm queer!" exclaimed Ian Hart-as-John in 1994's *Backbeat* movie – centred on The Beatles' visits to Hamburg. He was referring to Astrid Kirchherr, who had noted the brusque tenderness between Lennon and her boy-friend, Stuart Sutcliffe.

"No," replied Stuart. "She said she thinks we love each other."

"And what did you say about that?"

"I might have nodded."

His doubtful standing as The Beatles' bass guitarist was of less concern to Sutcliffe, a lapsed painter, than maintaining his old affinity with Lennon, the subject of at least two of his portraits. Their finely balanced scale of conflicting emotions – hurt, anger, and emotional dependence – during Stuart's final weeks with the group is encapsulated in a *Backbeat* scene in which the wise-cracking pair are so nearly robbed of speech that they are not able even to revile each other in their customary matey way.

Having said it at last – that he was going to leave The Beatles – Sutcliffe had read the omen of assault in Lennon's eyes, but if the latter's pent-up rage ever overflowed into violence against Stuart, it subsided. Somehow, they would be together again one day; Sutcliffe might even rejoin The Beatles. John, at least, did not regard this eventuality as unlikely, even if Paul, George and Pete did.

Stuart's consequent correspondence with John from Hamburg was in aptly glum existentialist vein, dwelling at length about how pointless everything was, and upon esoteric issues in which Lennon assumed the role of 'John the Baptist' and Sutcliffe that of 'Jesus Christ'. The most quoted and evocative lines from these letters came to be John's poetic 'I can't remember anything without a sadness/So deep that it hardly becomes known to me/So deep that its tears leave me a spectator of my own stupidity.'

Picking at these oblique lines for meaning, they are reminiscent of 'True lowliness of heart/Which takes the humbler part/And o'er its own shortcomings weeps with loathing' from 'Come Down O Love Divine', a Whitsuntide times that both boys from Church-going upbringings would have been familiar.

Inspired perhaps by these dialogues, Stuart began an ultimately unfinished autobiography-cum-novel entitled *Spotlight On Johnny*. Describing himself in the third person (as 'Nhoke'), Stuart disclosed that "when he stood up, he complained of a blackout and tremendous headaches." As this was happening in real life, he consulted German doctors who recommended treatments that could only retard rather than arrest the progress of what he could only refer to as "the illness".

TWO SIDES OF THE MOON

If 'In My Life' – on *Rubber Soul* – had been supposedly composed by John with Cynthia, his first wife, in mind, it was re-dedicated to Yoko Ono, his second, in a calendar within the couple's 1969 *Wedding Album* package.

George Harrison's vocal cords had been weakened to a tortured rasp on in-concert renderings during his 1974 winter North American solo tour when in *his* life, he loved *God* more. Not to be outdone, Keith Moon of The Who decided to half-recite one of the most nostalgic songs The Beatles ever recorded in a manner that the Germans would call Sprechstimme, on his only solo album, *Two Sides Of The Moon*, released in spring 1975. Moon's streets-of-Wembley intonation and untutored phrasing floated effortlessly over layers of treated sound, and what amounted to a backing choir and lone piano tinklings.

Another Lennon number was also selected for *Two Sides Of The Moon*. A leftover from 1974's *Walls And Bridges*, 'Move Over Mrs L' was perceived as a lyrical dig at his estranged spouse beneath a riff lifted from a 45 by Lord Rockingham's XI, resident group on *Oh Boy!,* a British ITV pop showcase in the late Fifties. Yet, still carrying a torch for Yoko and fearing it would upset her, Lennon tossed what was not his finest hour as a composer to Moon. While such a gift, however trite, was no longer the licence to print money that it had been in the Sixties, it was all grist to MCA's publicity mill.

A new Lennon recording of 'Move Over Mrs L' was to be the flip-side of his 'Stand By Me' single in 1975.

LOVE GONE WRONG

When The Beatles landed in New York in 1964, Mark David Chapman was eight and living with his parents and younger sister in Atlanta, Georgia. He compiled the first of many scrapbooks that kept track of The Beatles' ever-unfolding career. By the time Mark reached puberty, every nook and cranny of his bedroom was crammed with Beatles memorabilia and merchandise: pictures of them all over the walls, and piles of records with label variations, foreign picture sleeves and the canons of associated artists: the Word made vinyl in the comfort of his own home. His function then was to remain uninvolved directly, just absorb the signals as they came.

For hundreds upon thousands of hours, he'd filed, catalogued and gloated over his acquisitions, finding much to notice, study and compare. Mark could dwell very eloquently and with great authority on his interest, but couldn't grasp why fellow pupils at Columbia High School were not as captivated.

When he graduated in 1973, Chapman had experienced both LSD and, fleetingly, the glory and the stupidity of being in a pop group. He was also professing to be a born-again Christian. Two years later, he was working amongst Vietnamese refugees on a reservation in Arkansas, pleasing his superiors with his diligence and aptitude for the most onerous of tasks. No longer outwardly living his life through The Beatles, it was a period that Chapman would recognise as the nearest he'd ever come to contentment.

1978, however, was a climacteric year for him. His parents divorced, he parted with one girlfriend and met another (who he was to marry on the rebound). He sank into a deep depression that drove him to two suicide attempts. Somewhere along the way, the old Beatles craving reared up with a vengeance to the degree that he evolved a grave fixation about John Lennon.

By autumn 1980, he had decided that the chief Beatle's control of his life could not remain remote – especially now that Lennon was re-entering public life with the release of his first album in five years, *Double Fantasy*.

Mark may have preferred John's career to remain an ever-silent 'no return' saga. Perhaps he felt uncomfortable about a comeback that might make Lennon no longer his unknowing intimate, but common property again. Therefore, he finished his last shift as a security guard in Hawaii – signing off as 'John Lennon' – and appeared in New York as if from nowhere early in December 1980.

Twilight was falling on Monday, December 8 when John – with Yoko Ono – strolled out of the Dakota building. After assuming that all he had to do was autograph another copy of the new album, John Lennon walked on. Before the day was done, he'd be back near that same spot with his life ebbing out of him. Yards away, Mark Chapman would be standing with a smoking revolver in his hand.

Most people felt that John Lennon was killed simply because Chapman – who'd also been sniffing around Todd Rundgren – was as nutty as a fruitcake. This opinion was fuelled from the start by the police officers who detained the suspect at New York's Twentieth Precinct station. Yet Mark Chapman was to be confined not to a mental institution but gaol when, rather than seize the opportunity to deliver a headline-grabbing speech from the dock, pleaded guilty without fuss, saying tacitly that "I insist on being incarcerated for at least the next 20 years."

He continues to serve his sentence separated from other prisoners for the sake of his own safety, particularly when he seemed to be nearing celebrity as the subject of a video documentary, television interviews and numerous magazine articles.

However, an apparently remorseful and rehabilitated Chapman is, if freed, likely to become, advisedly, as reclusive as his victim was during the 'househusband years'. In jail, he'd blamed 'society' for his crime. He'd also refused written requests for autographs, remarking, "This tells you something is truly sick in our society. I didn't kill John to become famous, and I'm horrified by these people." Take that how you like.

BETTINA

The most common sources of artificial energy in Hamburg's Grosse Freiheit were beer and the amphetamine content of Preludin (after its principal compound, phenmetrazine), a brand of appetite suppressant for dieters. For purposes other than fighting the flab, supplies of Preludin – 'Prello' – tablets were stocked for employees' use in most of the district's establishments that kept Dracula hours.

Behind the bar at the Star Club appeared a photograph autographed, 'John Lennon, King of Prello'. There too stood Bettina Derlein, a blonde, full-breasted barmaid with a beehive hairdo. She was John's most constant girlfriend among a seraglio he accumulated during The Beatles' five seasons in Germany.

Derlein is not to be confused with Erika Huebers, who was to claim an irregular kinship between Paul McCartney and her daughter Bettina.

Bettina Derlein also worked in a club along the Herbert-strasse, the notorious 'Street of Windows'. "You couldn't see into it," remarked Ricky Richards, one of The Jets (who had preceded The Beatles as resident group at the Kaiserkeller in 1960) "because of great iron gates either end like the entrance to a concentration camp."

John would rag 17-year-old George Harrison about notices forbidding minors from entering the Herbertstrasse where unlovely old rascals, purchasing brief respite from frustration and loneliness, looked the sluts up and down like farmers at a cattle auction. There was, however, no subtext of financial transaction for visiting British rock'n'rollers. Indeed, when John needed extra cash, he would sometimes take his guitar to a favoured brothel to earn tips by entertaining the prostitutes and clients before and after they'd been about their business.

MAY PANG

From a well-to-do Chinese family living in New York, May Pang had been an office employee of Allen Klein, and thus, with deceptive casualness, entered the life of John Lennon. Among her tasks in 1970 was handling administrative matters relating to a pair of films made in New York by Yoko with assistance from John. They were so impressed by her efficiency that she was taken on as their personal secretary.

During her third year on the couple's payroll, the 22-year-old went beyond the call of duty after Mrs Lennon informed her that their marriage was floating into a choppy sea, and asked May how she felt about becoming John's mistress. Wasn't it a French homily that ran: "The chains of marriage are so heavy that it takes two to carry them, and often three"? As it was inevitable that John was going to stray, pontificated Yoko, let it be to someone they both knew and liked.

After an initial and understandable reluctance, May succumbed, and remained with Mr Lennon throughout the lengthy trial separation from his wife – to whom she sent progress reports. Overall, Pang – able to stomach conduct by him that Yoko found intolerable – was a standard bearer of calm amid the craziness of Lennon's 'lost weekend' – which, according to her, ended after his visit to a hypnotist, ostensibly, to wean him off cigarettes.

Nevertheless, May and John continued to meet for sporadic and discreet assignations after he returned to Yoko in 1975.

In 1983, *Loving John: The Untold Story*, May Pang's memoir of her life with the Lennons was published by Warner Books. Before the decade was out, she had married Tony Visconti, a record producer, whose clients had included T Rex and David Bowie. His first wife was Mary Hopkin, whose maiden single, 'Those Were The Days', had succeeded The Beatles' 'Hey Jude' at the top of the British charts in 1968. In parenthesis, Cynthia Lennon's one and only foray as a recording artist was on a 1995 revival of 'Those Were The Days'.

FRENCH CONNECTIONS

With George Harrison, Paul McCartney and others in tow, endeavouring to monopolise her art school boyfriend's time, Cynthia's heart would sink to her boots. However, she would periodically catch John eyeing her in a lustful fashion; perhaps because he had finally noticed that her blonde perm had gone to highlighted seed so that she now looked a bit like Brigitte Bardot, who had emerged as France's femme fatale, thanks to a combination of unruly sexuality and doe-eyed ingenuousness. "John's perfect image of a woman was Brigitte Bardot," concluded Cynthia, "I found myself fast becoming moulded into her style of dress and haircut."

She noted too that John also admired Juliette Greco, svelte and spectral high priestess of popular existentialism – and more the thinking man's French actress than Bardot. Her intellectual image and dark hair, stark make-up, black garb and habit of covering her figure in a tent-like sweater that tapered into form-fitting trousers was akin to that of Yoko Ono's 'look' when John first met her in 1966. "She was the one for John," sighed Cynthia, "It was pure instinct; the chemistry was right; the mental aura surrounding them was almost identical."

BRIAN AND JOHN

Much has been written about Brian Epstein's homosexuality and his erotic attraction to The Beatles, particularly Lennon. It was often the butt of unpleasant jibes by John over the years, such as suggesting that Epstein title his life story *A Cellarful Of Boys* – rather than *A Cellarful Of Noise* (Souvenir Press, 1964).

Brian "genuinely loved John", estimated The Beatles' US attorney Nat Weiss, "it was more than a sexual attraction," while Cynthia Lennon felt John, "aspired to Brian's finesse." Moreover, during a depressed, stressed and exhausted Epstein's spell – not the only one – in a residential London clinic, John sent a rueful bouquet and a card inscribed, "You know I love you and I really mean it." It caused Epstein to burst into tears.

Yet in his first autobiography, *Beatle!*, Pete Best states that Brian propositioned him one evening in 1962, "but there had been nothing nasty about it, nothing obscene, nothing dirty. It was a very gentle approach."

When The Beatles took a fortnight's break from a hectic schedule between April 27 and May 11, 1963, Brian – godfather to the newly born Julian Lennon – persuaded John to join him for a 12-day break in Spain. Paul McCartney's notion about the acceptance of such an invitation from a known homosexual was "John, not being stupid, saw his opportunity to impress upon Mr Epstein who was the boss of the group. He wanted Brian to know who he should listen to. There was never any hint that he was gay."

However, some within The Beatles' circle imagined that the two holidaymakers had an affair – which John denied emphatically at the time, to the degree of a drunken attack on Bob Wooler, the Cavern's principal disc jockey, at Paul's 21st birthday party, for a remark about 'the honeymoon'.

Brian too insisted that "It is simply not true" when asked about the matter by Don Short of the *Daily Mirror*.

"I think he enjoyed the fantasy of the trip," added Nat Weiss, "But I think it would have been spoiled by anything physical. I don't believe it was consummated – but it was genuine."

In any case, as it was with Pete Best, Epstein "wouldn't have done anything to frighten John off," stressed Brian's personal assistant, Wendy Hanson. "John was a womaniser – and Brian was a very sensitive person. He'd never push himself on anyone."

Nevertheless, ever the iconoclast, Lennon, routinely unfaithful as both a boyfriend and husband, may have decided to experiment for much the same reason as French sex symbol Serge Gainsbourg, who admitted in print that, yes, he'd once had a homosexual experience, "so as not to remain ignorant". In a 1983 memoir, *In My Life*, Lennon's childhood friend and fellow Quarry Man Pete Shotton wrote that John himself had admitted that there had been a half-hearted attempt at non-penetrative sex on one occasion in Spain, perhaps lending credence to Lennon's rationalisation that, "Well, it was almost a love affair, but not quite. It was never consummated – but it was a pretty intense relationship." This was also implied in 1991's *The Hours And Times*, a 60-minute celluloid dramatisation of the vacation – with Lennon played by Ian Hart, the same actor who portrayed him in *Backbeat*.

After the Spanish jaunt, there was no other indication that what passed between John Lennon and Brian Epstein was anything beyond friendship and business.

Who cares anyway?

MEET THE WIFE

John Lennon dismayed his female following when he headed a Mersey Beat list of performers thought to be married. However, the image of him held by most lovestruck pubescent girls in Inverness or Penzance was of the Poor Honest Northern Lad Who'd Bettered Himself as a pop singer with an electric guitar. How many of them wondered what his penis was like (or whether he even had one)? Ignorance was bliss – and worship of an idol without vice or blemish was in a way less harmful an analgesic than most to an otherwise mundane provincial existence of school, homework and Church youth club.

John was married, true enough, but it was to Cynthia, known then – erroneously as events were to prove – as the shrinking violet of The Beatles clique. The speed of events after take-off with 'Love Me Do' had not yet overwhelmed her as she coped with marathon fan vigils outside the Lennon family's Kensington bedsit; stifled giggles from those who'd winkled out the ex-directory number and even an attempted kidnap of Julian. Disguises, decoy tactics and secret destinations were to be as essential as spare underwear whenever the Lennons went on holiday. On one occasion, Cynthia had to be smuggled out of a hotel in a laundry basket.

"The change in him was like Jekyll and Hyde," sighed a still saddened and perplexed Cynthia in 1997. "John would have laughed at himself years before if he could have seen the future. Before he met Yoko, there was an item in *The Times* about her film, 'Bottoms' – myriad naked human buttocks in close-up – and John said, 'Look at this mad Japanese artist. What will they print next?!' So his attitude then was she was a nutcase – and I agreed. I'm not a conceptual artist. When I look at things, I like to understand what I'm looking at."

ONE VIRGIN?

When not yet an official Quarry Man, George Harrison had been happy just to be around John Lennon, three years his senior and fledged rock'n'roller with sideburns, who boasted about how he'd tilted successfully for the downing of some girl's knickers. George's heart would feel like it would burst through its ribcage whenever the Great Lennon lowered himself to actually speak to him, no matter how nastily. Had John then offered anything other than slights, exploitations and jokes at his expense, George might have been worried about his position as the lowest of the low in the Quarry Men hierarchy. It gave him a feeling of belonging.

When John bragged about, say, an encounter with a girl way out of his league, George did not dare to voice his disbelief – or the educated guess that John Lennon at 17 was probably still a virgin.

In the days before the birth pill and the Swinging Sixties, pre-marital sex was a much bigger issue. Through some undignified fumblings, John might have discovered that even the youth club's most arch proto-feminist – the sort who looked as if she couldn't wait for a game of ping-pong, followed by a chat about life-after-death over an orange squash – was screaming for sex as much as any bloke. He'd uncovered this secret at parties held when the host's parents were away overnight. The living room was transformed into a den of iniquity by dimming table lamps with headscarves and pushing back armchairs as a prelude to snogging and attacks of 'desert sickness' (a pre-Seventies euphemism for fondling: 'desert sickness' = 'wandering palms'). The soundtrack to this effused from the Dansette record player in the corner, surrounded by a scattering of brittle 78s and the plastic 45 rpm discs that were usurping them.

Yet it was in this exotic scenario that John noticed the coltish charms of his first true girlfriend. In one of Woolton's public parks, he and Len Garry, The Quarry Men's tea-chest bass player, established contact with two 14-year-old girls, Barbara Baker and her less attractive friend. No one knew if Barbara went all the way or was hanging on to her virginity. Initially, she 'walked out' with Len, but, if feigning indifference, seemed to be weighing up John out of the corner of her eye.

When Garry withdrew gracefully, and John and Barbara began going around together, he was emboldened one evening to plant an exploratory kiss on her lips. During subsequent frolics over the year in which they 'went steady', matters took a serious and abandoned turn – or so John told the lads. The more sceptical of his cronies imagined that he might have got to 'third base' after a lot of effort, but only a 'cheap' girl didn't 'save herself' for her future husband. Anyway, girls only went all the way if they really loved you – and, even then, a true daughter of the Fifties would usually have none of it while yet unwed.

Now married and living in Cheshire, Barbara Baker has always politely declined to be interviewed about what went on between her and John Lennon.

WHERE'S YOUR WIFE?

The first indication that John and Yoko were an 'item' was when he brazened it out by escorting her to London's Old Vic Theatre on June 18, 1968 to catch a National Theatre adaptation of his slim 1964 volume, *In His Own Write*. "Where's your wife?" shouted a hovering press person. "I don't know," snarled Lennon.

A worried *Beatles Monthly* passed Yoko off as John's "guest of honour."

'LOVE'

After 'She Loves You', 'You've Got To Hide Your Love Away', 'It's Only Love' and 'All You Need Is Love', John composed just plain 'Love' in 1970 as one of his many paeans to Yoko Ono. It was recorded for his *John Lennon: Plastic Ono Band* LP, and issued as a posthumous single in 1982, reaching number 27 in the UK charts.

In the early Sixties, Ono directed a six-minute film also titled *Love* – which consisted of a couple engaged in athletic sexual intercourse in tight close-up.

THAT OLD GANG OF MINE

When auditioning unsuccessfully to join The Texans – later, Rory Storm and the Hurricanes – in 1957, Harrison as a 14-year-old had played and sung Gene Vincent's arrangement of a song from the Twenties, 'Wedding Bells'. Its hookline ran, "Those wedding bells are breaking up that old gang of mine."

"The old gang of mine was over the moment I met Yoko," concurred John Lennon. "It was like when you meet your first woman, and you leave the guys at the bar and you don't play football anymore and you don't go play snooker and billiards. Maybe some guys like to continue that relationship with the boys, but once I'd found the woman, the boys became of no interest whatsoever, other than they were like old friends – but it so happened that the boys were well known and not just the local guys at the bar."

GROUPIES

John's overt public attachment to Yoko put paid to him being a star in the sense of sending teenage girls into paroxysms of screaming ecstasy. Nevertheless, a special 'Groupies' edition of *Rolling Stone* in 1969 concerned female music-lovers renowned for evading the most stringent security barriers to impose themselves on rock stars. The more free-spirited of these 'groupies' remained interested in John Lennon sexually. "It'd be a privilege for him to even notice me," said one.

THE 'MEMBER' OF THE BRITISH EMPIRE

The sleeve for *Unfinished Music No. 1: Two Virgins* showing photographs of the pair naked, back and front, pledged John to Yoko more symbolically than a mere engagement ring ever could. While it demonstrated that they didn't look much different from anyone else, the intention of the Two Virgins was more to do with magnifying the gap between its makers and the common herd – or in their mind, "us two and you lot".

Most of "you lot" were too perplexed to give an Art Reply when Yoko explained that *Two Virgins* was an Art Statement. Months before the eventual release date in November 1968, the sleeve had been postponed while Lennon's appalled advisors tried to talk him out of it. They had not associated penis display with Lennon who, only three years earlier, had seethed, "You don't do that in front of the birds!" when he, Cynthia and the Harrisons had been confronted by a drunken Allen Ginsberg wearing only underpants – on his head – at a London soiree held on the beatnik bard's birthday.

Yet, although he "didn't dig their music" – sounds not thought of generally as pop music – Ringo Starr swooped unquestioningly to Lennon's defence. "It's just John being John. It's very clean," he remarked. Paul had been persuaded to write a commendation (if it was one) for the *Two Virgins* cover – that called Lennon and Yoko 'saints' – but he and his new girlfriend, Linda Eastman – a showbiz photographer from a family of US attorneys – were, reportedly, most offended by the whole business.

It wasn't as if Lennon and Ono had invented full frontal nudity, Swinging Sixties style. Female pubic hair had been seen by movie-goers for the first time in 1966, courtesy of Jane Birkin, the actress listed as 'Blonde' in the closing credits of Michelangelo Antonioni's slow-moving *Blow Up*. When *Two Virgins* appeared, the 'hippy' musical, *Hair*, had already opened in New York and transferred to London. Its murkily lit 'nude scene' was there for all to see the very day after stage censorship was abolished via 1968's Theatres Act. This would also allow a presentation by Black Widow, a rock band from Leicester that featured a bare lady prostrate beneath singer Kip Trevor's sacrificial sword amid chilling screams and abundant spilling of fake blood.

Generally speaking, however, even the most scantily-clad female on the jackets of the budget label Hallmark's Hot Hits series of carbon-copies of then-current smashes wore more than girls did for a summer's afternoon on Margate beach.

Yet a Hot Hits photo – especially the one on which a blonde in a bikini grips a phallic fishing rod – was far more erotic than *Two Virgins* – and so was *Oh, Calcutta!*, a post-*Hair* revue that ran at the Roundhouse in Chalk Farm, embracing nakedness in clear light. In London's underground stations at the same time, a poster promoting a newly released flick, *Till Death Us Do Part* – based on the BBC comedy series – had an unclothed Warren Mitchell-as-Alf Garnett in pride of place – albeit covering up his member with hands and tobacco-pipe – and a caption thanking John Lennon for 'pioneering this form of publicity'.

It resonated too at the reception following Cilla Black's wedding in 1969 to her long-time fiancee, Robert Willis. Reading a congratulatory telegram from John and Yoko, the bride got a cheap laugh by adding the addenda 'Stay nude!' (rhyming and scanning 'Hey Jude': get it?).

In parenthesis, Arthur Ballard, John's former art tutor, painted a self-portrait of himself with his girlfriend. Entitled 'Punch And His Judy', it was in similarly self-revelatory vein to the cover of *Unfinished Music No. 1: Two Virgins*.

SEVEN YEAR ITCH

On a night flight from Delhi, after he and Cynthia left the Maharishi's yoga-ashram in Rishikesh, she instigated a discussion about seven year itches and extra-marital affairs. She was rather taken aback when her husband implied that he had been tempted by "the need to experiment". He didn't go into distressing details then, but, a few weeks later, Cynthia arrived home unexpectedly to find him 'with' Yoko Ono. Nevertheless, the marriage – which, thought Cynthia, "had been rolling along nicely with no fireworks" – wasn't over immediately, and, while she did not erupt with anger, Mrs Lennon fled the house to spend a few days taking stock at a friend's house in London.

On her return to Weybridge, she implored John gently to help her grasp what it all meant. Thinking aloud with the same questions coming up again and again, she seemed to be groping for some excuse to explain his conduct. After one particularly cliff-hanging silence came a frank exchange during which John confessed to have had erotic congress with over 200 other women since the wedding in 1962.

MARGO

Tony Dangerfield, one of Lord Sutch's Savages during their residency at the Star Club in 1962, recalled John Lennon knocking about with a rather portly German female called Margo. She was, apparently, not too fussy who she obliged as long as he was British and in a beat group. "It was funny to witness tearful goodbyes," chuckled Colin Manley of The Remo Four, "only to see someone's sweetheart holding hands with a member of the next group to arrive fresh from England."

Cognisant of the situation, Lennon learnt not to spoil a no-strings dalliance by getting jealous and sulky with Margo and other of his frauleins who needed someone who didn't care any more than he did.

Back on Merseyside, Cynthia might have guessed what he'd been up to abroad from signals that penetrated the tacit vow of silence that has persisted among bands of roving minstrels for as long as omerta has among the Mafia. Yet outlines were not to dissolve in a compartmentalised love-life for years until John met someone so self-possessed that, like Margo, she wasn't troubled about anything as tedious as wives or girls-next-door.

OH! CALCUTTA!

For the 1968 stage show, *Oh! Calcutta*, John contributed a comedy sketch about schoolboys masturbating together. His career summary in the printed programme ran: 'Born October 9, 1940. Lived. Met Yoko Ono 1966'.

THELMA PICKLES

The girl who preceded Cynthia in John's affections was Thelma Pickles, another art student. She was the one who, during a very public spat in Ye Cracke, the pub where the unconventional Arthur Ballard held some of his tutorials, snapped back at Lennon's ravings with "Don't take it out on me just because your mother's dead!"

After a few months, the two drifted apart. Some linked Thelma romantically with Paul McCartney for a while, but she married (and divorced) Roger McGough, who with John Gorman and Mike, Paul's brother, formed Scaffold, an ensemble that mingled poetry and satirical sketches, and were to score a UK Number One in 1968 with vexingly catchy 'Lily The Pink'.

Thelma was among the producers of the ITV series *Blind Date*, hosted by Cilla Black, prior to an emigration to Australasia.

TOSHI AND TONY

Yoko Ono's first husband was Toshi Ichiyanagi, a student at New York's Julliard School of Music. He was, more or less, 20-year-old Yoko's first boyfriend too.

Toshi was not, however, a hit with Ono's well-connected parents, Eisuke and Isoko, mainly because he was of decidedly proletarian upbringing. Their raising of this and other objections when their daughter announced that she wanted to marry the boy, led to Yoko leaving both her all-girls finishing school and the family home to live with him. Nevertheless, though Yoko's father – like mother Isoku – absented himself from the ceremony, he paid for the reception in a capacious city ballroom, and persuaded the Japanese consul general to make careful comment in an after-dinner speech.

The newlyweds moved into a loft conversion in downtown Manhattan, where Yoko – probably a virgin on her wedding night – soon allowed herself affairs with other men after convincing Toshi that theirs was an 'open relationship' whereby each would tolerate the other's physical infidelities. As a result, Yoko's first abortion was not to be her last as her espousal to Toshi muddled on.

Moreover, it become clear that Yoko's art and Toshi's avant-garde compositions weren't going to pay the rent. By

1960, he was tinkling piano in a cocktail bar, and she was a waitress in a Greenwich Village restaurant. Despite her husband's urgings to the contrary, she would not sponge off Isoko and Eisuke.

Dogged by financial insecurity, Mr and Mrs Ichiyanagi stayed together only because neither had sufficient motivation to do otherwise. Nevertheless, a joyless partnership drifted quickly into open estrangement, and, with Yoko unwilling to revive it, Toshi quit the apartment, the city and the country to attempt a new beginning in Japan.

As there was no sign of any formal dissolution of the marriage, Yoko's worried parents – who had now revised their previously unfavourable opinion of Toshi – hoped that the emotional chasm between daughter and son-in-law wasn't too wide for either to negotiate. To oil the wheels of reconciliation, Eisuke proffered Yoko the use of an 11th-floor apartment he had maintained in Tokyo.

The consequent reunion was correlated with Yoko's near-suicidal depression and her incarceration in a mental hospital. One afternoon, a hitherto unknown well-wisher strode into the ward. He was Tony Cox, a jack-of-all-trades from the New York art world, who wanted to write the first substantial newspaper article about Ono's activities. Flattered by the solicitude of this young man – who could speak fluent Japanese and was sufficiently taken with the Fascinating Older Woman to continue visiting her – Yoko was persuaded to re-encounter the outside world, sooner rather than later.

Cox became a frequent dinner guest at the Ichyanagis, who, so he perceived, were merely two old friends who used to be lovers. Toshi, therefore, felt less anger than amusement when Tony replaced him as Yoko's bedmate. For a while, the three dwelt in the flat as a menage a trois, but a disagreement over financial arrangements led Toshi to seek accommodation elsewhere.

When Yoko's parents heard of this latest folly, they urged her to kiss and make up with Toshi, even as the decree nisi was confirmed. There came a graver complication when Yoko became pregnant with Cox's child, and was not torn between resentment and panic. This time, she wanted to both give birth to and rear the baby.

In the week in 1963 when her decree absolute came through, Yoko wed Tony Cox without bothering to tell her parents. Appalled when he found out, Eisuke ordered Mr and Mrs Cox out of his Tokyo apartment. This was regrettable rather than disastrous as they soon found a cheap place in the aptly named Foreigner Village in Shibuya, a suburb that attracted overseas students.

Tony kept the wolf from the door as a film extra and teaching English to native business folk – and so did Yoko for as long as she was able before the arrival of her daughter, Kyoko Chan, on August 8, 1963.

ELEANOR BRON

An actress possessing both beauty and sparkling conversation, Eleanor Bron was 10 years John's senior. She had been – as far as there had been one – the female lead in *Help!*, and, of all The Beatles, she'd certainly been particularly pally with John.

As a teenager, he'd been something of a sexual braggart, perhaps masking a hesitancy with regard to women – as well as more generalised insecurities – by brutalising himself, coming on as the rough, untamed Scouser that he never had been. This habit was tempered by age, but still peeped out as it did during an episode of moody discontent with Cynthia when he admitted with quiet pride that – to coin a tabloid expression – 'intimacy had taken place' between himself and Bron.

Eleanor may have found it hard to hide a fascination with John – and there may have been long, dangerous moments when they spent a few hours alone together in The Beatles' Beverley Hills abode prior to a show at the Hollywood Bowl in August 1965. Nevertheless, she has always maintained that their friendship had no romantic edge to it – and there was no mention of anything untoward with Lennon in the auto-biographical content of her *Pillow Book Of Eleanor Bron: An Actress Despairs* (Methuen, 1987).

A TWIST OF LENNON

Through a solicitor, John attempted to stop the publication of his former wife's autobiography, *A Twist Of Lennon* (W.H. Allen, 1977). After failing to do so, he attempted damage limitation via a front page feature in the *Daily Express* by alleging that during his estrangement from Yoko Ono in the mid-Seventies, Cynthia had asked him to re-marry her. This was a sleight of verbal judo hinged on his misinterpretation of a remark made in his presence by Cynthia that she wished that Julian could have had a sibling.

Yet Cynthia's account of her years in The Beatles's inner circle was not the stuff of serialisation in one of the more lurid Sunday newspapers, but an honest, sympathetic and unsensational, if rather melancholy, presentation that concludes by exonerating John from blame for the breakdown of their marriage.

LIFE . . .

MENDIPS

John Lennon's childhood home 'Mendips', 251 Menlove Avenue, was built in 1933 as a three-bedroomed semi-detached house near the corner of Menlove Avenue and Vale Road in the Liverpool suburb of Woolton. In the mid-Eighties, a sign appeared outside reading OFFICIAL NOTICE. PRIVATE. NO ADMISSION. MERSEYSIDE COUNTY COUNCIL for the benefit of foreign visitors, mostly from the USA and Japan, pouring huge amounts into the English Tourist Board's coffers for conducted tours Beatle shrines around Merseyside.

However, in the Nineties the house was acquired by the National Trust who offer guided tours as part of a combined visit that also includes 20 Forthlin Road, the former home of the McCartney family.

BRITISH SOIL

When he departed from London's Heathrow Airport for the United States on Tuesday, August 31, 1971, how could John Lennon have known that he'd never return to his land of birth again? The closest he came, domestically if not geographically, was during his so-called 'househusband' years when, encouraged by his busy wife, he began spending lonely holidays progressively further beyond the shores of North America.

These included a stay in Hong Kong – before its secession from the British Empire – where, because it was one of the last places you'd expect to find an ex-Beatle, he discovered how pleasurable it was to be just another anonymous English tourist.

It was the same in summer 1980 when he spent several weeks in what was still the British Crown Colony of Bermuda. Among his activities there was watching the Queen's birthday parade in Hamilton, the island's capital, visiting a botanical garden that contained a freesia called Double Fantasy and – purportedly – composing some of the songs for what became the album of the same name.

BELT UP

Around 1969, John Lennon was seen in a black coat made entirely from human hair, apart from a woollen lining. It resembled the shaggy garment that Frank Zappa donned for the front cover of The Mothers Of Invention's maiden album, 1966's *Freak Out!*

Though Lennon said he would not wear animal skins, he made an exception when he disembarked from an aeroplane flight en route to one of his and Yoko's Bed-Ins. He was photographed by the waiting media in a brown leather belt to hold up the trousers of an otherwise all-white outfit. It was intended as a deliberate focus for criticism so that, according to karmic law, there would be balancing positive coverage for, hopefully, his and Yoko's peace campaign.

A HARD DAY'S NIGHT

The expression 'A Hard Day's Night' – the title of both The Beatles first film and the associated Lennon-McCartney A-side – was not original. It was coined obliquely by US singing actress Eartha Kitt in her self-composed 'I Had A Hard Day Last Night', B-side of 1963's 'Lola Lola' (EMI Columbia BD 7170).

JAPANESE TEARS

Paul McCartney spent nine days as Prisoner No. 22 in a Tokyo gaol, following his arrest on January 16, 1980 at Narita airport after a polythene bag of marijuana was discovered in his suitcase. A story persists that Yoko Ono, overwhelmed with spite after a strained telephone conversation with McCartney two days earlier, had – with her husband's approbation – prodded nerves to endure that when Paul and the other members of Wings reached the customs area, Paul, then a known and regular smoker of marijuana, would be the one to open his suitcase. Straight up! A mate of mine told me.

LOWRY LOOKALIKE

A pencil sketch by L.S. Lowry was sold for £25,000 to an anonymous collector in an auction by Bonham's of London on June 14, 2005. It was drawn in 1964, and depicted five standing figures, one of whom was noted to bear a striking resemblance to John Lennon, albeit a John Lennon anticipating the hirsute 1969 vintage, rather than a contemporaneous representation of the clean-shaven Moptop.

Caroline Oliphant, director of Bonham's picture department, commented, "I couldn't say if the new owner was a Beatle fan. There was a conversation about the similarity between the singer and the figure in the drawing, but at the time when the drawing was done, Lennon would not have looked like that."

Lowry, who died in 1976, was the subject of 'Matchstick Men And Matchstick Cats And Dogs', a 1978 British chart-topper by Brian & Michael (alias producer Kevin Parrott and songwriter Mick Coleman) with St Winifred's School Choir.

CONSTRICTED

When living in the Surrey stockbroker belt with Cynthia and Julian, John tended to absorb the latest avant-gardenings second-hand from Paul, resident in the heart of the capital, and unhobbled by marriage and fatherhood. "John was so constricted living out in Weybridge," lamented McCartney. "He'd come to London and say, 'What've you been doing?' and I'd say, 'I went out last night and saw Luciano Berio. That was quite cool.'"

The concert by the electronics composer at London's Italian Institute on February 23, 1966 had been too much effort for Lennon to drive the long and gradually more hated miles from Surrey.

"I've got this new Stockhausen record. Check this out," Paul would crow too, adding "I think John actually said, 'I'm jealous of you!' He just needed to get out of Weybridge, watching telly. It was his wife's fault. She just didn't understand how free he needed to be."

LENNON, WHERE'S YER TROOSERS?

On an annual holiday with Scottish cousins, the teenage Lennon, affecting a piping Highland trill, went shopping in Durness in a kilt he'd found in a chest-of-drawers. That he wisnae a bona fide Scot became obvious when he forgot to take his change in a tobacconists.

WINSTON TO ONO

While continuing to paint himself into a corner with Yoko, John went so far as to change his middle name by deed poll from 'Winston' – which he'd always disliked anyway – to 'Ono' on April 22, 1969 in a brief but formal ceremony, with Senor Bueno de Mesquita, the Commissioner of Oaths, officiating, on the flat roof of Apple's central London office.

Technically, however, he was re-registered – to his apparent annoyance – as John Winston Ono Lennon. However, if you tally all the o's in John Ono Winston Lennon and Yoko Ono, it comes to nine, John's lucky number (see LUCKY NUMBER).

BACKBEAT AND IAN HART

Backbeat vied with *Four Weddings And A Funeral* as the British movie of 1994. 'John Lennon' was played by Ian Hart – who had already portrayed a slightly older version of the same character in *The Hours And The Times*, a 60-minute film, shot in period monochrome, about Lennon and Epstein's 1963 holiday in Spain. It was shown on British television in 1992.

From Scala Productions, the makers of *Letter To Breshnev* and *The Crying Game*, *Backbeat* was on general release from April 1994.

The action took place against a backdrop of Liverpool's Regional College of Art and The Beatles' lengthy and ground-breaking residencies in Hamburg clubland in the early Sixties. The plot concentrates specifically on the often volatile relationships between John Lennon, his fated best pal Stuart Sutcliffe, and Stuart's girlfriend, Astrid Kirchherr. In this respect, Ian Hart, Steven Dorff (Stuart) and Sheryl *Twin Peaks* Lee all delivered moving performances that encapsulated the conflicting loyalties involved.

There were also lashings of sex, drugs and rock'n'roll (issued on a soundtrack album). Yet Ringo was hardly mentioned, and Paul, George and a brooding, malcontented Pete Best – and a hilarious Tony Sheridan – were almost incidental figures. Beatle trainspotters also alighted on several liberties taken with known fact. For all that, however, Backbeat captured a true feeling of 'being there', and is likely to stand as the most atmospheric evocation of both the young Beatles and the Hamburg scene that you're ever likely to see.

TITTENHURST PARK

When Tittenhurst Park, John and Yoko's 26 room Tudor mansion near Ascot, was put on the market in September 1973, it was purchased within a fortnight by Ringo Starr. John had recorded his *Imagine* album in the eight-track studio that had supplanted all but the pipe-organ in what had once been the main building's private chapel. The familiar promo film for the title track was shot in the drawing room.

HOLLAND

When 'I Feel Fine' was released in the Netherlands, Dutch Parlophone was in the final months of using the old logo – with the firm's name in large capital letters across the top of the label, and an additional '45' prefix at the start of the catalogue number. The second pressing stuck to the same fundamental design, except that it was printed in a more compact typeface. This is most noticeable on the song title. The Dutch 'I Feel Fine' also had a push-out rather than fixed centre.

CROSBY'S COCAINE CRASH

Portly Dave Crosby, former Byrd and the 'Crosby' in Crosby, Stills & Nash, slipped into a drug-induced slumber whilst motoring down the San Diego Highway on March 28, 1982. Uninjured after crashing into the central partition, he was arrested after police discovered a quantity of cocaine and associated freebasing 'works' plus a pistol that Mr Crosby said he'd purchased in the aftershock of John Lennon's shooting.

111

BEATLEMANIA

Viewing figures were at their highest when, straight after the prescribed hour of religious programmes on October 13, The Beatles inaugurated an edition of ITV's *Sunday Night At The London Palladium*, the central height of British show-business aspiration, with a teasing burst of 'I Saw Her Standing There' during a single rotation of the Palladium's revolving stage. Before the four reappeared for five numbers that they could hardly hear themselves play, the seated majority of teenagers fidgeted through endless centuries of formation dancing, US crooner Brook Benton, singing comedian Des O'Connor and the celebrated 'Beat The Clock' interlude, in which a woman was scolded by compere Jimmy Tarbuck for producing a large toy beetle from her handbag, thereby starting off another orgy of screaming.

The next day, the media was full of the 'overnight sensation', and the *Daily Mirror*'s Vincent Mulchrone came up with the word Beatlemania. The phrase stuck, particularly after it was the blanket description used to summarise The Beatles' fabled appearance in the Royal Command Performance three weeks later on November 4, 1963, notable for John Lennon's chirpy "rattle yer jewellery" instruction to the royal balcony.

POSERS

To workmanlike local groups like Cass & The Cassanovas and Derry & The Seniors, The Silver Beatles had been derided as 'posers', what with Lennon and McCartney's pretensions as composers, and Lennon and Stuart Sutcliffe's use of long words and mention of the likes of post-impressionist painter Modigliani and the Danish philosopher Kierkegaard into conversations.

They'd once been involved too in a fusion of poetry and

rock with beat poet Royston Ellis, who'd judged them to be "more of the bohemian ilk than other young northerners of the time". To a degree, John, Paul, Stuart – and, as far as he was able, George – played up to it. In one incident, they dumbfounded a member of another outfit in the dressing room by pretending to be reading Russian poetry to each other, each intoning and murmuring appreciatively in mock seriousness.

The Beatles' general 'arty' aura was a subliminal lure for Hamburg's young aesthetes, but, in a wider world, British pop stars – as opposed to British pop music – had started to move up in highbrow circles on their own soil, following Adam Faith's intelligent and eloquent showing on BBC television's inquisitorial interview programme, *Face To Face* in 1960.

However, the notion of the music as a viable means of artistic expression wasn't taken seriously amongst prominent intellectuals until the coming of The Beatles. In the first instance, 'quality' newspapers like *The Times* and *The Observer* were concerned almost exclusively with the hysteria that accompanied Beatles performances on the 'scream circuit', putting sniffy inverted commas around their name, followed by 'the Liverpool "pop" group' or similar explanatory phrase.

Then William S. Mann – who wrote for *The Gramophone* and usually covered classical music for *The Times* – entered the fray after a rather patronising fashion on December 27, 1963, the day after a prosy *Times* end-of-year cultural summary – attributed to 'Our Music Critic' – discussed John and Paul's 'Aeolian cadences', 'chains of pandiatonic clusters', 'sub-mediant key switches' and 'melismas with altered vowels'. Finally, the two were lauded as 'the outstanding composers of 1963' – two days before Richard Buckle of the

Sunday Times had them as 'the greatest composers since Schubert'.

On the horizon were Fritz Spiegl's *Eine Klein Beatlemusik*, a 1965 album of their hits arranged in the style of Mozart, a Beatles B-side, 'Yes It Is', analysed in *Music And Musicians* magazine, and comparisons of Lennon's prose in his first book, *In His Own Right*, to that of James Joyce and Edward Lear. To an enquiry about his use of 'onamatopaeia', Lennon – whose naivety may have been false – wondered what all this 'automatic pier' nonsense meant.

After flicking though *In His Own Right*, a Member of Parliament raised a question in the House of Commons about what he perceived as the poor standard of English language teaching in the north-west.

JOHNNY WINTER

Because he was an enthusiastic listener to Johnny Winter, a boss-eyed, albino Texan bluesman who'd had been catapulted from regional celebrity to the front page of *Rolling Stone*, Lennon contributed 'Rock 'N' Roll People' for 1974's *John Dawson Winter* album, a delayed reaction to a captivation with 1969's Grammy-winning 'The Thrill Is Gone', the only mainstream pop hit by B.B. King, one of the few surviving links between post-war blues and mid-Seventies rock.

TRANSPARENTLY NAKED

Kate Bush paid £4,000 for a perspex statue of John and Yoko as the 'Two Virgins' in a London rock'n'roll memorabilia auction in December 1981.

FATHERLAND

In his best-selling 1993 novel, *Fatherland*, Robert Harris mentions 'a piece by a music critic attacking the "pernicious

Negroid wailings" of a group of young Englishmen from Liverpool, playing to packed audiences of German youth in Hamburg'.

THE BIRTH OF THE BEATLES
According to one bizarre report, Pete Best was to play the teenage George Harrison in Dick Clark's made-for-TV *Birth Of The Beatles*. Actually, the drummer had been engaged as one of the project's factual advisors. The part of George went to a John Althan, while Stephen McKenna, another professional actor, took the more prominent role of John Lennon.

Covering the period from The Silver Beatles to the 1964 landing in North America, *The Birth Of The Beatles* was broadcast on British television three weeks after John's death. One of the more memorable scenes has 'Brian Epstein' explaining to McKenna in so many words that the parts of the group did not equal the whole – in which Lennon was the mind, McCartney the soul, Harrison the heart and Starr the flesh-and-blood.

VISA
John Lennon's US visa was revoked in March 1972.

MURALS
Three murals painted by John Lennon and Stuart Sutcliffe when they were art students were restored when the Jacaranda was re-opened in February 1996. Pete Best, who led the musicians performing on the night of the re-launch, commented: "Coming back here brings back memories, but they are good memories. There is nothing that makes me sad."

THE REVOLUTIONARY

Once, John had been active only after a detached, pop-starrish fashion in verbal support of pacifism, sharing the general disenchantment with the hippie counter-culture following the Sharon Tate bloodbath and the general dissipation of flower-power idealism. He said as much in an interview with *Student*, edited by future Virgin international corporation mogul, Richard Branson.

Yet Lennon had earned the approbation of this magazine's leftish readership partly through his pragmatic support of *Oz*, one of Britain's foremost 'underground' organs, after the saga of its notorious 'Schoolkids' edition climaxed at the Old Bailey. As well as testifying on behalf of the journal, he and Yoko composed and produced 'God Save Us' by Bill Elliot and the Elastic Oz Band, a 1971 single to help raise the defence costs for the celebrated obscenity trial. Elliot, the singer, was to be one of Splinter, a duo signed to George Harrison's Dark Horse label in 1974.

More far-reaching than 'God Save Us', however, was John's B-side to 1968's 'Hey Jude', 'Revolution'. However irresolute it would seem in retrospect, it was an assessment in song of many of the cultural, political and other undercurrents pertinent to the culmination of the Swinging Sixties. There was also both an alternative take and an item entitled 'Revolution 9' on The Beatles' eponymous double-album.

The longest track, 'Revolution 9' was included at the insistence of Lennon – who created almost all of it with Yoko. Only the recurring 'number nine' announcement lent it even vague orthodox form – though Lennon was to aver that "It has the basic rhythm of the original 'Revolution', going on with some 20 tape loops we put on, things from the archives of EMI. There were about 10 machines with people holding pencils on the loops. I did a few mixes until I got one

I liked. I spent more time on 'Revolution 9' than I did on half the other songs I ever wrote."

This patchwork of noises was assembled literally second by second from seemingly random sources, and was lauded, too, in the *International Times* as a send-up of John Cage's 'Fontana Mix', an 11-minute 'chance operation' tape collage recorded in 1958, and a classic of its kind. *Rolling Stone* called 'Revolution 9' 'an aural litmus of unfocused paranoia', but it reached a far, far larger audience than all its avant-garde antecedents combined – antecedents of which most of its buyers were unaware.

ELVIS

In 1975, John was seen at one of Elvis Presley's magniloquent pageants at 20,000 capacity Madison Square Garden, where he included songs that had fuelled the ex-Beatle's adolescent imaginings. Though the King was dismayingly portly in appearance, his voice remained intact. "If you half-closed your eyes," smiled Lennon, "it was heaven."

The two pop icons met just once – at Presley's Beverly Hills mansion in 1965. A prelude to this had been an after-hours session involving The Beatles and an outfit led by the King's former bass player, Bill Black, when both acts were in a Key West hotel a year earlier. There'd also been an exchange of presents when The Beatles dropped by the Hollywood office of Elvis' manager, Colonel Tom Parker.

Elvis received his English visitors like deified Caesar had the Gallic peasants. It was he who broke the silence, wondering whether The Beatles intended to stare at him all night. He'd met Herman's Hermits a few weeks earlier. They'd been shy too.

Then followed an obligatory blow with John and George on guitars, Elvis on bass, and Paul on piano. Three hours later, Presley bid The Beatles farewell, and gave them each a signed boxed set of his albums to date.

When Elvis returned to the stage in the later Sixties, John telegrammed his felicitations, but in an astounding and ramblingly respectful letter to President Nixon in the early Seventies, Presley asked to be enrolled as a Federal Agent in order to combat 'that hippie element' of which he considered Lennon to be a part.

When Elvis died, Lennon was asked for a comment and replied: "Elvis died when he went into the army."

3 GAMBIER TERRACE

Though not an official tenant, John stayed at 3 Gambier Terrace, located within earshot of the bells of both the Anglican and Roman Catholic cathedrals, and in the heart of what was then bohemian Liverpool. Dwelling there when The Beatles were in Germany in 1960, Johnny Byrne, now a television script writer, remembered 1960's cruel and bitter winter. "The water used to come up through the flagstones when it rained, and we were living on a loaf in which we made a hole and filled with a packet of chips, and which you carved up like a meatloaf.

"Outside were all these paintings of Lennon's. The landlord had come, and he and Stuart hadn't paid their rent, and the paintings were thrown out into the backyard where they were rotting. I went out there and got them, and I burnt I don't know how many to keep us warm.

"I hated Lennon. I cannot separate people and what they do from who they are. Lennon was unmitigatingly evil as far as I was concerned. Perhaps 'evil' is too strong a word, and I want to believe that people change, but he treated Cynthia abysmally. Even with all the pain of his background and all that, there was a type of total brutality in his attitude to people."

BOOTLEGS

John was a keen collector of Beatles bootlegs. One dated as far back as rehearsals in Liverpool in early 1960 with himself, Paul, George and Stuart Sutcliffe.

NUREYEV

On the Madrid stop of The Beatles' 1965 European tour, Lennon pulled swimming trunks over his head prior to greeting another hotel guest, ballet dancer Rudolf Nureyev, lately defected from Soviet Russia. He met fire with fire by deadpanning the subsequent conversational platitudes.

COPYISTS

In the mid-Sixties, it was common in even the most out-of-the-way town hall dance to witness a quartet that looked and sounded just like The Beatles, wearing collarless suits, sporting moptops that resembled spun dishmops whenever they shook their heads and went "oooooo", and making announcements in tortuous Liverpudlian accents freighted with apposite fab-gear-wack slang. Some either used insectile appellations – Termites, Moths, Grasshoppers and so on – or worked the word beat into their titles – Beatstalkers, Counterbeats, Beat-Chics, Beat Merchants ad nauseum.

After The Beatles had gone international, myriad similar local 'answers' crawled from the sub-cultural woodwork. A New Jersey quartet, The Knickerbockers actually scored in the US Top 20 with 1966's 'Lies', an uncannily precise duplication of the salient points of The Beatles' overall sound. No such luck came the way of more hastily assembled soundalike discs by the likes of The American Beatles, The Bug Men, John and Paul, The Manchesters, The Wackers and The Beatlettes (with 'Yes You Can Hold My Hand') – mostly by session musicians who probably bitched during coffee breaks about this Limey combo everyone's talking about.

Even Soviet Russia threw down a gauntlet with what translates as 'The Candid Lads'. In Japan, it was The Spiders while Los Shakers cornered Latin America. The latter outfit came closest to copying both the Look and the Sound, while the seven-piece Spiders ditched their covers of 'She Loves You', 'Help!' and so forth soon to develop an in-built and charmingly ingenue originality lacking in most other acts of their type. A few self-composed items, if dependent on what was going on in Swinging London, were delivered in Japanese; the earlier ones with an abandoned drive made all the more piquant in the light of official disapproval of pop, manifested in frenzied protest demonstrations when The Beatles 'polluted' the Budokan Hall, Tokyo's temple of martial arts, for three nights in summer 1966.

In reciprocation, The Spiders began a tour of Europe – which included a spot on *Ready Steady Go!* – the following October. Los Shakers, however, chose to consolidate their standing at home. Yet their take on British beat was more melodic than a lot of the genuine articles. Moreover, the pronounciation of their all-English lyrics is so anonymously precise that they wouldn't have been out of place in Hamburg's Star-Club or even the Cavern, circa 1963.

Still taking their cues from John, Paul, George and Ringo four years later, Caio (the 'John' figure), Hugo ('Paul'), Osvaldo ('George') and Pelin ('Ringo') adjusted to *Magical Mystery Tour*-esque psychedelia without quite getting the point, judging by 'The Shape Of A Rainbow' and 'I Remember My World', filling some of the dying minutes of a painstakingly-conceived turn-of-the-century CD retrospective containing all most UK pop-pickers will need to experience of Los Shakers.

For The Beatles themselves back in 1964, however, the most irritating repercussions of copying were isolated instances of local talent checkmating their originals in the charts. Off-the-cuff examples are Mississippi's Gants' lead singer, Sid Herring, sounding as Scouse as Lennon on a debut disc that xeroxed The Beatles' 1966 B-side, 'Rain' – and a New Zealand ensemble, Ray Columbus & His Invaders, issued a version of 'I Wanna Be Your Man' which sold more than those by both The Beatles – on a New Zealand-only A-side – and The Rolling Stones.

RUST NEVER SLEEPS

In the title track to a 1979 album, *Rust Never Sleeps*, Neil Young, was to whinge lines like 'It's better to burn out than to fade away . . .' that seemed to laud the banal live-fast-die-young philosophy involuntarily played out by Jimi Hendrix, Jim Morrison, Janis Joplin, Keith Moon, Sid Vicious and like unfortunates chewed upon and spat out by the pop industry. "For what?" inquired John during one of his last interviews. "So that we might rock? If Neil Young admires that sentiment so much, why doesn't he do it?"

INFORMATION ABOUT WHAT HE ATE

In *New Musical Express'* 'Lifelines' questionnaire early in 1963, John chose 'curry and jelly' as his 'favourite food'. In 1966, he was the first Beatle to at least try a meat-free diet. Later, he backslid, justifying himself in 1980 with, "We're mostly macrobiotic – fish and rice and whole grains – but sometimes I bring the family out for a pizza. Intuition tells you what to eat." He was then studying cookery books and baking bread; monitoring Sean's meals with a detail that dictated how many times each bite was to be masticated, and undergoing long fasts when only mineral water and fruit and vegetable juices entered his digestive system.

THE GOONS

Of all The Beatles, John Lennon was the loudest in praise of BBC radio's *Goon Show*. It was a development of the off-beat humour and topical parodies of an earlier series, *Crazy People*, which also starred Spike Milligan, Peter Sellers, Michael Bentine and Harry Secombe, veterans of entertainments organised by the Armed forces from their own ranks. Incongruous parallels, casual cruelty and stream-of-consciousness connections not only made The Goon Show different from mainstream series like *Educating Archie* and *The Clitheroe Kid*, but also ushered in that stratum of fringe-derived comedy that culminated in the late Sixties with *Monty Python's Flying Circus*. Aspects of *The Goons* became apparent too in the stylistic determination of such as Scaffold, The Bonzo Dog Doo-Dah Band and, less directly, The Beatles, particularly in their first two films, and in Lennon's associated slim volumes, *In His Own Write* and 1965's *A Spaniard In The Works*.

Many of their assorted oddments dated from the first broadcasts of *The Goon Show*, and a habit of John's that had intensified with exposure to the programme – of scribbling nonsense verse and surreal stories supplemented by Milligan-esque cartoons and caricatures. He was also among those irritating people who re-enacted *Goon Show* sketches the next day during the programme's high summer – which was reflected in UK hit parade entries in 1956 for its spin-off double A-sides, 'I'm Walking Backwards For Christmas'/'Bluebottle Blues' and 'Bloodnok's Rock'n'Roll'/'Ying Tong Song'. While these were released on Decca, solo records by Milligan, Sellers and Bentine – as well as two volumes entitled *The Best*

Of The Goon Shows – came to be issued by Parlophone, an EMI subsidiary, and produced by George Martin, elevated to headship of the label in 1954 at the age of only 29. By coincidence, the last Goon to scurry into the hit parade with a disc specifically designed to be funny was Peter Sellers in 1965 with his cod-Shakespearian recitation of The Beatles' 'A Hard Day's Night' – with 'Help!', preached like a sermon, on its B-side.

This lay in an unimaginable future back in 1959 when The Quarry Men's repertoire contained 'When You're Smiling (The Whole World Smiles With You)' sung by John in Harry Secombe's 'Neddy Seagoon' voice.

Lennon's liking for *The Goons* persisted for as long as he lived. When he was in the mood, their albums were on instant replay during his so-called 'househusband' years.

LUCKY NUMBER

It is the highest number that can be expressed by one digit. It is the number of cabalistic power (Hebrew), the number of perfection (Greek) and the superlative of superlatives (Sanscrit) – and the trinity of trinities (Christian). For Christians too, there are nine heavens, nine orders of angels and nine regions of hell.

Nine was also John Lennon's self-designated lucky number – even after a calamitous evening in a Las Vegas casino when he kept placing chips on that particular number on the roulette wheel.

He was born on the ninth day of the ninth month of the year – and so was his younger son. He died on what was the ninth day of the month, Greenwich Mean Time.

Though Yoko Ono was born on September 18, 1933, of greater significance to her Japanese parents was her birth number – which was nine on the basis of both the year and

1 + 8 + 2 + 1 + 9 + 3 + 3 adding up to 27, and two and seven equalling nine.

If you tally all the os in Yoko Ono and John Ono Winston Lennon, it comes to nine (see WINSTON TO ONO).

Among Lennon compositions are 'One After 909', 'Revolution 9' and No. 9 Dream' (which peaked at number 9 in the US charts). 'Imagine' spent nine weeks in the US Top 40 – as 'Instant Karma', 'Power To The People', 'Mind Games' and 'Beatles Movie Medley' did in Britain.

Finally, at the heart of 'When We Was Fab', a spin-off single from George Harrison's 1989 album, *Cloud Nine*, is an F augmented ninth chord – common to both his 'I Want To Tell You' from *Revolver* and Lennon's 'I Want You (She's So Heavy)' off *Abbey Road*. These two are adjacent if you list Beatles songs alphabetically.

MARTIN TAYLOR

As teenagers, noted British jazz guitarist Martin Taylor and his younger brother Bob saw The Beatles miming 'She Loves You' on television in 1963. "They came on with these funny haircuts, going, 'Ooooooh', and shaking their heads about," grinned Martin. "Bob and I were on the floor, holding our ribs; we thought it was the funniest thing we'd ever seen in our lives. We were laughing about it for weeks."

THE FOOL

In 1967, Lennon commissioned The Fool – four Dutch theatrical designers – to paint psychedelic patterns over the bodywork of his Rolls-Royce.

PRABHUPADA

In 1969, his Divine Grace AC Bhaktavidante Swami Prabhupada and his closest disciples – shaven-headed bhaktas dressed in orange sheets – in the Krishna Consciousness Society were accommodated in an annex in Tittenhurst Park, John and Yoko's newly acquired 80-acre estate between Ascot and Sunningdale. It was in these quarters that their hosts and George Harrison were conducted into the master's presence. Ono and the elderly Prabhupada did most of the talking – but his Divine Grace had a feeling that, during his Calcutta boyhood, he had known the then-unborn Lennon in a previous existence as a businessman-philanthropist.

By 1970, however, the Swami and his retinue had outstayed their welcome at Tittenhurst Park. Although Krishna devotees had been featured on the Plastic Ono Band's first single, 'Give Peace A Chance', their chanting of the familiar maha-mantra ('Hare Krishna Hare Krishna Krishna Krishna Hare Hare/Hare Rama Hare Rama Rama Rama Hare Hare') wasn't peaceful enough when it recurred at lengthy and regular-as-clockwork intervals on the Lennons' own doorstep.

THE GHOST GOES GEAR
The 1966 movie, *The Ghost Goes Gear*, featured The Spencer Davis Group, whose drummer, Pete York, seemed to have borrowed from the John Lennon's *Hard Day's Night* persona. In swimming trunks and admiral's greatcoat, Pete was very surreally Lennon-esque in his holding a bottle to his ear in comic dialogue with a hotel's room service.

A MIDDLE CLASS SWINGER
Lennon's first experience of LSD had been when a mischievous dentist – "a middle class swinger", he reckoned – concluded an otherwise pleasant evening round his house by slipping a mickey finn of acid into each of his dinner guests' coffee.

Learning they'd been spiked, John and Cynthia left hurriedly. In the Ad-Lib an hour later, the mental distortions of the drug became all too hysterically apparent as they crossed from reality into a wild dream.

Prior to his visit to the dentist, John had quizzed Brian Epstein about a 'trip' he'd taken. Brian could only elucidate in broad terms: it was a stimulating experience, but its effects varied from person to person, from trip to trip. For John, that initial paranormal sensation was the start of a fantastic voyage that would carry him to untold heights of creativity. Cynthia, however, surfaced from a quagmire of horror.

John underwent a second trip in California in the rented nerve-centre of The Beatles' next North American tour. Present too were Peter Fonda, members of The Byrds – and a journalist from *Daily Mirror*, who was ushered from the premises.

'She Said She Said', a Lennon composition on *Revolver*, was a memoir of this occasion. The finale of the same album, his 'Tomorrow Never Knows', also exuded knowledge of the 'psychedelic' inner landscapes of LSD. "Everyone from Brisbane to Bootle hates that daft song Lennon sang at the end of Revolver," complained the schoolgirls comic *Mirabelle*.

SUPERMARKET

With George Harrison and ex-Quarry Man Pete Shotton, Lennon was co-director of a Hayling Island supermarket until he resigned in 1969. The previous year, Shotton had been appointed manager of Apple's main boutique – which was closed in July after The Beatles decreed that all remaining merchandise was to be given away to the public, who, predictably, pounced on the shelves and hat-stands like hags at a jumble sale.

CHARLES MANSON

Awareness Records released *Lie*, an album by Charles Manson in 1970. The artist was, however, unable to promote the disc in person because, guilty of masterminding the Sharon Tate bloodbath by his 'Family' in 1969, he was serving a life sentence in California's San Quentin prison. Addled by drugs, demonology and group sex, The Family had had *The Beatles* double-album on instant replay as they prepared for the Tate murders, having deduced revolutionary directives in such as 'Helter Skelter', 'Piggies', and, especially, Lennon's 'Revolution' as well as such innocuous tracks as 'Rocky Racoon' and 'Blackbird'.

'Message' songs that Manson composed when inspired by the *White Album* were included on *Lie* which is less remarkable for its content than a sleeve that reproduces the cover of *Life* magazine but with the title altered to read *Lie* above a portrait of C. Manson, Esq. looking rather less than welcoming.

HAWAII

A holiday in Hawaii was cut short when the 'sexy Beatle' and 'the quiet Beatle' (as a local newspaper dubbed John and George), plus Cynthia and Harrison's fiancee, Pattie Boyd, were run to ground, and besieged in the Royal Hawaiian Hotel on Waikiki ocean front. Pursuing an exclusive, one brazen radio disc-jockey nosed through the babbling crowds outside in limousine, wig and tortuous Liverpool accent in an attempt to breach hotel security by impersonating Paul.

Finally, the Royal Hawaiian's advertising director put up the two couples in his Oahu beach house, but three brief hours of serenity there finished with a fresh onslaught of fans and reporters. Fleeing to Tahiti, John and George were delighted to roam the streets of Papeete virtually unnoticed, probably because the resort was in the last stages of its monsoon.

SEXY SADIE

In February 1968, the Lennons and the Harrisons were the advance guard of The Beatles' retreat to study meditation at the Maharishi Mahesh Yogi's yoga-ashram in the forested foothills of the Himalayas. They were both relieved and disconcerted to find, after a long and bumpy ride from New Delhi, not a compound of mud huts, but whitewashed, air-conditioned chalets, fully equipped to US standards, with an attached post office, laundry and dining room.

Among 60 other seekers of nirvana were Mia Farrow, Donovan and Mike Love of The Beach Boys. Famous and obscure, all would assemble clothed against the morning heat in the open-air amphitheatre for lessons that included practical demonstrations such as the apparent suspended animation that the Maharishi – born plain Mahesh Prasad Varma – induced in one of the staff. He spoke too of levitation, but no Beatle was to be around long enough to witness any. Gradually, the talks became shorter, and periods for individual contemplation longer.

The balmy quietude of the campus also yielded new songs from the pop contingent, many of them musical observations of other students. Lennon's 'Dear Prudence', for instance, was about Mia Farrow's shy sister, who "wouldn't come out. They selected me and George to try and get her out of her chalet, because she would trust us. She'd been locked in for three weeks and was trying to reach God quicker than anybody else."

Back in Britain, John would compose 'Maharishi What Have You Done', restructured as 'Sexy Sadie' for the *White Album*, as a put-down of Varma. Lennon had perceived that the Maharishi was all too human, telling him so to his face after a Beatles hanger-on accumulated enough tittle-tattle to speak to Lennon about Varma's apparent claudestine and earthly scheming for the downfall of the knickers of a female student – a North American nurse – and propositioning her with the forbidden meal of chicken as other cads would with a box of chocolates. Deaf to protestations of genuine innocence after confronting the guru with his infamy, Lennon – and his wife, Cynthia – left before the day was out. When they got back to England, rock'n'roll revival was in the air, and The Beatles took heed with their next chart-topper, 'Lady Madonna', reminiscent of Fats Domino. After being sucked into a vortex of experiences deeper than just plain folks could ever have imagined, John had surfaced with the certain knowledge that rock'n'roll was healing, inspirational. It had saved Lennon's soul more often and more surely than any amount of sermonising from vicar or guru.

In one of his last interviews, Lennon would profess that he still practiced meditation, but at least one so-called insider would claim that this comprised the swallowing of temazepan-like relaxants to induce the side-effects of stream-of-consciousness monologues, directed as much to himself as anyone listening, and mood swings from almost manic euphoria to deep self-reproach.

JOHNNY REMEMBER ME

John Lennon loathed the galloping propulsion of 1961's 'Johnny Remember Me' by singing actor John Leyton, and agreed with the unanimous 'miss' verdict on BBC television's *Juke Box Jury*. Yet Brian Epstein's instinct for a smash was demonstrated amply by his bold requisitioning of 250 copies for his North End Music Stores of what was to be lauded as the hit song of 1961.

JUST COINCIDENCE?

Did you know that Jim Morrison of The Doors' birthday was December 8, and on that selfsame day in 1980, John Lennon was assassinated? Exactly two years later, country-and-western artiste Marty Robbins died in Nashville, aged 57. Five plus seven equals 12. The twelfth Doors album to be released was *An American Prayer*, a collection in which the quartet's living members added music to an extant tape of Morrison reciting poems, most of them alluding to death in differing degrees. Lennon's twelfth solo entry in *The Guinness Book Of Hit Singles* is '(Just Like) Starting Over', his last before the cruel release of his spirit. Elvis Presley's *Flaming Star* – with a title track lyric insisting that when a man sees one, 'his time has come' – entered the UK album list on the fifth day of the seventh month (making 12 again) two years to the day before Morrison – just like Elvis – suffered a fatal heart attack in a bathroom.

In *A Hard Day's Night*'s most surreal scene, Lennon – in swimming trunks – is immersed in a foam bath. He vanishes beneath the suds to the consternation of The Beatles' road manager (played by Norman Rossington). The plug is pulled and the water drains away, but there is still no sign of Lennon until he appears, clothed in a bathrobe, at the bathroom door.

TIM HARDIN

Tim Hardin, acclaimed singing composer of 'If I Were A Carpenter', 'Reason To Believe' and 'Misty Roses' – all better known for other artists' interpretations – died on December 29, 1980, a passing overshadowed by that of John Lennon, three weeks earlier.

BILL HARRY AND *MERSEY BEAT*

In 1954, Bill Harry commenced his studies at Liverpool's

Regional College of Art where he met Stuart Sutcliffe – who he then introduced to another friend, John Lennon. In 1961, Bill founded and edited *Mersey Beat*, the country's first independent pop newspaper. Among its aims was the fostering of local musicians' self-expression beyond just hammering out 'Bony Moronie' down the Cavern. As well as John's Goonish early prose – usually under the alias 'Beatcomber', after 'Beachcomber', a column in the *Daily Express*, *Mersey Beat* was responsible for innovations later adopted by the national music press – including the first gig guide and photographs taken on location or onstage rather than posed studio shots.

"In the late Fifties, Stuart Sutcliffe and I were on the Students Union committee," recollected Bill, "and we used to book John's group – who were then undecided about a name – as support act for Saturday night dances. We also put forward the proposal that the Union used its funds to buy PA equipment for them to use.

"I was planning a new magazine called *Storyville And 52nd Street*, divided between trad and modern jazz. Yet I remember walking down from the college one lunchtime, and thinking why do a jazz thing when there's John's band, Cass & The Cassanovas, Rory Storm & The Hurricanes and all the other groups I'd got to know.

"Soon I began making notes of what was happening locally because people didn't seem to be aware of it. Bob Wooler [Cavern MC] and I got together and worked out that there were over 300 groups in Liverpool of every variety – not just four-man guitars-bass-and-drums outfits, but duos, trios, octets, all girl bands and all black vocal. Incredible!

"The word got round what I up to, and a civil servant called Jim Anderson lent me 50 quid to start *Mersey Beat*. The first issue was out in July 6, 1961. I did all the distribution myself. First, I went to the three main wholesalers – including W.H. Smith – who took some. Then I arranged for all the different venues to take copies. Next, I went to see the managers of the music stores, among them Brian Epstein at NEMS, who, incidentally, knew all about The Beatles months before this reputed guy coming into NEMS and asking for 'My Bonnie'.

"One of the things I was trying to with *Mersey Beat* was get the musicians to express themselves, and bring a flavour of their world across to the readers, what it was like on the road, playing the gigs and so on – because I was always interested in dragging the potential out of creative people. That's why I used to have John writing his 'Beatcomber' pieces. I used to encourage artists to send me letters from all over the place. In The Beatles, John and Paul were the ones who wrote from Hamburg, Paris, wherever they were."

PAUL IS DEAD

Supporting a widespread rumour that Paul McCartney had been beheaded in a car accident in 1966, and replaced by a doppleganger were what some heard as "I buried Paul", uttered in a daft voice by John in the last seconds of 'Strawberry Fields Forever' – and at the end of 'I'm So Tired' on 1968's *White Album*, doesn't Lennon mumble "Paul is dead. Bless him, bless him, bless him . . ."?

All that actually happened was that, on the day in question, McCartney cut his lip in a mishap whilst riding a moped.

THE BUST

A fur-coated woman had hollered, "You are a very holy man," when John and Yoko had emerged from Marylebone Magistrates Court on November 28, 1968, where John had been fined £150 with costs after pleading guilty to possession of substances – to wit, 219 grains of cannabis resin – contrary to the provisions of the 1966 Dangerous Drugs Act, section 42. A charge of obstructing the police in the execution of a search warrant was dropped.

He and a pregnant Yoko had been recipients of a narcotics squad pounce the previous month after they'd found a temporary refuge from self-aggravated media attention in a one bedroom flat, rented from Ringo Starr, on the ground floor of Montagu Square, a long Victorian block near Regent's Park. Rather than respond to the relentless bell-push, Lennon dialled The Beatles' solicitor, Nicholas Cowan before a squad of six Scotland Yard officers and an Alsatian sniffer dog gained access. When Cowan's car engine died outside the block, John and Yoko's persecutors were on the point of escorting them to Paddington Green police station to be formally charged and fingerprinted.

John had interrupted the search with "Can I ask a question: as the stuff is all mine, am I to be the only one charged?" He was concerned about Yoko's status as a resident alien and her possible deportation. Unacceptable to Sergeant Norman Pilcher, the plain-clothes officer directing operations, however, Lennon's excuse that what he and his men were about to discover was the lost property of some earlier tenant, maybe Jimi Hendrix or beatnik novelist William Burroughs, a former drug addict.

The first Beatle of three to be 'busted', Lennon was no longer above the law, MBE or not. The rip-tide of the drama – "an offence of moral turpitude" – was to wash over his attempts in the next decade to settle permanently in the United States, but in 1968, he accepted it as part of life's small change – and he didn't find the furore completely unwelcome as it gilded his image as the most way-out pop star in the firmament. He even used for the back cover of *Unfinished*

Music No. 2: Life With The Lions, his second LP with Ono, a Daily Mirror photograph of him with his arm round a distressed Yoko in the midst of policemen and morbid inquisitiveness outside Marylebone Magistrates Court. It was, however, to come home to roost when Lennon as a drug miscreant was obliged to keep re-applying for an extension of his visa in order to remain on US soil, and generally making things difficult when he wanted to settle permanently in the States.

Furthermore, stung by the unwelcome publicity, genteel Brymon Estates Limited, who leased the flat, instigated legal proceedings against Starr to bar the Lennons and other undesirables from using the premises. Although their battle was lost before the Queen's Bench, the affair left such a nasty taste in Ringo's mouth, that he sold his freehold interest in the place.

Incidentally, years later, Pilcher of the Yard – who also busted George Harrison and various Rolling Stones – was to be jailed for six years in 1972 for corrupting the course of justice, which entailed planting incriminating substances on several people.

JOHN BRATBY

One of Britain's post-war 'Angry Young Men', 'kitchen sink' painter John Bratby's works included 'The Toilet', 'Milk Bottles', 'Back Garden, Hardy Road' and further vistas of domestic squalor and sordid scenarios from the inner city – just the thing to nail over your mantelpiece.

Yet he was much admired by The Beatles, notably John Lennon and Stuart Sutcliffe – who, as art students, went through a phase of aping the expressionist style and "realist" content of a self-fixated and faintly unpleasant talent who

pioneered an art form that caught a mood of cultural radical-
ism that would first climax in the Swinging Sixties.

CAVERN COUNTRYSIDE COMEBACK

After the Cavern became as famous a Liverpool landmark as
the Pier Head, a shoal of further Caverns sprang up in other
regions until the Merseybeat craze petered out. However,
with the success of *Backbeat*, and The Beatles' own *Anthology*
documentary on Britain's small screen, an enterprising hotel
manager named Paul Cassin has resurrected the idea in the
subterranean restaurant club of the Swan Hotel in Thaxted, a
jewel of a village set amid the rolling hills, windmills and
mediaeval churches of rural Essex.

The new Cavern is, nonetheless, lent an authentic sheen
by dim lighting, arched ceiling and displays of memorabilia
that includes one of Ringo's drum kits. Yet, rather than the
mere soup and roll of yore, patrons' stomachs can be pam-
pered with such varied dishes as 'Kingsize Taylor's Rump
Steak' and 'Linda and Mac's Vegetarian Selection'. If you
fancy fish, there's the 'Pacemakers' Mersey Trawl' and, in
honour of the old club's arch-bouncer, 'Paddy Delaney's
Marinated Bake'. One of three 'Big Three Burgers' might hit
the spot if you only want a snack, and 'Epstein's Irish Cream
Bash' is among many 'Sweets For My Sweet'.

There were plans too for another contemporary Cavern
to be established in a 4,000 square feet establishment off
London's Leicester Square.

A pub called 'The Cavern' stands in the centre of a shopping arcade in New Malden, where London bleeds into
Surrey.

LENNY BRUCE

For those outside his native USA who've ever heard of him,

the late Lenny Bruce is remembered vaguely as some sort of blue comedian, trading in humour rather than humour. Nonetheless, under the auspices of Apple Records, John Lennon was the principal advocate of a subsequently jettisoned idea of marketing a 24-album retrospective of his in-concert monologues – with titles like 'White Collar Drunks', 'The Steve Allen Show', 'Don's Big Dago', 'How To Relax your Colored Friends At Parties' and 'Commercials' – in hip restricted code. A glossary booklet was to be included in the package.

FRIAR PARK

Richard Reed was an architect who restored Friar Park, George Harrison's mansion in Henley-on-Thames. "George was the most normal and friendly of men," commented Richard in 2002. "He introduced me to John Lennon, who was shorter than expected and not as pleasant as George. He just shook my hand and turned away."

JOHN KONGOS

Inspired by The Beatles – especially Lennon – this singing multi-instrumentalist left his native South Africa for London in 1966. After leading a group called Scrub through several flop singles, he was signed as a solo artist by Dawn Records who released 1969's *Confusions About Goldfish*. A transfer to Fly two years later gave Kongos – now an almost exact *Wedding Album*-period John Lennon lookalike, right down to round-lensed spectacles – a fleeting taste of pop fame when 'He's Gonna Step On You Again' and 'Tokoloshe Man', its uncompromising lyrics born of the socio-political unrest back home – each bounded to number four in the UK charts in 1971. John Lennon's only UK hit that year was with the similarly-motivated 'Power To The People'.

FAMILY . . .

THE MORNING AFTER IN BRITAIN

On December 9, 1980, Cynthia Lennon was staying with Maureen Starkey, Ringo's first wife, in her home in London's Maida Vale where they learned about John's death via Ringo from the Bahamas in the graveyard hours.

Shortly afterwards, Cynthia's third husband, John Twist – with whom she ran a restaurant, Oliver's Bistro, in Ruthin, North Wales – telephoned too. He did not tell a sleeping 17-year-old Julian – then a pupil at a local school – immediately. In the grey or morning, however, he read a statement, composed by Cynthia – then being driven back to Ruthin – to a waiting media: "I would like to say how terribly upset we are at the sudden and tragic death of John Lennon. Julian is particularly upset about it. It came so suddenly. Julian remained very close to his father in recent years, and is hoping to follow a career in music. He looked to John for guidance.

"For myself, I have always held John in the deepest regard since the divorce, and have always encouraged his relationship with Julian."

By the evening, Cynthia and a leather-jacketed Julian were flying from Heathrow to New York.

Only three days earlier, Lennon had made one of his regular Transatlantic calls to Aunt Mimi in the blue-curtained breakfast room of the house he bought her, overlooking the harbour in Poole, Dorset. She had been half-expecting a visit before Christmas. "You could never set a time with John. He seemed happier than he had in a long time," she commented hours after Yoko rang with the news at 7 a.m. "What could make someone do it," she asked, "to such a kind, happy, generous man? He was never 40 years old to me. He was just my John. My husband thought he had been put on this earth for his benefit. We did not have any children of our own. He was our son. I still can't believe it."

WATER EVENT

Coinciding with John's 31st birthday on October 9, 1971, Yoko's hastily organised 'Water Event' at New York State's Everson Museum of Art began a three-week run. A toilet customised to emit 'Working Class Hero' when flushed was among exhibits that filled three halls. The preview climaxed with a party at which – with Phil Spector on piano – the omnes fortissimo choruses of olde tyme rock'n'roll were mixed up with Beatles numbers.

TIME

Dave Clark's *Time*, a West End musical, was praised mostly for its spectacular visual effects. Its soundtrack featured Julian Lennon's overhaul of 'Because', a 1964 British B-side that was a US hit for The Dave Clark Five.

In 1988, the three surviving Beatles and Yoko Ono had slapped a writ for damages against the Five's drummer-leader's video company because clips of The Beatles had been shown on Channel Four's re-runs of ITV's *Ready Steady Go!*. There were also allegations that, likewise without permission, Clark was selling video compilations of Beatles material from *RSG!* footage.

CYNTHIA LENNON, ARTIST

In 1999, John's former wife exhibited her paintings at the KDK Gallery down London's Portobello Road. At the preview, Julian was there supporting his mother and Phyllis McKenzie, friends since student days in Liverpool when they breathed the air round others occupying that wide territory between realism and abstract expressionism. Phyllis leaned closer to the latter form than Cynthia – who included her own illustrations in her 1978 autobiography, *A Twist Of Lennon*.

The originals were on display in KDK for most of the summer, along with further visual mementos of her life at the storm centre of Sixties pop as well as later pictures bereft of such reference. Cynthia Lennon was not nominated for that year's Turner prize. Nevertheless, her work had a charm that begs the question: does only the surname prevent her from being an Artist In Her Own Right?

In attendance too at the preview were Jurgen Vollmer and Julia Baird, one of John's half-sisters.

MOTHER-IN-LAW

John's Japanese mother-in-law, Isoko Ono, shuffled off this mortal coil on January 23, 1999, aged 88. Yoko attended the funeral in Tokyo, sitting next to Eisuke, her ailing father, who'd been driven from his and Isoko's final home in Fujisawa, nearly 40 miles away.

CHARLES LENNON

John's uncle Charlie was half of an informal trio with John's parents, Freddie and Julia. With Charlie on mouth-organ and piano, and Julia on banjo, they used to sing Italian love songs in harmony during those 'musical evenings' before television became an indispensable domestic fixture.

Until his death, Charlie was a familiar and talkative figure, propping up the bar in the John Lennon pub, opposite the reconstructed Cavern and the Cavern Walks shopping mall.

He was also a frequent guest at Liverpool's Merseybeatle weekends, centred on the Adelphi Hotel near Lime Street railway station. He could usually be prevailed upon to sing to assembled fans, sometimes choosing his own composition, 'Ships Of The Mersey'.

SEAN AND ELIZABETH

Twenty-eight-year-old Sean Lennon was briefly the boy-friend of Elizabeth, daughter of Mick Jagger and Jerry Hall. "Sean looks so much like John now," beamed an approving Jerry, "and writes beautiful poetry." A chip off the old block, Sean held his own when fingering piano during musical soirees, known as 'Jerry's Jam Sessions', at the Jagger's home in Richmond, Surrey,

UNCLE NORMAN

At the age of 77, Norman Birch, John's uncle by marriage, was knocked down and killed by a car outside his Liverpool home on October 30, 1991, a few miles from where Julia Lennon, John's mother died in the same manner. Norman was the second husband of Julia's younger sister, Harriet. Her first, an Egyptian named Ali Hafez, died during a visit to the dentist.

'ME DAD'

With Billy Butler, Bob Wooler was the most omnipresent disc-jockey at the Cavern. After Brian Epstein suggested a formal meeting after a half-day closure on Wednesday December 3, 1961 at NEMS to discuss his possible manage-ment of The Beatles, they arrived late, and were accom-panied by 29-year-old Wooler, who John introduced rather doubtfully as 'me Dad'.

MIMI AND LOUISE

Louise Harrison, George's mother, was as fanatical about The Beatles as any Cavern dweller young enough to be her grandchild. Without embarrassment, she'd be down there, clapping and cheering, foremost among those blamed by John's Aunt Mimi for encouraging 'the stupid fool' and his so-called group.

MELTDOWN

On Sunday June 19, 2005, 72-year-old Yoko Ono appeared at London's Queen Elizabeth Hall as part of the South Bank's Meltdown festival, curated by Patti Smith.

To a tape loop of birdsong and female sexual ecstasy, Ono stepped through a screen depicting a 'sir and ma'am' mid-western US family with a black plastic bag over her head. Reaching the central microphone, she launched into a free-form monologue, 'I Want You To Remember Me', backed by a five-piece unit that included Sean on bass. Throughout the performance, she wore a number of different hats, selected from a small table. Musically, the set was drawn principally from her 2001 album, *Blueprint* – though she encored with 'Walking On Thin Ice' accompanied by special guests, The Pet Shop Boys. During one number, a member of the audience shouted, 'Liverpool: champions of Europe!' Ono did not respond.

The previous year, she scandalised the city when, as part of Liverpool's Biennial – as a tribute to John's mother – she plastered the city centre with images of some woman's mammaries and pudenda.

HALF-BROTHERS

After divorcing John's mother, Freddie Lennon remarried and fathered two further sons. David was born in 1969, and

Robin four years later. Both live in Brighton, and have never had any direct association whatsoever with their world-famous half-sibling (apart from David's visit with his parents to Tittenhurst Park when he was a babe-in-arms).

Born in 1947, Pauline, their mother, was 35 years younger than her husband, and seven years younger than stepson John. After Freddie died of cancer in 1976, she remarried.

THE GODFATHER

Before he mutated into a cross between Liberace and a male Edna Everage, Elton John, Sean Lennon's godfather, was first known to John as Reg Dwight, who kept the wolf from the door principally as a singing pianist for EMI's Music For Pleasure budget label, circa 1969–1970. His lack of individuality as a vocalist was ideal for xeroxing the hits of others. "Can you tell the difference between these and the original sounds?" asked the cunningly tacky sleeve notes to Reg Dwight's *Piano Goes Pop*, a 1994 compilation of such efforts. Indeed, you can.

JOHN LENNON'S DEATH

John Lennon died on November 21, 1968. He was the son of the soon-to-be ex-Beatle and Yoko Ono. His middle name was Ono, and he died at birth in Queen Charlotte's Maternity Hospital in London.

JOHN, PAUL, GEORGE, RINGO – AND CYNTHIA

In the August 1964 edition, *Confidential*, Hollywood's most scurrilous showbiz gossip periodical, assured readers that Cynthia Lennon had once been considered as The Beatles' lead vocalist. However, she hadn't even acquiesced to supplying onstage passive glamour as Dorothy Rhone, Paul

McCartney's former girlfriend, had when he persuaded her to sit on a bar-stool in the midst of the onstage Beatles.

Nevertheless, *Confidential*'s deathless claptrap aside, there was a Cynthia Lennon US Fan Club that found plenty to fill the pages of a monthly newsletter. "They wrote about what I wore to film premieres, and what I said," smiled Cynthia. "They were really sweet. I was only a housewife, but a very special housewife to them until divorce divorced me from The Beatles."

JULIAN AND CHUCK

"Doesn't he look like his Dad?" Chuck Berry had asked rhetorically when Julian Lennon was among special guests at *Hail! Hail! Rock 'N' Roll*, a televised concert in Berry's honour, organised by Keith Richards, at the Fox Theatre in St Louis in 1986.

In the early Seventies, Chuck's publisher, Morris Levy, had sued Julian's father for inserting a doctored line from Berry's 'You Can't Catch Me' in 'Come Together' on *Abbey Road*. By way of compensation, John revived 'You Can't Catch Me' and another Berry opus on 1975's *Rock 'N' Roll* LP. He also performed two numbers with Chuck when he and Yoko were guest hosts for a week on a US television chat-show in 1972.

HOLIDAY IN PARIS

A 21st birthday cheque from John's rich Aunt Elizabeth – known to him as 'Mater' – and Uncle Bertie Sutherland in Durness, Scotland was blown on a fortnight in Paris with Paul from September 29 to October 15, 1961. There, they witnessed a performance by black leather-clad Vince Taylor, a Hounslow youth who had spent his early youth in California. Some – including Screaming Lord Sutch – reckoned that Taylor had everything it took – except the voice – to be not only a second Gene Vincent, but a contender for Presley's crown. However, following 'Jet Black Machine', his only UK chart entry, he focussed on France where he surfaced as the darling of *le ye-ye*, a Gallic species of rock'n' roll enthusiast.

John and Paul also linked up with Jurgen Vollmer, a visiting exi from Hamburg, who convinced each to restyle his hair in a heavy fringe like Jurgen's own. After a decade of quiffing, it wouldn't cascade naturally into a pilzenkopf immediately, but the two wore it boldly around Liverpool on their return – and George steeled himself to do the same. It became known locally as a 'Beatle cut'.

'Mater' was proud to have played a part, however indirect, in the saga, but was disconcerted by her nephew's behaviour after he met Yoko, and gave him a tight-lipped reception when the pair visited in July 1968 with Julian and Yoko's daughter, Kyoko. He spoke to Mater of his hopes of obtaining custody of Julian after the divorce from Cynthia. "You've ruined all chances of that," retorted his aunt. "You've made your bed, now lie in it."

GRANDMOTHER MARY

Nicknamed 'Polly', Mary McGuire was John's paternal grandmother. Through a combination of lingering Victorian custom and hit-or-miss birth-control methods, they became the parents of eight children. A sister and five brothers survived infancy. The family lived in the Toxteth district of Liverpool. After Jack's death in 1921, Freddie, the fourth son, was placed in an orphanage, but was permitted to stay with his illiterate and poverty-stricken mother during school holidays.

PERCUSSION
Julian and Sean Lennon joined Steve Winwood onstage in New York during his 1983 world tour. Julian bashed a tambourine while his half-brother shook jingle-bells.

ON HIS MOTHER'S SIDE
Annie, John's maternal grandmother's surname was Millward until she married George Stanley, an amateur musician who worked in a dockside clerking office, in 1906. The couple's first two children died in infancy, but there followed five daughters. The fourth of which was Julia, John's mother, born on March 12, 1914. She lived at the family home until – and for periods after – she married Freddie Lennon in 1938.

NOT SUCH A SHRINKING VIOLET
Who could begrudge Lennon's ex-wife not fighting incentives to cash in on The Beatles' ticket? In 1996, while it may not have reactivated the Cynthia Lennon Fan Club, the release of a debut single, a revival of Mary Hopkin's chart-topping 'Those Were The Days', had precipitated a more far-reaching reassessment. Produced by Isle of Man neighbour Chris Norman, formerly of Smokie, for his own Dice Music label, 55-year-old Cynthia turned in a surprisingly appealing vocal – though perhaps not so surprising considering since from the age of 10 until she was 14, she was in the Hoylake Parish Girls Choir, and ended up as soloist.

"As an adult, I had no aspirations to be a singer," she said. "I didn't even sing around the house or in the bath, but a fax came through from a German record company who wanted to get in touch with Julian. So Jim, my partner, 'phoned back and said sarcastically, 'Julian's not here, but you can have his mother' – a throwaway comment that they answered in all seriousness, 'We can't do anything unless we know whether she can sing.' My voice had dropped about two octaves – probably because of all the cigarettes I smoke – but I'm game for anything nowadays, so I taped a selection of songs a capella. Chris asked to hear it out of curiosity, and said, 'Let's give it a whirl.'

"Chris thought 'Those Were The Days' would be a good song for a person of my age, and very pertinent, looking back – though I resisted a temptation to sing 'Once upon a time, there was a Cavern' on disc. For weeks after the session, I was on cloud nine. I was so pleased with it – and it was so creative for me. Six months earlier, if somebody had told me a record of mine was going to be on the radio, I'd have fallen about on the floor in hysterics, but – what's John's expression on *Double Fantasy*? – 'Life is what happens when you're busy making other plans.'

"At nearly every interview I've done, I've got one of the same two questions. 'Don't you think you're jumping on the bandwagon?' 'Won't people think you're cashing in?' I've tried for intelligent answers that don't sound aggressive, but no one other than me will ever understand. 'Cashing in' is earning a living as far as I'm concerned. Why should you feel guilty for working?"

BIRTHDAY
Ringo Starr presented Julian Lennon with a white horse on his 19th birthday celebration at London's Stringfellow's night club.

JULIA
Julia, John's natural mother, was killed on July 15, 1958 by a car with a policeman at the wheel who was late for his shift.

John was touched when 15-year-old George Harrison – admittedly forced by his own mother – arrived on the front door to offer his commiserations.

Julia was survived by boyfriend John Dykins and their two daughters, Julia and Jacqui.

Her first-born was to compose and record three songs dedicated to her, 'Julia' (on the *White Album*) and 'Mother' and 'My Mummy's Dead' (on *John Lennon: Plastic Ono Band*).

BABY'S HEARTBEAT

The content of *Unfinished Music No. 2: Life With The Lions*, John's second LP with Yoko, was concerned principally with Yoko's miscarriage in November 7, 1968. John's tape-recording of the dying foetus's heartbeat was one of the tracks. It was also offered to and rejected by *Student* magazine as a giveaway flexidisc.

John and Yoko's own pounding hearts underpinned their repeated utterances of each others name's for 20 minutes on autumn 1969's *Wedding Album*.

LENNON ON THE ROAD

Cynthia Lennon was the novelty headliner of *With A Little Help From Their Friends*, a revue that you shouldn't have missed but probably did, judging by the half-capacity audience at any given theatre en route round Britain. Other 'insiders' on the bill were more hardened to both poor turnout and general stage exposure than Cynthia – notably The Merseybeats, who appeared with her ex-husband's group more times than anyone else.

Sub-titled "A celebration of The Beatles by those who were part of the story", this package was not a convention-like evening of selective reminiscences, but a musical spectacular coalesced by scripted patter and short cameos like

Cynthia's then-boyfriend Jim Christie scuttling on as 'Brian Epstein' during a spot by the soundalike Silver Beatles, who focus on their blueprint's apogee as a local attraction.

The Silver Beatles captured the required ramshackle grandeur. Other *With A Little Help From Their Friends* antics, however, appear lame or peculiar in cold print today – such as a sketch in which matronly Cynthia was embraced by The Silver Beatles' Andy Powell as youthful 'John' in his high-buttoned suit – but they made sound sense in the context of proceedings that closed on an emotional high with the assembled cast joining the Merseybeats and a jubilant audience, blasting up chorus after rowdy dah-dah chorus of 'Hey Jude'.

At the last hurrah in Eastbourne's Congress Theatre, a palpable wave of goodwill had washed over Mrs Lennon the instant she walked centre-stage before a backdrop mock-up of the graffiti-covered Cavern wall. The customers, typically English, loved Cynthia for being a survivor – and for reaching her half-century in such great shape too. Moreover, from being a softly spoken outcast after the world and his wife were confronted with a John they'd never known before in 1968, Cynthia, if no Ken Dodd, proved a self-assured, likeable compere – and dropped sufficient reserve to open the second half with 'Those Were The Days'. Shorn of the Welsh soprano's incongruous maidenly innocence, Cynthia's pining for past times was as poignant as 'Free As A Bird'.

SHOWBUSINESS ANCESTORS?

Most families tend to forge a real or imagined genealogical links with someone at least vaguely famous. Thus John Lennon claimed affinity with a Liverpool-Irish grandfather, Jack Lennon (1855–1921), who'd emigrated to North America, and been in a touring revue called Andrew

Robertson's Kentucky Minstrels prior to returning to Merseyside as a pub entertainer.

Furthermore, Julia, John's mother, plinked the banjo, and taught him a few less-than-full guitar chords before she died.

John kept quieter about The Lennon Sisters – Dianne, Janet, Kathy and Peggy – who came to national attention in the USA on light orchestral supremo Lawrence Welk's weekly television show, all scripted grinning and harmless fun. When the Sisters were signed to Coral – Buddy Holly's label – in 1955, they became known as singers of catchy tunes with jaunty rhythms, as demonstrated by their US Top 20 entry the following year with 'Tonight You Belong To Me' with Welk and his orchestra – though it peaked several positions behind a version by Patience and Pridence. Later Lennon Sisters releases included 'Teenage Waltz', 'Sad Movies' – and a 1964 album, *Great Folk Songs*, attributed to The Lennon Sisters & Cousins.

FREDDIE CASHES IN

In the mid-Sixties, The Beatles' renown was such that any direct connection with them was a handy bartering tool to rake in a bit of loot. After 18 years as the most shadowy figure in John's life, his father, Freddie Lennon, then a kitchen porter in a Surrey hotel, reappeared with his hands open in March 1964 on the Twickenham set of *A Hard Day's Night*, The Beatles' first movie. After a short conversation with a bemused John, he left and some money was – through John – mailed to his place of work.

Freddie capitalised further by selling his life story to some-thing-for-everybody *Titbits* magazine, and then recorded a self-composed single, 'That's My Life (My Love And My Home)', coupled with 'The Next Time You Feel Important' (a revival of a number by 'Forces Sweetheart' Vera Lynn) for

Pye late in 1965. He was accompanied by some former Vernons Girls – who'd released a 45 entitled 'We Love The Beatles' in 1964 – and, glad of the session fee, Folkestone's Loving Kind, veterans of poorly waged spots low on the bill of round-Britain package tours on which they were never sure of sleeping in proper beds each night. Their lead guitarist was Noel Redding, later bass player with The Jimi Hendrix Experience.

'That's My Life' received a modicum of airplay, and made an appearance in pirate Radio London's 'Fab Forty'. John cornered one of the station's executives at a New Year's Eve party to protest about the championship of the record – and, allegedly, Brian Epstein – at John's instigation – prodded nerves to curtail any further headway. Freddie was determined to tell his boy about what must surely be some mistake, and arrived at Kenwood, the mock-Tudor mansion in Weybridge where John, Cynthia and Julian now lived. Outside a locked front door, Freddie would be at a loss to understand his son and heir's deafness to his pleas. So began a family feud that would never quite resolve itself.

LENNON VERSUS WYMAN

Bored tabloid journalists came up with a non-story that 'Lennon's', Cynthia's short-lived Covent Garden restaurant – serving dishes such as 'Penny Lane pate' and 'Rubber Sole and chips' – was in fierce competition with ex-Rolling Stone Bill Wyman's Kensington eaterie, 'Sticky Fingers'.

MOTHER BY PROXY

"Lennon's no hero of mine," glowered Johnny Byrne, now a TV scriptwriter, but one of Liverpool's arch-beatniks in the early Sixties, "His one saving grace was that Stuart Sutcliffe – a painter who I respected enormously – liked him, and Stuart knew Lennon in a way that no one else did at the time."

A blue abstract by the late Sutcliffe was given to John after he and Bill Harry paid a surprise visit to the Sutcliffe family home in Sefton Park after a Beatles concert at the Liverpool Empire on November 8, 1964. Stuart's mother also returned *How To Draw Horses*, a book John had won at primary school and lent to Stuart. "John kissed us all and was most tender and affectionate," said Mrs Sutcliffe – Millie – who would tend to claim him vicariously as a son by proxy. That was, nevertheless, the last the Sutcliffes ever saw of John Lennon. His aunt, however, stayed in touch until Millie died in Tunbridge Wells on December 8, 1983 – three years to the day after John had been shot dead.

THE HEAD OF THE 'FAMILY'

During a dinner party at Ringo and Maureen's home in Ascot, circa 1973, the company almost leapt out of their skins when, suddenly, George Harrison declared his deep love for Maureen. Calculated to wound his own wife rather than compliment a bright-red Mrs Starkey, the bombshell would reverberate beyond the tense dining room. Yet Maureen's later reciprocation of her guest's affection wouldn't pain Ringo as much as he'd imagined it would. It would have hurt more if George had been underhanded about it. What did it matter? Ringo and Maureen were washed up anyway. If anything, John – as self-appointed Beatles paterfamilias – was more annoyed, ringing George from the States, purportedly, to chastise him for this 'incest'.

SEASON OF GLASSES

A depiction of Lennon's blood-stained spectacles on the sleeve were among the more dubious items that assisted Yoko Ono's 1981 *Season Of Glass* to the edge of the US Top 50.

A less-publicised opportunity to keep herself in the public eye arose in 1993 when she sanctioned an exhibition in Los Angeles entitled "Family Blood Objects" which contained bronze casts of Lennon's bullet-ridden shirt, and replicas of his shattered glasses. These could be bought as a joy forever for, respectively, $25,000 and $18,000 each.

NO RELATION

As production exercises only, console boffin Joe Meek was behind 'I Learned To Yodel' – an attempt to board the bandwagons of both The Beatles and Frank Ifield, a yodelling balladeer at the height of his fame in 1963 – by a certain Jimmy Lennon and his Atlantics, issued in January 1964. Such was the glamour of The Beatles too that *Mirabelle*, a schoolgirls' comic, appointed as features editor a lad named Pete Lennon, largely through his surname too.

In 1970, Punch, a record label of no great merit, released 'Ram You Hard', a single of reggae persuasion by John Lennon & The Bleechers. Around the same time, an IRA terrorist named John Lennon made brief headlines. I don't think it was the John Lennon or even a relation either.

Mrs Sheila Lennon is the manager of a pharmacy in Reading, Berkshire. Her Japanese sister-in-law's maiden name is Ono.

WEDDING NIGHT

On the evening following his and Cynthia's wedding, John was performing with The Beatles at Chester's Riverpark Ballroom.

CAMBRIDGE 1969

Before she met John, Yoko had found a niche in the furthest extremes of avant-garde jazz through vocal gymnastics that owed much to the free choral babbling and odd tone clusters of Schoenberg and Penderecki – whose best-known work, The Devils Of Loudon, has Satan sniggering from within a nun's bowel – as well as seitoha (Japanese clasical music). Her flexibility was not dissimilar to that of Subbulaksmi, an Indian diva seen frequently on Western stages, and, more appositely, Hagiwari, the blind female koto virtuoso and singer, recepient of Juyo-Mukei-Bunkazai, one of the highest cultural posts the Japanese government could assign.

Purely on the strength of sonic vibrations, some of Yoko's sung offerings bore uncannily close resemblance to certain popular classical pieces. On ITV's Classical Brit Awards, 37-year-old mezz-soprano Cecelia Bartoli's excellent rendition of Vivaldi's 'Anchi'il Mar Par Che Sommerga' aria could have been lifted by time-machine from one of the milder recitals by Yoko Ono in the company of respected free jazzers, notably Ornette Coleman, using her voice as a front-line horn on a par with the alto saxophonist's honking daredevilry.

It was there for all to hear during a performance on a Sunday in March 1969 at the Lady Mitchell Hall in the University of Cambridge with Lennon at her feet, back to the audience, either holding an electric guitar against a speaker – causing tinnitis-inducing spasms of feedback – or twiddling with some electronic device to create bleeps, flurries, woofings and tweetings to complement peep-parps from Danish saxophonist John Tchikai, the clatterings of drummer John Stevens (of The Spontaneous Music Ensemble) and Yoko's screeches, wails, kitten-esque mewlings and Nippon jabber – as if its abstract sentiments couldn't be expressed through expected melodic and lyrical articulation. Titled 'Cambridge 1969', the result – all 27 minutes of it – filled one side of

Unfinished Music No. 2: Life With The Lions, Yoko and John's second album, one of only two releases on the Apple subsidiary, Zapple.

On the night, the ensemble had been cynosures of an unnerving stare from what looked like a gigantic photograph of about five hundred silent and undemonstrative students. A minority absorbed it in a knowing, nodding kind of way, whilst blocking out an impure thought in the tacit question: 'How could anyone like this stuff?' Mal Evans (on 'watch') apart, everyone onstage, even Beatle John, was an artist after all, and it became obvious that the greater the effort needed to appreciate this squiddly-bonk music, the more 'artistic' it must be.

After clapping politely when the row ceased, the highlight of the night was the opportunity afterwards to chatter about how 'interesting' it all was, this 'spontaneous music' that was an avenue to drop names like 'Edgard Varese', 'Ornette', 'John Cage' and 'Luciano Berio'. There had once been a time when many venues had been closed shops to The Beatles because their music was unpalatable to jazz fans, the sort of attitude John couldn't stomach: that air of pitying superiority towards those that didn't like it, or enjoyed it for what was derided as 'the wrong reasons'.

THE BIG SISTER

George Harrison's sister, Louise – who emigrated to the USA in 1956 – was invited from her Illinois home to New York's besieged Plaza Hotel where The Beatles were staying during their first visit to North America in February 1964. "We were going to meet at the airport, but it would have been difficult for us to link up what with all the media descending on it. George booked a room for me at the Plaza, but he had such a bad throat that the hotel physician, Dr

Gordon, suggested that using the already present sister made more sense than hiring a nurse."

Thanks to Dr Gordon and Louise's ministrations, George was able to go the distance on *The Ed Sullivan Show* with The Beatles. "My first impression of the other three," recalled Louise, "was that I felt like I had an extra bunch of brothers. As the only daughter of four children, I'd gravitated more towards football with the lads than girly pastimes. As a result, I was very much at ease. Paul was the diplomat, very gracious. He'd been doing tape-recordings on the plane, funny fake interviews. Ringo was delightful too – and so was Cynthia Lennon – but I was scared of John because of his sarcasm, his biting sense of humour, really nasty. I mentioned this to mum, but she said that basically he was OK. When he behaved like that, he was covering up for his own insecurities. It was an interesting lesson to me – because it made me better able to cope with a wide variety of people on the right level – because you can understand and empathise with their frailty, and, consequently, they respond to you in a much nicer way."

AUNT YOKO

Not long after her husband's murder, Yoko Ono soon returned to her status as a subject of barbed invective. Some of it was prompted by what had been understood about her grip on the purse-strings of John's fortune and her inter-related attitude towards both long-time employees and his blood relations. For instance, her and Lennon's tarot reader – albeit useless in the light of what occurred on December 9, 1980 – was directed to vacate his apartment in the Dakota, and Julian Lennon was to receive assorted – and, according to him, long overdue – monies only after much to-ing and fro-ing of solicitor's letters.

There was no love lost between him and his father's relict.

While noting her and Sean's attendance at the funeral of Lennon's 88-year-old aunt, Mary "Mimi" Smith in December 1991, others from John's side of the family felt the same. "Dad bought his half-sister Julia and her family a house to live in," grimaced Julian by way of example. "As soon as Dad passed away, Yoko went and took their home that had been given them by him, and then gave it to charity with no compensation for them."

A PHOTO OPPORTUNITY

The ease with which Julian Lennon secured a British Top 10 hit in 1984 might be the most renowned instance of affinity to The Beatles kick-starting a musical career. In April the following year, he and his backing musicians played three nights in a theatre in New York. During this brief residency, Julian and his mother were spotted at a dining table, sharing the proverbial joke with his half-brother and Yoko Ono. "It was after Julian's first appearance in New York," clarified Cynthia Lennon, "and he and I, Yoko and Sean were there – so for the photographers, it was a classic coup, but though we both wed the same man and both had a child by him, we were and still are worlds apart."

WIDOW'S WEEDS

Ono and Sean had had no qualms about walking onstage after Elton John sang his tribute, 'Empty Sky (Hey Hey Johnny)', at a Madison Square Garden concert in August 1982, but there'd been an earlier, if less conspicuous, indication that Yoko was rising from a half-death of Dakota seclusion, comfort eating and, as a newly bereaved Japanese wife was supposed to do, scissoring off 30 inches of the black frizz that had hung like a cloak over her shoulders since God knows when.

When an invitation arrived for her to collect a Grammy for *Double Fantasy* at the National Academy Of Recording Arts and Sciences, Yoko laid out an all-white trouser suit, made the most of what was left of her hair and had a cosmetic miracle performed on a careworn face. She wouldn't let John down. In the summer of 1981 too, she'd become actively involved in the creation of Strawberry Fields, a two-and-half-acre garden memorial to John in Central Park (which was to open formally in 1984), and had undertaken her first media interviews since *Double Fantasy*.

When going through such motions, she revealed the existence of a boyfriend in Sam Havadtoy, a Hungarian interior decorator and antiques dealer, 20 years her junior. Not long after John's death, Havadtoy had been commissioned to renovate Yoko's properties in New York and Florida. With Sean's approval a key point in his favour, Havadtoy was to be Yoko's "constant companion" for longer than all of her three husbands put together.

She was also back in the office, doing deals on the telephone – and in the studio recording a new album, *Season Of Glass*, with most of the crew who'd been on *Double Fantasy*, though they weren't as willing participants as they'd been when John had been there too. Yoko also hired and then dispensed with the services of Phil Spector – who'd only agreed to help for old times' sake.

The following September's *It's Alright (I See Rainbows): An Air Play By Yoko Ono* embraced a milder shock tactic on the back cover, whereby a spectral John stands via trick photography, next to Yoko and Sean in what looks like a recreation ground. This particular collision of art and commerce was meant to stress Ono's belief that Lennon remained with her spiritually.

The day-to-day mundanities of selling records always

boiled down to Lennon and The Beatles – which was why *It's Alright* missed the chart, and *Milk And Honey: A Heart Play* – with remaindered *Double Fantasy* items sung by John its chief selling point – came within an ace of number one in Britain and elsewhere. Even the associated *Heart Play: Unfinished Dialogue* – 40 minutes of Yoko and, crucially, John chatting to *Playboy* magazine – harried the lower regions of the US list late in 1983.

Lennon was kept before the public too via Yoko's compilation and marketing of 1986's *Skywriting By Word Of Mouth*, a slim volume of his latter-day prose. If less directly involved, her input had left its mark on a television film, *John And Yoko: A Love Story*, which tied-in with the fifth anniversary of his passing.

She was to have a far more pronounced hand in *Imagine: The Movie* and its soundtrack from her exploratory soliciting of Warner Brothers to her frame-by-frame scrutiny of hundreds of hours of footage, familiar and otherwise, from the Dakota archives such as the early Seventies sequence from Tittenhurst Park that would be used every time the title opus song was re-promoted as a chartbusting single, most recently during 1999's Christmas sell-in.

SEAN AND LIVERPOOL

When visiting England in January 1984, Sean Lennon and his mother flew to Liverpool airport, which droned by the windswept mud banks of the Mersey. On this, Sean's first visit to the Holy City, they were driven by limousine along the A561, lined with chimneys belching the chemical waste that fouled the air and waterways, and slum overspill estates including the one in Speke where George Harrison had grown up.

Elsewhere too, Sean, after checking in at the Adelphi, the

city centre's plushest hotel, was now old enough to feel pangs of received nostalgia for locations to which he'd hitherto only drunk in second-hand as germane to his sire's legend during a walkabout accompanied by a camera crew as if he and his mother were visiting royalty. Chaperoned by a record company executive, they were filmed seeing Penny Lane, Quarry Bank school, the art college and the patch of unofficial countryside along Mathew Street where a 'Cavern' was to be reconstructed next to the Cavern Walks shopping mall, and opposite the John Lennon pub where Charlie, Sean's great-uncle – John's late father's brother – was to regale tourists on The Beatles' scent with endless reminiscences about what John got up to in nineteen-fifty-forget-about-it.

If not as conspicuous, the principal flag-waver on John's mother's side of the family was frail Aunt Mimi, who happened to be staying with a sister in Rock Ferry on the other side of the wide, bleak Mersey. This was convenient for a duty-call from Yoko and Sean.

The pilgrimage to the north-west concluded with a gift from Yoko of a six-figure sum to Strawberry Fields Orphanage. The place closed on May 31, 2005.

JOHN'S STEP-DAUGHTER

Yoko Ono's second husband, Tony Cox, resurfaced in her life in January 1986 via an article based on an interview with him in the USA's glossy *People* magazine. Nine years earlier, it read, he and Kyoko, the only issue of their marriage, had been roped into the Church of the Living World in Los Angeles. Cox then pledged himself to The Walk, an extreme 'prepare-to-meet-thy-doom'-type sect, that preached that John, Yoko and their sort were 'the personfication of evil'.

If unsettled by her former spouse's disobliging comments

in print, pragmatism ruled as Yoko appealed through an open letter in *People* – signed 'Love, Mummy' – for Kyoko, now 23, to make contact.

Kyoko was 39 when she deigned to reply. Next, a permanent reunion with her mother started with a guarded conversation from Denver, Colorado, in November 1997, a few days before the birth of Emi, Yoko's first grand-child. Encouraged by her husband, a devout Christian, Kyoko was amenable to a face-to-face meeting, which took place in New York several months later.

Joint heirs to Yoko and the late John's multi-million dollar estate, Kyoko and Sean are as different vocationally as a sister and brother could be. She's a teacher while he's followed his father into showbusiness.

BATTLE OF THE GIANTS: JULIAN AND SEAN

The toast of the New York club scene in the mid-Nineties was Cibo Matto, a duo of expatriate Japanese feminists – singer Miho Hatori and general instrumental factotum Yuka Honda, who happened to be Sean Lennon's then-girlfriend. Quite an accomplished musician himself now, Sean went on the road with Cibo Matto as bass player, having formed Ima (Japanese for 'now'), a trio that backed his mother on both her new album, *Rising*, and the 1996 tour that promoted it. The stock Oldest Teenager In The Business, Yoko remained as au fait as Sean and Yuka with the latest sounds, dancing away the night of her seventieth birthday to The Strokes, Moby and, of course, Cibo Matto and Ima.

Though possessing a degree in anthropology from Columbia University, Sean secured a recording contract partly on the strength of his talismanic surname, thus furnishing his pop career with the same best and worst start as half-brother Julian, whose 1998 album, *Photograph Smile*, was in the shops the same month as Sean's 13-track *Into The Sun* debut. Produced by Yuka, it was, he reckoned, "about the happiness of being in love and the craziness that goes with it".

Conducting himself with observed good humour when Sean's effort was deemed by most to be a more profound critical success than his own, Julian said he liked *Into The Sun*, qualifying this with: "He knows he's comfortable for the rest of his life. It's not like he feels a hunger, but he's talented." He laced this with a flavouring of sour grapes so piquant that a story persists still of Yoko pulling strings to have *Photograph Smile* dropped from radio play-lists.

JOHN'S JAPANESE IN-LAWS

On the threshold of his 30th birthday in 1932, Eisuke Ono began a courtship of 21-year-old Isoko Yasuda to the bemusement of her Buddhist parents, worried about both Eisuke's Christianity and, to a greater degree, his apparent aspirations to make a living as a pianist.

Mr and Mrs Yasuda kept the distressing information from the family matriach, Isoko's maternal grandmother, widow of Zenjiro Yasuda, who'd founded the Yasuda Bank – which, specialising in property investment and insurance, had thrust tentacles into Europe and North America. His nepotism had been quite naked. Son-in-law Iomi Teitairo – Isoko's father – had been groomed as his successor, and the old man may have pulled strings to have Iomi elevated in 1915 to the Japanese equivalent of a earldom, albeit on condition that he changed his surname by deed-poll to Yasuda.

Isoko was the youngest of eight offspring of Iomi Yasuda and Teruko, Zenjiro's eldest child. The family dwelt within a stone's throw of the royal palace on Tokyo's loftiest hill, and possessed a motor-car long before nearly every everyone-who-was-anyone had one too.

In alliance with his own parents, the Yasudas prevailed upon Eisuke to shelve any notions about a musical career, and to follow in his father-in-law's footsteps as a banker. So it was that Eisuke Ono came to wed Isoko Yasuda, and buckled down to work at the Yokohama Specie Bank. One materially appealing part of the deal was that he would commute from a comfortable home on the vast estate of his bride's lately bereaved grandmother.

It was here at 8.30 on the snowy morning of February 18, 1933 – the Year of the Bird – that Eisuke and Isoko's first baby – a daughter – entered the world. It would have been more desirable if their eldest had been a son, but they were satisfied that Isoko's labour had been straightforward and that the newcomer was robust. They named her Yoko – which means "Ocean Child" – as she was a Pisces.

While her father was a remote figure in her infancy, her dutiful rather than doting mother trusted nappy-changing, feeding and other mundane aspects of her child's rearing to various of the 30-odd servants, who aped the manners of those in the palace by, for example, kow-towing in and out of the mistress's presence.

Among Yoko's earliest recollections of Eisuke was him measuring the span between the tips of her fingers and her thumb, and pronouncing that it wasn't long enough for her to be a keyboard player of any great merit. Nevertheless, he hired a piano teacher and was delighted to hear that he was getting his money's worth as Yoko was both keen to learn and self-contained enough to disassociate the music from the drudgery of daily practice.

Eisuke was more impressed with Yoko's speaking and singing voice when she acted out Japanese folk myths and narrative ballads that she had picked up from the servants, much to the disgust of her mother, who hoped that her daughter would absorb the English language as well as tap-dancing, Shakespeare and further disparate aspects of Western culture after she started at the creme-de-la-creme Gakushuin or Peers' School, where her classmates were to include Akihito, the Crown Prince.

Yoko hoped so too – because she was and would always be anxious about parental approval, even when she had, ostensibly, escaped from their clutches. Thus she endeavoured to exhibit no resentment when Isoko's selective and hard-won attention focussed on a new baby, Keisuke, a boy born in December 1937, as, in the name of Akihito's father, Emperor Hirohito, Japan's involvement in the forthcoming war loomed.

The tension would climax with the Japanese assault on Pearl Harbour, and as it grew, all signposts for the Onos pointed to perhaps the last place you'd expect to find them – New York, where Eisuke had been ensconced for weeks in the Yokohama Specie's Manhattan outlet where he'd been so overwhelmed with work that members of his own family could only speak to him by appointment via his secretary.

A local accent began to peep out of Yoko's pronunciation of the tongue she was encouraged to speak in the classroom both in the USA and, to a lesser extent, after the Onos, in the fever of mobilisation, were able to slip away unchallenged in the New Year.

Technically, there were five of them. Isoko was pregnant again, and her final confinement would produce Setsuko, a sister for Yoko and Keisuke, just before Christmas 1941.

All the members of Yoko's immediate family, parents and siblings, were alive when she met and married John Lennon in the late Sixties.

FRIENDSHIP . . .

STUFFED DOG
As a house-warming present when he moved to Weybridge, Ringo Starr received a stuffed dog in a glass case from John.

THE NEXT DAY
On BBC television's evening news on December 9, 1980, George Martin was asked if he considered Lennon a great musician.

"He was a great man," replied the diplomatic Martin.

Another George – Harrison – let it be known that "After all we went through together, I have – and still have – great love and respect for John. It is an outrage that people can take other people's lives with a gun when they haven't got their own lives in order."

Accosted by a camera crew, Paul McCartney, almost at a loss for words, had uttered: "John was a great guy. I won't be going to the funeral. I'll be paying my respects privately. I want everyone to rally round Yoko." To this, he tacked on: "It's a drag," and mentioned that he would carry on as scheduled with a day's work at a studio console.

On the printed page, he seemed too blithely fatalistic, but McCartney felt curiously empty, having assumed that there'd always be another chance for him and John to face each other with guitars in hand. What with Wings in abeyance, and John back in circulation again, the notion of 'Lennon-McCartney' – as opposed to 'Lennon and McCartney' – hadn't been completely out of the question.

When pressed for a comment, Mike McGear of The

Scaffold, Paul's brother, felt that "John's death has robbed a whole generation. The last years of his life were dedicated to worldwide peace, and he ends up being gunned down." On tour in the Far East, fellow Liverpudlian Cilla Black was "shattered. To me he will always be the eternal rocker."

Another old pal from Merseyside, Allan Williams conjectured "how strange and tragic how three people connected with The Beatles have died so young: first Stuart, then Brian and now John."

In common with everyone else who cared too, Gerry Marsden remembers the very moment he received the news. In the Marsden household on the Wirral, he was wrenched from sleep at 5 a.m. on that shifty morning by Liverpool's Radio City. His reaction was akin to that of George Harrison down in Henley-on-Thames. With phlegmatic detachment, Gerry "went back to sleep. It wasn't the kind of information I expected to turn out to be true."

On waking up, Gerry, like Paul McCartney, decided that "the only thing to do was to carry on with some kind of routine to get rid of the shock." He chose not to cancel a business meeting in Bradford in the teeth of constant attempts to reach him by the media. Yorkshire Television landed the biggest scoop by persuading Gerry to sing 'Imagine' on *Calendar*, an early evening magazine.

Earlier that same day in London, Mick Jagger was "absolutely stunned. I knew and liked John for 18 years, but I don't want to make a casual remark about him at such an awful moment for his family and his millions of fans and friends." Similarly, on behalf of The Who, Roger Daltrey's "heart goes out to his family, wife and sons."

Most succinct of all, however, was that of Jerry Lee Lewis, who'd been chatting over transatlantic telephone to British record producer Guy Stevens when the news leapt from the radio he'd had on in the background: "I don't believe it. I don't fucking believe it."

THE FIRST GEORGE KNEW OF JOHN

At Dovedale Primary School, John was in the same form as Peter, one of George Harrison's elder brothers (as well as comedian Jimmy Tarbuck and television newsreader Peter Sissons). However, George was first aware of John as a boy who lived in one of the posher houses on his Saturday morning delivery round for Mr Quirk, a local butcher.

MICK JAGGER

On hearing rumours of Mick Jagger's forthcoming wedding in May 1971, John Lennon chuckled, "He can't afford it. The Stones would be all over!"

PHOTOGRAPH

After Ringo Starr's self-composed (with George Harrison) 'Photograph' topped the US Hot 100 in December 1973, John mailed an affable telegram asking his old drummer to "write me a number one tune".

BIRDS OF A FEATHER

Partly through their manager Georgio Gomelsky's friendship with Brian Epstein, The Yardbirds secured a support spot at The Beatles' 1964 Christmas residency at London's Hammersmith Odeon. Though their lead guitarist passed the time of day with George Harrison along backstage corridors, George "didn't really get to know" the youth who was to be both his best friend and his first wife's second husband.

John Lennon, however, came to seek the particular company of The Yardbirds at the Odeon, recommending a revival of 1962's 'Any Day Now (My Wild Beautiful Bird)' by US soul singer Chuck Jackson as their third single.

However, drummer Jim McCarty's most vivid memory of Lennon was during an intermission when he observed John standing at the top of a fire-escape at the back of the building in the teddy-bear suit he wore for a comedy sketch that filled part of the show. The Beatle was considering the purchase of one of a fleet of limousines from a London showroom. As it was inconvenient for a pop star such as Lennon to visit the garage during opening hours, the proprietor had arranged for the vehicles to nose past the twilit foot of the metal stairway.

In the event, 'Any Day Now' was not recorded by The Yardbirds, who preferred million-selling 'For Your Love' (though this choice precipitated blues purist Clapton's departure from the group). In August 1965, however, 'Any Day Now' was the debut single by The Alan Price Set. Though it was a 'turntable hit' on pirate radio, it missed the British Top 50.

WRONG TURNING

In 1976, when all four ex-Beatles happened to be on the same land mass at the same time, they were tempted to call the bluff of Lorne Michaels, producer of *Saturday Night Live* – a TV satire transmitted from New York – who said that if they agreed to play together before his cameras for the prescribed Musicians Union fee of $3,000, he'd squeeze them onto the show. He didn't mind, apparently, if John, George and Paul wanted to "pay Ringo less".

As they were all fans of the show – a sort of North American cousin to *Monty Python's Flying Circus* – "they decided to rebound on us", according to its host, Chevy Chase, "and appear on the show. I never dreamt they'd take up our offer."

Depending on whose account you read, unfortunately – or, perhaps, not so unfortunately – Lennon and McCartney ordered a taxi, but decided they were too tired. Alternatively, Paul, Ringo and George arrived for the show, but John's chauffeur drove to the wrong studio, thereby capsizing what might have been, had they kept their nerve, the ultimate practical joke.

THE FOURMOST

John Lennon was a periodic attendee at a London Palladium season in May 1964, starring Cilla Black and fellow Merseysiders, The Fourmost. With Paul McCartney, John had composed Cilla's first Top 40 entry ('Love Of The Loved') and The Fourmost's first two ('Hello Little Girl' and 'I'm In Love'). The Fourmost were also offered 'It Won't Be Long', opening track of *With The Beatles* – as Gerry Marsden was 'Hello Little Girl'.

JOHN AND JONES

After The Beatles had experienced The Rolling Stones for the first time – at Richmond's Craw Daddy club on April 21, 1963 – John was keen to pick up tips from Brian Jones, their self-appointed leader, on how to improve his mere "blowing and sucking" on the harmonica.

The two became friends to the extent that they were spotted sharing the proverbial joke at the *Fourteen Hour Technicolor Dream* on April 29, 1967, a 'happening' to raise funds for the underground newspaper, *International Times*. During one of the few intermissions, the promenading audience was treated to a turn by Yoko Ono and a female model, rendered supine by some narcotic or other, seated on a step-ladder with a spotlight shining on her. John and Brian watched Yoko hand onlookers a pair of scissors each, and directed to cut away the other woman's garments. Not everyone was impressed. "Yoko Ono's happenings were boring," grimaced *IT* associate John Hopkins. "She was the most boring artist I've ever met."

John had told Brian about Yoko at the Ad-Lib where, on another night, Jones, the worst for drink, felt able to confide his fears about being sidelined by the other Stones. "They're destroying me," he babbled to John one night in the Ad-Lib. "I started the band, and now they keep trying to squeeze me out." The arch-Beatle stared appraisingly and with not a little exasperation: "Look, I get sick of Paul sometimes, of the way he's forever trying to dominate me. You have to stand up to these ego maniacs. You can't just get smashed out of your box. Look, how about if I ask you to play sax or something on some Beatles records? That'll make them sit up and take notice, won't it?"

Gathering strength from this proposal, Jones progressed from joining in the omnes fortissimo choruses to 'Yellow Submarine' to honking woodwinds on two Beatles B-sides, 'Baby You're A Rich Man' and 'You Know My Name (Look Up The Number)'.

After Brian left the Stones in summer 1969, he made a half-serious attempt over several telephone conversations to cajole John to quit the disintegrating Beatles and join him in the formation of a 'supergroup'. Lennon, however, changed the subject.

"Well, he was different over the years as he disintegrated," was John's final analysis after Brian drowned a few weeks later. "He ended up the kind of guy that you'd dread he'd come on the phone – because you knew it was trouble. He was really in a lot of pain – but in the early days, he was all right."

JIMMY NICOL

It had been necessary for Ringo Starr, suffering from pharyn-gitis and tonsillitis, to be hospitalised for 12 days at the start of The Beatles' 1964 world tour. The three functioning musi-cians with George Martin and Brian Epstein resolved the dilemma by hiring Jimmy Nicol, one of the workmanlike but individually uncredited Ghost Squad on *Beatlemania*, a cheap Pye LP of anonymous Beatles covers. Moreover, he had adopted a moptop, and was drumming presently with Georgie Fame's backing Blue Flames.

In Abbey Road's Studio 2 on the afternoon before opening night in Copenhagen, Jimmy ran through the set during two hours of curt tuition, mainly from John Lennon, who, smiled Nicol, "gave me a great build-up" onstage throughout the assignment.

Rather than remain huddled under bedclothes, Starr was touched by a telegram of the "miss you" variety from the other three and, not wishing to inconvenience them more than was necessary – or miss any of what was still great fun – he rose after not much more than a week in bed, the minimum time advised by the doctor. He caught up with The Beatles in Melbourne, Australia, watching them per-form with Nicol at the city's Festival Hall that evening.

Afterwards, there was a party to thank Jimmy and welcome back Ringo, who was to complete two remaining dates in Melbourne, another in Sydney, three in New Zealand, and two nights back on the mainland in Brisbane from where, on July 1, 1964, The Beatles would fly back to England.

It was from Brisbane too that Jimmy Nicol returned home on June 16. By cruel contrast to his 12 days as a Beatle – when "it seemed that the whole population had turned out to meet us" – he'd been greeted only by his wife and infant son when he landed at Heathrow.

Jimmy had never been entirely comfortable socialising with The Beatles. "The boys were very kind," he would reminisce, "but I felt like an intruder. You just can't get into a group like that." He spent most waking hours off-duty with support acts such as Sounds Incorporated – in whose ranks then, incidentally, was Trevor White, destined to play 'Ringo Starr' in the Australian production of a musical, *Lennon*, in 1988.

Later, when The Beatles and Jimmy (now leader of The Shubdubs) found themselves booked one night in the same British theatre, neither party made the effort to pop over to the other's dressing room for a chat.

FRANK ZAPPA

The discerning Frank Zappa of The Mothers Of Invention regarded *Abbey Road* as "probably the best mastered, best engineered rock'n'roll record I've heard", albeit adding "which has nothing to do with the material on the album."

Lennon and Zappa were introduced on June 6, 1971, the afternoon before the Mothers appeared at the city's Fillmore East auditorium. The two hit it off immediately, and John was invited – with Yoko – to perform with Frank and his group that evening.

The Lennons came onstage for the lengthy final encore. One side of their 1972 double-album *Sometime In New York City* embraced this guest spot with Zappa. It contained a driving revival of 'Well (Baby Please Don't Go)', a 1958 B-side by The Olympics, which, also with Lennon on lead vocal, had been in The Beatles' repertoire from 1960 to 1962.

A different mix and edit of the performance was to be included on Zappa's 1992 album, *Playgroup Psychotics*.

ADRIAN HENRI

During the Nineties, small fortunes changed hands for Stuart Sutcliffe oil paintings, not in the murmur of museums or art gallery committee rooms but in the unrefined bustle of pop memorabilia auctions. Nonetheless, at a 1990 Sutcliffe retrospective at Liverpool's Bluecoat gallery, poet and painter Adrian Henri, an art college friend of both Sutcliffe and Lennon, acknowledged that "Some of the self-directed Hamburg abstracts look as good today as when they were painted and as relevant. His posthumous reputation doesn't need the glamour of his former band to enhance it."

Henri's painting The Entry Of Christ Into Liverpool depicted The Beatles, and a poem, 'New York City Blues (For John Lennon)' was selected for *Adrian Henri: Collected Poems* (Allison & Busby, 1986).

WHO BROKE FIRST?

It's unlikely Ringo Starr looks back on the making of the *White Album* with much affection, although there was no discernable animosity at first. However, according to engineer Ken Scott, under Paul McCartney's instructions during brass overdubs to 'Mother Nature's Son', "Everything was going really well, and then John and Ringo walked in – and, for the half-hour they were there, you could have cut the atmosphere with a knife." Since the advent of Yoko Ono, and John's co-related growing indifference to Beatle activities, McCartney's attempts to motivate the group had backfired, his boisterous determination translated as barely tolerable bossiness.

An irksome lecture from Paul about a fluffed tom-tom fill was the delayed-action spark that inspired Ringo to stalk out of Abbey Road mid-session. Sooner than any Beatle imagined, he'd testify in court he'd had a surfeit of Paul's schoolmasterly perseverance, while the withdrawn John let him get away with it. That their weary drummer's resignation was more than a registered protest or one of his infrequent fits of pique became clear with his verbal notice to John – who Starr still regarded as 'leader' – and then Paul. Yet neither they nor George dared credit this extreme strategy by the recognised standard bearer of group stability.

During a fortnight in the Mediterranean on Peter Sellers' yacht, the stress of the preceding weeks evaporated, and, for all that had driven him from the group, it made abrupt sense to ring up and report for duty again. Half expecting a row, the returned prodigal was greeted at Abbey Road with a drum-kit festooned with remorseful flowers and 'welcome back' banners.

A second departure took place – for much the same reasons – when The Beatles were in the throes of recording *Let It Be*. One bone of contention was George's progress as a composer. Whereas John could get away with 'Revolution 9' and Paul with 'granny music', a gradually more irritated Harrison, like a travelling salesman with a foot in the door, had to make a pitch with his most enticing samples: "The numbers I think are the easiest to get across, and will take the shortest time to make an impact."

The *Let It Be* movie was to contain "a scene where Paul and I are having an argument and we're trying to cover it up," observed George. "Then in the next scene, I'm not there." Not knowing why this was, the reviewer for *The Morning Star* was still aware of "George Harrison's shut-in expressions".

An outcome of the incident was that McCartney could no longer assume that he held the group in the hollow of his hand. Soon, with his maiden solo album underway, he'd be preparing a press release that almost-but-not-quite proclaimed his departure from The Beatles. He'd also be setting wheels in motion for the formal dissolution of Messrs. Harrison, Lennon, McCartney and Starkey as a business enterprise. Yet months before the writs were served, the group had, to all intents and purposes, broken up. John, more preoccupied with Yoko than the group, tendered privately his own resignation well before Paul.

SINGULARGE

As the completion date for *A Spaniard In The Works*, John's second book of verse, stories and drawings, loomed, he picked the brains of others. George Harrison assisted with 'The Singularge Experience Of Miss Anne Duffield', a send-up of Arthur Conan Doyle.

In reciprocation, Lennon lent the most sympathetic ears when Harrison presented two compositions for possible inclusion on the soundtrack of *Help!* A week prior to the recording dates in February 1965, the pair spent half the night polishing up 'I Need You' and 'You Like Me Too Much'.

"Well, it was 4.30 when we finally got to bed," enthused George, "and we had to be up by 6.30. What a fantastic time!"

Much as Harrison appreciated his help, Lennon began to resent his tacit obligation: "He came to me because he couldn't go to Paul. I thought, 'Oh no. Don't tell me I have to work on George's stuff too. It's hard enough doing my own and Paul's.'" To John, George was "like a bloody kid, hanging around all the time. It took me years to start considering him as my equal."

THE QUARRY MEN

John's skiffle outfit, The Quarry Men, consisted of friends and friends-of-friends messing about for the hell of it. Most members weren't that dismayed when engagements were confined mainly to wedding receptions, youth clubs, Church fetes and street parties, or when circumstances obliged them to leave – because the group was seen as a vocational blind alley, a folly to be cast aside on departure from school to the sadder real world.

However, pianist John Duff Lowe's growing inclination to remain a Quarry Man was mostly because of geography: "I lived in West Derby, on the opposite side of Liverpool to all the others. Whereas Paul could easily bike round to John's house, it was a journey on two buses for me. I didn't tend to get involved during the week. Also, my parents – like all parents then – were paranoid that I was going to turn into a teddy-boy, pushing bottles into people's faces and creating mayhem in the clubs. The uniform indicated someone who was looking for trouble – and John used to dress in what you'd loosely describe as teddy-boy gear. He gave the impression of being like that, but he was actually quite a nice guy.

"George Harrison came into the group a week after me. Prior to us, the band had Rod Davis on banjo, Eric Griffiths on guitar, Pete Shotton on washboard, Colin Hanton on drums, Len Garry on tea-chest bass, John Lennon and, right at the end of the skiffle era, Paul McCartney.

"George was playing in other groups, and I was getting fed-up with the hour-long journey from West Derby to rehearsals, and my girlfriend used to moan. Also, A-levels came along – plus parental pressure. The Quarry Men wasn't that special a thing."

Yet the power structure whereby George Harrison was to be subordinate to John and Paul for as long as they stayed together was founded during The Quarry Men era – so you'd read when the myth gripped harder – on the handshake that had now formalised the Lennon-McCartney songwriting partnership.

ONLY YOU

Mastered in 1993, a hitherto un-issued album by Harry Nilsson contains an arrangement of The Platters' 'Only You' – a rediscovered duet with Lennon, circa 1975. Ringo Starr's single of the same song reached the British and US Top Thirties in 1974.

FAME

Omnipresent in the States in the mid-Seventies, David Bowie was attempting to re-invent himself as a blue-eyed soul man when recording 1975's *Young Americans* LP. It was through this that John Lennon made his most iconoclastic contribution to that decade's popular culture. As his 'lost weekend' approached its Sunday evensong, he'd been invited to a Bowie session for a resuscitation of 'Across The Universe' – from *Let It Be* – in New York. There, he ended up co-writing 'Fame', *Young Americans'* infectious US chart-topper, with David and an awestruck Carlos Alomar, a highly waged guitarist of urgent precision and inventiveness whose apprenticeship in James Brown's employ qualified him for the house band at the trend-setting Sigma Sound complex from which had emanated Philadephia's feathery soul style earlier in the decade.

All three writers of 'Fame' would be present at a Grammy awards ceremony at the Uris Hotel in New York on March 1, 1975 (with John sporting a label badge that read just ELVIS).

However, when the album had just been pressed, John took Paul and Linda McCartney to David's apartment to hear it. According to the latter's then-girlfriend, Ava Cherry, the visit was rather confrontational: "There was this tense feeling. I don't think Linda liked David very much, and the feeling was mutual." The dialogue deteriorated further when, after listening to the new record twice through, Paul snapped, "Can we hear something else?" This request was all the more barbed because of John's friendship with Bowie and his pronounced creative investment in *Young Americans*.

THE NURK TWINS

During the Easter holiday of 1960, Lennon and McCartney spent a week down south in McCartney's married cousin's pub, The Fox and Hounds, on the junction of Westbourne Road and Gosbrook Road in the Berkshire village of Caversham – between Reading and Henley-on-Thames – even performing as a duo, The Nurk Twins, in the public bar on April 23.

JOHN AND ROY

Of 'Please Please Me', John recalled that, in its downbeat lyric and nascent slowish tempo, "It was my attempt at writing a Roy Orbison song." The faster version that was the making of The Beatles also raked up Orbison in its flights of falsetto.

When a jet-lagged Orbison arrived for the first date of his 1963 tour with The Beatles, he'd barely sat down in his dressing room at the Slough Adelphi when Lennon and Brian Epstein asked if he'd got a minute: "They said, 'How should we bill this? Who should close the show? Look, you're getting all the money, so why don't we – The Beatles – close the show?' I don't know whether that was true or not, whether I was getting that much more than they were. It wasn't that much – and the tour had sold out in one afternoon."

No one could pretend that Roy was the foremost cause of

this quick profit. The Fab Four's 'From Me To You' would be at number one for the duration of the tour. Nevertheless, Orbison was no lamb to the slaughter. "He'd slay them," gasped Ringo, "and they'd scream for more." Underlying the inherent good nature of British pop's most optimistic period, however, was Roy's memory of the opening night when "John and Paul grabbed me by the arms, not letting me go back on to take my curtain call. The audience was yelling, 'We want Roy! We want Roy!', and there I was, being held captive by The Beatles, saying, 'Yankee, go home' – so we had a great time."

THE LAST HE SAW OF PAUL

When his former songwriting partner, six-string in hand, attempted to visit the Dakota – after spending the previous evening there – on Sunday April 25, 1976, he was sent away by a harassed John. "That was a period when Paul kept turning up at our door," sighed John. "I would let him in, but finally I said, 'Please call before you come over. It's not 1956, and turning up at the door isn't the same anymore. You know, just give me a ring.' That upset him, but I didn't mean it badly." Without formal goodbyes, the two friends went their separate ways, and were never to speak face-to-face again.

While John was to conduct Paul's brother Mike into the Dakota's inner sanctum too, he could not bring himself so much as to put his head round the door when Paul with George and Ringo met Yoko in the same building to discuss further the division of the empire.

LORD WOODBINE

A walk-on part in The Beatles' fairy tale brought Lord Woodbine, a popular and, when in the mood, hilarious confidant within their circle – to a wider public than he might have warranted in the ordinary course of events. There have always been at least fleeting mentions of him in biographies of the group, and he was represented in the *Backbeat* biopic by actor Charlie Caine, resplendent in sharkskin suit and Sinatra-esque snap-brim hat.

As plain Harold Phillips, he'd arrived from Trinidad in 1948 to settle in an area of central Liverpool where a Scouse bohemia intermingled with a Scouse Harlem. Ennobling himself as 'Lord Woodbine' – after the cheap cigarettes he chain-smoked – he was established quickly as "one of a great line of Liverpool characters," smiled Bill Harry, "full of cheek and audacity, but fun to know." Harry recalls organising a "plane trip for Cavern regulars to Hamburg in 1963. Loitering at the airport with passport at the ready, Woodbine occupied a last-minute spare seat. He spent most of the subsequent weekend buying up contraband to sell at inflated prices back home. On the return flight, he spread his booty amongst pliant fellow passengers, retrieving it after they'd passed through customs.

More legitimate occupations included that of builder-and-decorator, calypso singer and barman in Toxteth's rougher shebeens (where he defused unrest by brandishing a cutlass). In the late Fifties, he formed The All-Steel Caribbean Band, who were resident in his own New Colony Club. He also booked The Beatles, who often turned up with only half their equipment or a member short.

Other ventures were in partnership with Allan Williams, proprietor of The Jacaranda, a coffee bar a convenient stone's throw from both the art school and the labour exchange. As a change from the juke-box, The All-Steel Caribbean Band played evening sessions in the basement. After Woodbine left, the ensemble remained there as The Royal Caribbean

Steel Band until 1960 when they were noticed by a German sailor. It was on his recommendation that, with Deutschmarks and spicy imagery of free-spirited frauleins, they were poached by a Hamburg club agent.

Quite unashamed of their perfidy, the Band wrote to Woodbine, telling of the recreational delights of their new domicile. Sniffing a business opportunity, he and Williams found themselves on the Reeperbahn soon afterwards. With amused contempt, they listened to inept native rock'n'rollers before instigating exploratory talks with local promoters about bringing over more accomplished Liverpool groups. This new enterprise began that summer with a season by Derry Wilkie & The Seniors at Bruno Koschmider's Kaiserkeller.

Back home, all The Beatles' future seemed to hold was odd engagements at less public venues. 'Odd' was the word for the week in July 1960 when, twice nightly, they tried to keep their minds on their job accompanying the cavortings of a Mancunian stripper at Williams and Woodbine's New Cabaret Artists Club, a well-concealed ledger in their accounts.

Because they'd so gamely gone through this tasteless assignment, their employers were convinced that the group was no longer, as George Harrison would say, "hopefully messing about". Therefore, when Koschmider requested a group for another of his clubs, Woodbine drove an overloaded minibus through the inky firs of Lower Saxony, with a human cargo consisting of the five Beatles as well as Williams and his wife plus a brother-in-law who'd taken what was to be a much-syndicated photograph of the passengers – minus Lennon, too comfortable in the front seat – at the Arnhem War Memorial.

Giddy and stiff outside the Kaiserkeller, youths and adults

were conducted down the strasse to the dingier Indra where The Beatles began that first season in Hamburg, transforming themselves from clumsy provincials to a peerless live act and a potential chart proposition.

Lord Woodbine, however, was all but lost to the archives of oblivion. If well-placed to grow fat on Beatlemania, he choose instead to continue living on his wits around Toxteth. Yet while he sold a rather bitter story to *The Observer*, Lord Woodbine – perhaps surprisingly – never guested at any of the Beatles Conventions that became annual fixtures throughout the globe from the mid-Seventies – and, unlike others less qualified – resisted further incentives to cash in on The Beatles' ticket.

He perished with his wife Helen in a house fire on July 5, 2000.

CAVEMAN

In 1979, Ringo Starr took the title role in Caveman, a movie with a plot that begins in one zillion BC on October 9, John Lennon's birthday.

MY SWEET GEORGE

During one of his last interviews, John Lennon sighed, "George could have changed a few notes and nobody could have touched him – but he let it go and paid the price." This was a reference to George Harrison being found guilty of 'sub-conscious plagiarism' in 1976 when his million-selling 'My Sweet Lord' was deemed to sound too much like 'He's So Fine' by The Chiffons, a black vocal quartet from the Bronx, who were the epitome of the US 'girl group' sound of the early Sixties.

Times got harder for The Chiffons during the British

Invasion, though they gave a good account of themselves when on the supporting bill of The Beatles' first US concert.

BEST OF THE BEATLES

Muttering a few guilt-ridden platitudes when they passed along a backstage corridor in Liverpool in 1963, Lennon has been the only Beatle to speak to Pete Best since his sacking the previous year. Nevertheless, it had been 'John who?' that her shaving husband in the bathroom had spluttered when Kathy Best had shouted the news from the wireless that December morning in 1980 on Merseyside.

With brother Roag supplementing his drumming, the forgiving Pete would dust off his kit, and, with an eponymous group, play a set – that would embrace a Beatles B-side, 'I'll Get You' – in a John Lennon Memorial Concert with other Merseybeat musicians, belying their daytime occupations as pen-pushers, charge-hands and captains of industry.

By 1991, Pete was calling his group after his now very collectable 1965 LP, *Best Of The Beatles*. They were working at the Cavern on the very evening – July 6, 1992 – that Ringo Starr's All-Starr Band were appearing at the Liverpool Empire.

In deference to the years before the coming of Ringo, the first *Anthology* package contained items with Beatles who'd left the fold one way or another before 'Love Me Do'. Such inclusions were of no use to Stuart Sutcliffe, mouldering in a Liverpool parish cemetery for 35 years – but Pete Best could foresee a fortune in royalties. It was huge enough for him to resign from the civil service and concentrate fully on leading an outfit he'd dared to name Best Of The Beatles. *Anthology* also helped broaden Pete's group's work spectrum to a busy 1996 schedule, covering 18 countries as well as bigger UK venues than before – Margate Winter Gardens, Southport

Floral Hall, Barnsley Civic, Sutton Secombe Theatre, you name 'em.

Highlights of the show were Beatles favourites and the livelier crowd-pleasers from a new Pete Best album, *Back To The Beat*. Among its selections were some numbers Best had penned himself. Interviewed by a national newspaper just prior to the release of 'Free As A Bird', he described them as "what The Beatles would sound like if they were around in the Nineties."

VENUS AND MARS

During sessions in New Orleans for the 1975 Wings album, *Venus And Mars*, Paul telephoned John in California and found himself asking if his old colleague wanted to lend a hand. Lennon didn't materialise but, after *Venus And Mars* had been mastered, Paul flew over for an evening of coded hilarity and nostalgic bonhomie in John's place.

JOHN AND GEORGE IN THE MID-SEVENTIES

Lennon sent first-night flowers when George Harrison's troubled 1974 North American tour opened in Vancouver, and the two chatted affably enough at one subsequent post-concert party. At another, however, everything turned red as hell for Harrison, and he rounded on Lennon, and the flat of his hand shooting out in an arc to make glancing contact with John's spectacles.

These clacked onto the ground, and while John was grubbing for them, George was loud enough to be heard in Liverpool. His tongue-lashing streamlined what had become, in Lennon's estimation, "a love-hate relationship of a younger follower and older guy. I think George still bears resentment towards me for being a daddy who left home."

This time, the animosity sprang specifically from John's procrastination over signing some papers relating to The Beatles – and that John hadn't taken up an open invitation to join George onstage one night during the tour to do a turn as a surprise treat for the fans.

No more the tough guy that he'd never been, Lennon "saw George going through pain – and I know what pain is – so I let him do it."

The hatchet was never quite buried, and, as the months turned into years, only infrequent postcards filtered between Harrison and Lennon. Other than that, they knew each other only via hearsay and stray paragraphs in the press – and John was to be wounded by the glaring omissions of him from George's pricey autobiography, *I Me Mine*.

DESERT ISLAND DISCS

Among Paul McCartney's eight choices when a castaway on BBC Radio Four's *Desert Island Discs* in 1982 was 'Beautiful Boy (Darling Boy)', track seven, side one of *Double Fantasy*.

THE FIRST SINGLE

It was a purported McCartney-Harrison opus, 'In Spite Of All The Danger', that was to grace one side of the first Beatles-associated disc, an ego-massaging pressing in June 1958, taped and cut while-you-wait on shellac in a studio customised on the ground floor of a terraced house in Liverpool's Kensington district where a cluster of new streets would one day be named in three of the participants' honour – John Lennon Drive, Paul McCartney Way and so forth – a quarter of a century later.

The Quarry Men – by then, John, Paul, George, John Duff Lowe and Colin Hanton – shelled out for only one 'In

Spite Of All The Danger'. They also waxed an unimagina-
tive arrangement of 'That'll Be The Day' with Lennon as
Buddy Holly.

"We rehearsed quite a long time for the recording
session," recalled Lowe. " 'That'll Be The Day' was the
A-side. It was John's idea, but we all chipped in to pay for it.
The studio was just a back room with these huge machines
on the table, no overdubs, one microphone in the middle of
the room, and a piano. The guy – Percy Phillips – cut the
acetate out, there and then, and we walked out with one
copy. It didn't even have a proper sleeve; it was put in a
78 rpm Parlophone sleeve.

"Nobody used it for any other purpose than lending it
round. I ended up with it. Even after The Beatles had
become well-known, none of them then bothered to try and
get it back."

The disc was in John Duff Lowe's possession when The
Quarry Men faded away, sometime in 1959. Within a year
of Lennon's death, however, he let it be know that he pro-
posed selling 'That'll Be The Day'/'In Spite Of All The
Danger' to the highest bidder, which happened to be Paul
McCartney.

JOHN PEEL

Then a compulsive filler-in of forms, John Lennon voted
BBC Radio One presenter John Peel – who was among
those who took the stand at the Old Bailey during the *Oz*
trial – Top Disc-Jockey in *Disc And Music Echo*'s Valentine
Awards readers' poll. In reciprocation, on Radio Four's
morning news on December 9, 1980, Peel estimated that
"John Lennon was the engine room of The Beatles, and he
probably had more effect on people's lives than almost any
other person in the last 20 to 30 years."

I'M THE GREATEST

Until the sessions for 'Free As A Bird' and 'Real Love', the eponymous Ringo Starr album of 1972 would be the nearest the former Beatles would ever come to a reunion on disc, embracing as it did compositions and active participation by all four, albeit not at the same time. Lennon's main contribution, 'I'm The Greatest', a made-to-measure semi-autobiographical opus, came close as it featured himself, Starr and, after he telephoned to invite himself along, George Harrison at Los Angeles' Sunset Sound Studio. Present too were Klaus Voorman (on bass) and Ringo's producer, Richard Perry. Paul McCartney had been amenable to pitching in too, but was refused a US visa owing to a recent conviction for possessing narcotics, which had been seized during a European tour with Wings.

TONY SHERIDAN

Nothing would draw Tony Sheridan from his Teutonic haven until a repromoted 'My Bonnie' – this time by 'The Beatles with Tony Sheridan' – spread itself thinly enough to sell a purported million by 1964. In its wake came the exhumation of connected items thrust out on albums with titles like *The Beatles' First*, *Ain't She Sweet* and *This Is The Savage Young Beatles*.

There were also sufficient resulting offers and promises for Sheridan to go to Britain to promote a new LP (*Just A Little Bit Of. . . .*). During the visit, Tony renewed his acquaintance with The Beatles – for "talk of old times, laughs about some of the German raves and best wishes for the future," so he told *Melody Maker* – at Brian Epstein's London apartment after a shoot for *A Hard Day's Night*. This hail-fellow-well-met reunion, however, was not repeated a few months later when the group and Tony were staying in the same hotel during the Australian leg of The Beatles world tour. To the one newshound who asked him why not, Sheridan – now a world expert on heraldry – said he "wasn't trying to jump on their bandwagon", though he continued to look up individual members, bar John Lennon with whom he was not to speak again after 1964.

THE REBIRTH OF THE QUARRY MEN

In the mid-Nineties, John Duff Lowe re-launched not so much The Quarry Men as A Quarry Men. A 1994 debut album, *Open For Engagements*, mixed 'Twenty Flight Rock', The Del-Vikings' 'Come Go With Me' and further items from the 1958 edition's repertoire with some startling new material, more *Sgt. Pepper* than olde tyme rock'n'roll.

"In 1975, I'd moved to Bristol," he explained. "We always had a piano, and I used to play a lot – so I never lost interest in music. In 1991, I received a call from Mike Wilsh of The Four Pennies who, until then, hadn't realised that I lived only two miles away from him. I was rehearsing with The Four Pennies within three or four days. I spoke at a Merseybeatle convention in Liverpool in 1992, and, the following year, we played at a party at the Cavern as The Quarry Men, and, later that year, were asked to do a recording by Tony Davidson who had done one with The Four Pennies.

"That all came to nothing, but early this year, John Ozoroff, The Four Pennies' guitarist wanted to do a solo album in a Bristol studio. Three tracks were done with me on keyboards, and we decided to turn it into a Quarry Men album – to be put out on my own Kewbank Records.

"It was mastered at Abbey Road by Nick Webb, who, incidentally, was assistant engineer on *Yellow Submarine*, the *White Album* and *Abbey Road*, and he also does a lot of Paul McCartney's mastering now.

"Of the original songs on it, John Ozoroff tended to come up with the words and a basic tune, and then we'd work on arrangements and demo them on my four-track. There's a tribute to John Lennon, 'John Winston'. John (Ozoroff) was inspired to write it after we did another Merseybeatle event in 1993. Rod Davis came over from his home in Uxbridge to play rhythm guitar on the sessions."

This band dissolved when another Quarry Men came into being before the decade was out. Davis and others still alive from the Woolton fete line-up were heard 43 years after the event on *Get Back Together*, 15 tracks of rocked-up skiffle from the opening 'Mean Woman Blues' through to the apposite 'Lost John' valediction. As lead singer, Len Garry coped better with, say, 'Have I Told You Lately That I Love You' than 'Twenty Flight Rock', but, on his solitary vocal, 'When The Sun Goes Down', Rod Davis – hedging his bets – was as uncannily close to the Donegan template as John Lennon was on 'Putting On The Style' on the rediscovered tape of the Woolton bash where the Lennon-McCartney partnership began.

Overall, there wasn't as much grit as I'd have liked – but perhaps that's not the point for incorrigible old rockers with no other cards left to play. If nothing else, *Get Back Together* – with a teenage Lennon in pride of place on the front cover – sounds like it was fun to record, even if this particular brand of fun isn't a thing that money can't buy.

GERRY AND JOHN

The best-known example of the Merseyside group scene's esprit de corps was a merger of The Beatles with Gerry & The Pacemakers – as 'The Beatmakers' – one evening at Litherland Town Hall. However, after both outfits melted into Brian Epstein's managerial caress, and transcended

Liverpool's scruffier jive hives, local singer Johnny Sandon would note that: "The friendliness and comradeship between different groups seems to have lessened. Groups don't help each other now. If one group suffers misfortune, the others are glad."

As the leader of the first Liverpool combo to top the singles charts in all four of Britain's national musical weeklies, Gerry Marsden felt entitled to joke, "How does it feel to be Brian's number two group then?" when bumping into John Lennon at NEMS. Around the same time, joint press interviews were convened in a London hotel for Marsden and Lennon as principal spokespersons for the Merseybeat movement.

Shortly after the first *Beatles Monthly* was published, a similar periodical devoted solely to Gerry & The Pacemakers was considered a worthwhile market exercise for a while. Both outfits remained on terms of fluctuating equality as Gerry's second offering, 'I Like It', wrenched 'From Me To You' from the top. After The Searchers did likewise to the latest by Elvis Presley in August, they, Gerry, The Beatles and Billy J. Kramer slugged it out for hit parade supremacy for, more or less, the rest of the year.

The first signs of danger were to rear up in spring 1964 when Gerry's 'Don't Let The Sun Catch You Crying' stalled at number six, a true comedown by previous standards. After that, Gerry, with and without his Pacemakers, plodded a known path from a professional maturity to his very name becoming a millstone around his neck at times, making the most of every opportunity that came his way. Among these was his securing of the male lead in the West End musical, *Charlie Girl*, that ran and ran after an opening night dignified by the presence of John Lennon in the audience.

While the two weren't to remain in regular touch,

Marsden was among the few old mates able to reach Lennon during his reclusive 'househusband' period. "I didn't see John for many years while he was in the States," reminisced Gerry, "or hear much about him other than what I read in the papers. Then once, when I was appearing in New York, I called him after a decade of not communicating, and it was just as if the days of the Seamens' Mission in Hamburg hadn't gone."

In 1985, Gerry included 'Imagine' on *The Lennon-McCartney Songbook*, a vinyl long-player that was less Lennon-McCartney than Lennon and McCartney.

SOLIDARITY

While he was to confess later that *Two Virgins*, like the rest of John and Yoko's antics in the name of Art, didn't "give me any pleasure", Paul McCartney showed at least cursory solidarity by accompanying Lennon and his inseparable Ono to an appointment with EMI chairman Sir Joseph Lockwood to discuss the distribution of *Two Virgins*. Paul also permitted the inclusion of a shot – by his new girlfriend, Linda Eastman – that almost-but-not-quite revealed all of himself too in the pull-out poster that was part of the *White Album* packaging.

With himself on drums, piano and bass and John on vocals and guitar, McCartney and Lennon would be the only Beatles heard on 'The Ballad Of John And Yoko', the group's final British number one.

MY STARRS!

According to Ringo Starr, Lennon has transcended to some pop heaven "up there with Jimi Hendrix, Elvis and all the rest of them." For years after December 8, 1980, journalists would smile archly when Ringo began interviews by addressing an unseen Lennon before assuring them that "he's watching over us, you know."

PAUL AND STUART

When both were Beatles, Paul McCartney and Stuart Sutcliffe "hadn't much in common," recounted Paul, "and there was always jealousy within the group as to who would be John's friend. He was the guy you aspired to. Like, you got an Oscar if you were John's friend."

Lennon's personal bond with his fellow art student was tighter than that with McCartney: "John and Stuart went to this sort of grown-up thing together. George and I were school kids. We were younger – so I think age was something to do with it. The girls at the college were objects of desire etc., etc., and they could talk about it. I'm totally guessing now, but I think John was a little bit political, and he might have felt that to let one of us in would be bestowing too many favours – so that Stuart might have been a little more neutral than choosing George or me. There was a little separation by the fact that he was John's mate."

RAM

With a few lines suggested by Allan Klein, 'How Do You Sleep?' on *Imagine* was a riposte to what Lennon had perceived as a lyrical attack on him in 'Three Legs', a selection on Paul McCartney's 1971 album, *Ram*. Around the same time, a McCartney interview in *Melody Maker* headlined 'Why Lennon Is Uncool' prompted a bitter rejoinder from John in the readers' letters page the next week.

Adding injury to insult, Ringo – who damned *Ram* with faint praise – had drummed on *John Lennon: Plastic Ono Band*, while George had endorsed Lennon's venom by gladly picking guitar and dobro on 'How Do You Sleep?' "I liked being on that side of it, rather than on the receiving end," sniggered George, who received a backhanded compliment in John's claim that, to the 'rubbish' of *Ram*, he preferred Harrison's triple-album *All Things Must Pass*, albeit with the qualification, "It's all right, I suppose. Personally, at home, I wouldn't play that kind of music, but I don't want to hurt George's feelings."

Lennon's public reviling of Paul and his 'granny music', and McCartney's more veiled digs at Lennon continued after the 'Three Legs'–'How Do You Sleep?' episode. "'Imagine' is what John's really like," Paul informed *Melody Maker*. "There was too much political stuff on the other album."

"So you think 'Imagine' isn't political?" parried Lennon the following week in the same publication. "It's 'Working Class Hero' with sugar on for conservatives like yourself."

LITTLE RICHARD
When The Beatles mixed socially with Little Richard at the Star-Club in spring 1962, Billy Preston, his organist, would "remember how excited they were to meet Richard. In Hamburg, they'd always be with him, asking him about America, the cities, the stars, the movies, Elvis and all that." Richard himself would inform his biographer, Charles White, that "I developed a specially close relationship with Paul, but me and John couldn't make it. John had a nasty personality."

By the middle of the decade, Richard was to have cause to be thankful to The Beatles when they revived his 'Long Tall Sally' on disc. In 1976, his publisher claimed breach of copyright in the group's arrangement of 'Kansas City' on the 12-year-old *Beatles For Sale* LP – because they'd inserted a vignette of his 1958 B-side, 'Hey Hey Hey Hey', into the proceedings.

THANKSGIVING

In 1980, over dinner in New York, Ringo picked John's brains for feasible numbers for a new album because "he knows me better than anyone else in the world, better than the other two, so he really becomes involved – playing, singing, doing everything he can."

For John, "it was like a brother relationship," May Pang would recollect sadly. "It's so hard to explain, but it was just that he had great love for all of them – for George, for Ringo and for Paul."

As well as promising to be there when recording began in January 1981, Lennon sent Starr demos of four new compositions – including 'Nobody Told Me', which was to be selected for Yoko and the late John's 1984 album, *Milk And Honey* – but, to this day, Ringo has forbidden himself from recording any of them.

COMING UP

In May 1980, John was to grin at his own vexation on hearing himself humming 'Coming Up', Paul McCartney's latest hit, while turning a thoughtful steering wheel. Next, a personal assistant was directed to bring him a copy of the related album, *McCartney II.* That it was such an improvement on the 'garbage' of its *Back To The Egg* predecessor, the old striving for one-upmanship was reawakened in John, and was among factors that spurred a return to the studio to make *Double Fantasy*, his first album in five years.

JOHN, KLAUS, GEORGE AND RINGO

Over the years, less plausible candidates than either Brian Epstein, Stuart Sutcliffe, Pete Best or George Martin have nurtured a close enough affinity to John, Paul, George and Ringo to be rated – by either themselves or those with vested interest – as a 'Fifth Beatle'. Off-the-cuff examples of what is a faintly ludicrous notion anyway are New York disc-jockey Murray the K (later, 'the Sixth Rolling Stone' too) – because he almost-but-not-quite blagged his way into rooming with George Harrison during the first US visit – and Jimmy Nicol, Ringo's replacement for part of a world tour later that year.

Then there was Harry Nilsson, referred to in *Beatlefan* and further post-1970 fanzines as a 'quasi-Beatle' – and Klaus Voorman, a friend since their first visit to Germany. After experiencing the group at the Kaiserkeller one evening, he had threaded through to the bar to congratulate them, and to show Lennon – identified correctly as the group's leader – a record sleeve he had been commissioned to design for the German release of 'Walk Don't Run' by The Ventures.

John hardly looked at it before passing it back. "Show him," he said, indicating Stuart Sutcliffe. "He's the artist round here." Sutcliffe had at least the good manners to take an interest. After he left The Beatles, Stuart sold his bass guitar to Klaus, and gave a few pointers on how to play it.

While retaining his boyish good looks, Voorman's subsequent journey to middle age wasn't peaceful. By 1965, he had forsaken the security of graphic design to thrum bass in his first group – with Gibson Kemp and ex-Big Three guitarist Paddy Chambers. As Paddy, Klaus and Gibson, they secured a recording deal with Pye and a season at a night spot, frequented by London's 'in-crowd'.

In with the most exclusive in-crowd of them all, Klaus gave Ringo guitar lessons, and landed the plum job of crafting the sleeve of The Beatles' *Revolver* album. His liaison with Gibson and Paddy was nowhere as lucrative. Three consecutive flop singles contributed to the sundering of the trio in May 1966. Chambers joined The Escorts, Gibson the executive body of a record company, while Voorman served

The Hollies briefly before filling a vacancy created by Jack Bruce (later, of Cream) in Manfred Mann, in which he doubled on flute.

Well before Manfred Mann's break-up in 1969, Klaus found it convenient to live permanently in London from whence he turned out to assist on records by the Lennons, George Harrison and Ringo Starr, reacting instinctively whenever each ex-Beatle warmed-up for a take with some rock'n'roll classic half-remembered from the Kaiserkeller.

Inevitably, rumours of the impending formation of a Beatles had him like the stock Hollywood chorus girl, thrust into a sudden headlining role. See, as writ-happy Paul was persona non grata, the other three were going to try again as John, Klaus, George and Ringo. 'New Beatle Goes Into Hiding!' *Melody Maker* bawled that spring when Klaus and his wife spent a few days at George's country estate in Oxfordshire. *Disc* saw him less as McCartney's successor than "a natural replacement for Stuart Sutcliffe, the Beatle-Who-Died".

This was backed up with a convincing quote from Bill Harry: "Stuart was an artist from Liverpool who went to Hamburg. Klaus was an artist from Hamburg who came over here. It's always been obvious that he was particularly ideal to be a Beatle. Like Stuart, he's more of an artist than musician, and The Beatles have always admired his work. He would add another dimension to them. There is a charisma about him. He has a fantastically interesting face. He's a thinker."

The plot diluted after Harrison, Lennon and Starr issued a statement refuting any reformation involving Klaus or anyone else. The nearest their Hamburg crony was to come to Beatlehood was as one of the all-star band assembled by Harrison for the Concerts For Bangla Desh in New York in

1971, and on a 1973 Starr track that also happened to feature John and George.

COPYCAT KILLING

Lennon's murder summoned fears among his intimates of a copycat killing, especially as the homicidal Mark David Chapman had been photographed stalking Bob Dylan. Most immediately, Alsatians tugging at leashes gripped by sentries were in evidence around Ringo Starr's mansion in Hollywood – where visitors were not admitted unless they'd telephoned beforehand with the precise time of arrival.

"John's shooting definitely scared all of us," confessed George Harrison, "When a fan recognises me and rushes over, it definitely makes me nervous." George's trepidation would be justified when a paranoid schitzophrenic – from Liverpool of all places – stabbed him in his own home decades later.

For The Rolling Stones, the repercussions of Lennon's slaying would be compounded when, in the queue outside Seattle's Kingdome during an Eighties tour, a deranged woman attracted the attention of patrolling police by brandishing a revolver and spluttering about how she was going to worm her way to within point-blank range of Mick Jagger.

WORK . . .

RAMROD

John Lennon was no genius instrumentalist. Nevertheless, he functioned fully – most of the time – according to his capacity within the context of The Beatles.

As Baudelaire reminds us, "No task is a long one but the task on which one dare not start". Perhaps one subliminal effect of guitarist Bert Weedon's plebian-sounding forename was that it made his *Play In A Day* tutor manual – first published in 1957 – seem less daunting to John Lennon who, on acquiring his first guitar, began by positioning yet uncalloused fingers on taut strings while poring over 'When The Saints Go Marching In', 'Simple Blues For Guitar' and further exercises prescribed in Bert's book. Unlike George Harrison and Paul McCartney, however, he did not advance to pieces by the likes of Charlie Christian and Django Reinhardt in its *Play Every Day* companion.

Weedon's 'Guitar Boogie Shuffle' was to be the first solo guitar instrumental by a Briton to reach the domestic Top 10, and was learned note-for-note by George Harrison, whose comparative expertise stunned John when this pale slip of a lad made his pitch to join The Quarry Men in either February or March 1958.

One of John's few party pieces on lead guitar was, however, not anything by Bert Weedon, but 'Ramrod', a 1958 instrumental A-side by Duane Eddy & The Rebels. It was surrendered to Harrison after Lennon allowed him to join The Quarry Men. However, the concept of John cementing George's twanging with rudimentary chord-slashing soon became a misnomer. Lead and rhythm guitars came to merge in frequent interlocking harmony, evolved over hundreds of hours on the boards. As Lennon elucidated, "I'd find it a drag to play rhythm all the time, vamping like Bruce Welch [of The Shadows] does, so I always work out something interesting to play, although I never play anything that George could do better." (When George was a day away from being deported from Hamburg for violating the under-18s curfew, he spent much of it giving John a crash course in lead guitar the Harrison way, as the group seemed quite willing to continue in his absence. Also, John was to play lead guitar on 'You Can Do That' and 'Get Back'.)

Finally, John was no slouch as a keyboard player either – though he "only learnt to play to back myself". He was hunched, for example, over a Vox Continental organ when necessary during The Beatles' final tour, and, later, handled the fiddly 'Imagine' piano riff with ease.

RAPE

Among several films by John and Yoko screened at London's Institute of Contemporary Arts in September 1969 was *Rape*, a disturbing hour or so of an obtrusive cameraman following an increasingly more alarmed foreign student around London. It was broadcast on Austrian television on March 31, 1969.

HELP!

On March 13, 1965, The Beatles caught the 11 a.m. flight to Salzberg near the Austrian Alps location of a shoot for their second film, provisionally titled *Eight Arms To Hold You*. They stayed at Obertauern's Edelweiss Hotel. Directed by Richard Lester – also responsible for *A Hard Day's Night* – the movie, renamed *Help!*, also starred Leo McKern, Victor Spinetti and Eleanor Bron.

ELEANOR RIGBY

At the height of the antagonism between himself and McCartney after the sundering of The Beatles, Lennon would claim to have written a "good half" of 'Eleanor Rigby', the track on which Paul shone brightest on *Revolver*. However, with the candour of early middle age, he qualified this with an admission that the number had been "Paul's baby, and I helped with the education of the child."

DRUMS

When Ringo was absent for a fortnight during sessions for the *White Album*, John, Paul and George managed between them a composite drum part for 'Back In The USSR', and were about to minister likewise to 'Dear Prudence' when he returned.

In both cases, it had nothing to do with Lennon's joking "Ringo wasn't even the best drummer in The Beatles." Instead, corner-cutting pragmatism had ruled as it had when a session drummer was on hand to ghost the drumming on 'Love Me Do'. This was standard practice and no conscious slight on Starr's – or Pete Best's – ability as an instrumentalist. Nevertheless, when asked in 1992 if he ever felt sorry for Pete, Starr insisted, "No. Why should I? I was a better player than him. That's how I got the job. It wasn't on personality."

John was to qualify this later with "Pete Best's a great drummer, but Ringo's a great Beatle."

PHIL SPECTOR

Of all The Beatles, John Lennon and George Harrison had been the keenest on the record productions of a self-important young New Yorker named Phil Spector. He'd was hot property in the early Sixties for his spatial 'wall of sound' technique, whereby he'd multi-track an apocalyptic melange

– replete with everything, bar the proverbial kitchen sink –
behind artists who'd submitted to his masterplan. Styled "the
Svengali of Sound", Spector was known mainly for hits with
beehive-and-net-petticoat vocal groups, The Crystals and
The Ronettes.

In the wake of the British Invasion, Spector was among
many top US record-business folk who crossed the Atlantic
to stake claims in the musical diggings. He said he wanted to
work with The Beatles – and several years later, he – rather
than a disinclined George Martin – was drafted in to make a
silk purse of what was to become *Let It Be*.

As heard on numerous bootlegs – and *Let It Be: Naked*, an
official release in 2003 – the raw material resulted from the
disintegrating Beatles' harrowing weeks of loose jamming,
musical ambles down memory lane and hitting trouble
whenever they came up against each other's new compositions – as well as the bickering, discord and intrigues that
make pop groups what they are. The idea had been to tape
nothing that couldn't be reproduced onstage. "It would be
honest," so George Martin had understood, "no overdubbing, no editing, truly live, almost amateurish."

In keeping with this unvarnished production choice – as
well as a flagrant spirit of self-interest – anything that needed
too much thought got a thumbs-down. The strained atmosphere was alleviated slightly with the recruitment of organist
Billy Preston, who joined in the famous afternoon performance – The Beatles' last ever – on the flat roof of Apple's
central London storm centre.

Afterwards, the participants decided that their musical
appetites had been ruined by sessions that, overall, had
resulted in music that was lacklustre, raucous or just plain
terrible, depending on the mood of the hour. They were
tempted to jettison the frayed miles of *Let It Be* tapes, but, at

the urging of both John Lennon and Allen Klein – Spector's manager too – chose instead to let Phil apply his skills to salvaging whatever he could from it.

"George Martin had left it in deplorable condition," groaned Spector, "and it was not satisfactory to any of them. They did not want it out as it was. So John said, 'Let Phil do it,' and I said, 'Fine. Would anybody like to work on it with me?' 'No.' They didn't care."

Spector's superimposed much orchestral and choral gran-diloquence in many areas, but adopted a relatively unvar-nished approach on several tracks – notably 'Get Back', the first spin-off single. Moreover, he made pragmatic use of his wall of sound trademark to smother Lennon's poor bass playing on 'The Long And Winding Road'. Furthermore, on 'Across The Universe', John singing out of tune. John: "Instead of getting a decent choir, we got fans from outside – Apple Scruffs or whatever you call them. Phil slowed the tape down, added the strings. He did a really special job." He certainly made the best of a bad one.

Present at some of the overdubbing sessions, George Harrison was impressed too – so much so that he, like Lennon, continued working with Spector after The Beatles disbanded.

MATCHBOX
Surfacing on bootlegs from the John Lennon/Plastic Ono Band sessions were off-the-cuff renditions of 'Honey Don't' and 'Matchbox', Carl Perkins numbers recorded by The Beatles (with Ringo Starr on lead vocals).

FLUTES
The two-flute coda of John's 'You've Got To Hide Your Love Away' on 1965's *Help!* LP was the first occasion when

auxiliary musicians were hired for a Beatles session. It was also the first all-acoustic track the group ever recorded. "That's me in my Dylan period," he would admit. "I am like a chameleon, influenced by whatever is going on."

'You've Got To Hide Your Love Away' and 'Yesterday' on the same album was also a mild reflection of a major artistic differences between Lennon and McCartney. John was fond of Bob Dylan, but Paul preferred Paul Simon, a New Yorker then doing the rounds of British folk clubs. 1965's *The Paul Simon Songbook* caught on with those who found Dylan too harsh, especially now that the 'poetic' gentleness of the writer of 'Blowin' In The Wind' was being buried in rapid-fire surrealism with no trace of war being wrong and fairer shares for all.

I'M SO TIRED

In 'I'm So Tired' on the *White Album*, Lennon quoted the title of 'Got My Mind Set On You' from James Ray's 1962 album, *If You Gotta Make A Fool Of Somebody*, as he had a line from Elvis Presley's 'Baby Let's Play House' to begin 'Run For Your Life' on Rubber Soul.

George Harrison wrote a song entitled 'Got My Mind Set On You' which was recorded by his ad-hoc group The Travelling Wilburys in 1988.

DEPUTY

One lunchtime, Gerry Marsden deputised for an indisposed John Lennon at a Beatles Cavern bash, where it was noticed that, like John and The Searchers' John McNally, he had copied Tony Sheridan's high-chested guitar stance.

MASSACRE

In the Quarry Men era, Lennon allowed George Harrison to handle the lead vocal of 'Three Cool Cats', a Coasters

B-side, electing to just provide responses to key lines with McCartney. John had gone off the song after the trio of Marty Wilde, Cliff Richard and Dickie Pride had, in his opinion, 'massacred' it on the ITV pop showcase, *Oh Boy!*

In 1961, Lennon 'gave' 'Roll Over Beethoven', one of his favourite Chuck Berry numbers, to George. It was selected to start side two of 1963's *With The Beatles* LP.

BERYL MARSDEN

John promised a Lennon-McCartney song, 'Love Of The Loved', to Liverpool chanteuse Beryl Marsden (no relation of Gerry), but Brian Epstein insisted that it go to Cilla Black after she was signed to his NEMS Enterprises management company. Later, Beryl was enlisted into Lee Curtis & The All-Stars – into which Pete Best had been absorbed after he left The Beatles.

In May 1989, Marsden's unscheduled three-song spot at a local charity concert that reunited many Merseybeat acts, confirmed that she should have represented Liverpool womanhood in the Sixties charts rather than a lesser talent like Cilla Black.

BEING FOR THE BENEFIT OF MR KITE

Abbey Road studio assistants muttered darkly but said nothing out loud when, say, dials went into the red or George Martin razored a tape of Sousa marches in unequal lengths and instructed somebody to stick it back together randomly for the instrumental interlude in Lennon's 'Being For The Benefit Of Mr Kite'.

"The whole song is from a Victorian poster for a fair that must have happened in the 1800s," recalled John, the song's principal composer. "I bought it in a junk shop."

Elsewhere on *Sgt. Pepper's Lonely Hearts Club Band*, vocals floated over layers of treated sound, and gadgetry and constant retakes disguised faults. A mere 10 hours – the time spent recording their first LP – was no longer considered adequate for one Beatles track by 1967.

STAGE ACT

John Lennon spoke proudly of The Beatles' stage act in 1963: "What we generated was fantastic. There was nobody to touch us." Nevertheless, he would cite the subsequent tours as a principal reason why "we never improved as musicians. We always missed the club dates – because that's when we were playing music."

During the global aftermath of domestic Beatlemania, the group went into further decline through cranking out the same 30 minutes' worth of unheard songs night after night into the teeth of the screams and the jelly-babies and other votive offerings cascading onto the stage like hailstones. As bootleg recordings from this period reveal, they were taking numbers too fast, transitions from choruses to middle eights were cluttered, and lead guitar breaks wantonly slap-dash. For devilment, they'd mouth songs soundlessly or the three front-line Beatles would slam sickening discords while Ringo just as deliberately stamped the bass drum on the off-beat. For the wrong reasons, concerts could still be a laugh. "We must have been hell to work with," grinned George Harrison from another decade. "We'd always be messing about and joking, especially John."

Once, Harrison took the trouble to tune both his and Lennon's guitars. Now neither could care less about the wavering bars of bum notes and blown riffs. "Don't try to listen to us," groaned John to a support group at Hamburg's Ernst Merke Halle in 1966. "We're really terrible these days."

The final show – unless you count the performance on the roof of Apple's London headquarters in 1969 – was at San Francisco's Candlestick Park on August 29, 1966. No better or worse than any other show they'd given on that particular US tour, they ran through this final half-hour any old how, with Ringo repeating a verse of 'I Wanna Be Your Man' and George fluffing his guitar runs as Paul tried to make a show of it. "Nice working with you, Ringo," cracked John shortly before the four posed for an on-stage photograph as a keepsake, and then piled into the nostalgic finale, 'Long Tall Sally', which had been in and out of the set since the days of The Quarry Men.

GOODNIGHT VIENNA
The title track of Ringo Starr's 1974 LP, *Goodnight Vienna*, was composed by John – who also attended the session. It embraced a riff reminiscent of 'Money', and lines such as "I feel like an Arab that was dancing through Zion."

A spliced-up medley of this and its reprise – as "It's All Down To Goodnight Vienna" – was to touch the lower end of the US Top 30 the following July.

To preserve a rough-and-ready edge, each version kicked off with a tempo announcement, and the reprise closed the album like some cocktail-lounge combo with an accordion, winding up for the night.

Lennon also played guitar on another track on the same LP, 'All By Myself'.

CONSERVATIVE
After Paul McCartney's first date as a Quarry Man – believed to be October 18, 1957 in Liverpool Conservative Club's New Clubmoor Hall functions room – he rose quickly through the ranks, coming to rest as Lennon's second-

in-command, and in a position to foist revolutionary doc-
trines, principally the songs he'd begun to compose, onto the
status quo. The affront to the older John's superiority was
such that he contemplated starting writing himself.

ABDICATION

John's unofficial abdication as de facto leader of The Beatles
may be traceable to his murmured 'you say it' before Paul's
count-in to the reprise of the title song of *Sgt. Pepper's Lonely
Hearts Club Band*.

TWIST AND SHOUT

Soon to be regarded as The Beatles' signature tune, 'Twist
And Shout' had been literally an eleventh hour addendum to
an overworked outfit's debut long-player, made to cash in on
their 'Please Please Me' breakthrough.

Present with them for the 'whole day' it took them to
record the entire album on February 11, 1963, *New Musical
Express* scribe Alan Smith was to maintain that it was he who
suggested 'Twist And Shout' during the final coffee break of
the sessions, after hearing The Isley Brothers blueprint the
day before. It had, however, been in The Beatles' repertoire
since 1962.

Just as the studios were about to close for the evening, the
fatigued group picked up their instruments and smashed out
the raver that had stopped the show on their last night at the
Star-Club the previous December, Lennon rupturing his
throat with a surfeit of passion on what was, after all, only
doggerel about an already outmoded dance. A second take
was started and swiftly abandoned.

'Twist And Shout' became one of those tracks that emerge
as being Worth The Whole Price Of The Album. It
remained in The Beatles' stage set – sometimes in truncated

form – until 1965 when John moaned that he was "sick of it".

As a US single, it reached number two in the Hot 100 in March 1964. In Britain, it was the title track of an EP that reached the singles Top 10 at the same time as a version by Brian Poole & The Tremeloes peaked at number four, and The Isley Brothers original slipped in at number 42, and was gone by the following week.

LENNON LEAD VOCALS ON BEATLES BRITISH A-SIDES, 1962–1970

'Please Please Me'
'From Me To You' (duet with Paul McCartney)
'She Loves You' (duet with Paul McCartney)
'I Wanna Hold Your Hand' (duet with Paul McCartney)
'Ain't She Sweet'
'A Hard Day's Night'
'If I Fell' (import)
'I Feel Fine'
'Ticket To Ride'
'Help!'
'Day Tripper'
'Strawberry Fields Forever'
'All You Need Is Love'
'The Ballad Of John And Yoko'
'Come Together'

AWOL

Lennon absented himself from The Beatles' final recording date – to tie up a *Let It Be* loose end – on January 3, 1970. In skittish mood between takes, George Harrison indulged in a little taped tomfoolery at John's expense: "You all will have read that Dave Dee is no longer with us, but Micky, Tich and I would like to carry on with the good work that's always gone down at [Studio] number two."

RICKENBACKER

In autumn 1960, Ricky Richards of The Jets went with John Lennon to the Musikhaushummel shop in Hamburg to help him choose the instrument that he would still be using at the height of Beatlemania. He liked it for its unusual sharp-finned, short-armed shape.

The Rickenbacker was then the only US electric guitar available in Germany – though it was based on a hand-tooled acoustic prototype by German-Swiss artisan Adolph Ricken-backer who, on emigrating to Los Angeles to establish a manufacturing firm in 1925, marketed the solid-body elec-tric that would stimulate the company's period of greatest prosperity, thanks largely to John.

LONNIE DONEGAN

In the last major interview before his death, Lonnie Donegan spoke of the national impact of his breakthrough with 'Rock Island Line' in 1956: "I was shocked at all the skiffle clubs that had opened everywhere, and the thousands of guys trying to imitate Lonnie Donegan. It was uncanny how much John Lennon sounded like me on that Quarry Men tape that turned up a few years ago."

GOT TO GET YOU INTO MY LIFE

During their last season at Hamburg's Star-Club in 1962, The Beatles shared the stage with, among others, Cliff Bennett & The Rebel Rousers, a group from West Drayton, Middlesex. The northerners were to have an important bearing on Cliff's future, most crucially when John Lennon and Paul McCartney promised to give him a leg up by writing him a song if their group got famous before his did.

Destined for a walk-on part during The Beatles' subsequent conquest of the world, Bennett's boys were to be managed by Brian Epstein, who had been impressed by their interpretation of The Impressions' 'Talking About My Baby' when they were supporting The Beatles at London's Prince of Wales Theatre in 1964. By October, Cliff's seventh single, 'One Way Love', was heading for the domestic Top 10. However, its follow-up, 'I'll Take You Home', was to be his last Top 50 strike for two years.

Nevertheless, on the bill of the German leg of The Beatles final world tour, Bennett's set contained 'Got To Get You Into My Life', presented to him in a dressing room earlier in 1966 by its composers, Lennon dah-dah-ing a horn section with McCartney on guitar and vocal. This James Brown pastiche – "best song I ever recorded" – was to be Cliff's biggest smash, reaching Number Six in autumn 1967.

The following year, Bennett covered 'Back In The USSR' from the *White Album*.

NEW AGE

During his "house husband years", John Lennon's recreational listening included New Age, which left its mark as more than a trace element in the easy-listening cauldron that was *Double Fantasy* and *Milk And Honey*.

Marketed too as 'Adult Contemporary', New Age is the only wave of essentially instrumental music to have reached a mass public since jazz-rock in the mid-Seventies. Adjectives like 'restrained', 'shimmering', 'caressing' and 'atmospheric' crop up in critiques of the genre. Not meant to 'go anywhere', the sound at any given moment matters more than individual pieces – and individual performers whose photographs appeared but rarely on album artwork. Such anonymity compounded New Age's non-directional criteria in which moods commensurate with relaxation and pursuits of the mind are investigated undynamically and at length in a manner akin to, significantly for Lennon, Indian ragas, Japanese koto music and Scottish pibroch themes.

Its serene and often majestically slow 'classical music' effect appealed mainly to adults with high disposable incomes. You hear it today in hip dental surgeries, TV commercials for mineral water, painting studios, health food stores, massage parlours and what used to be known as 'head shops'. Moreover, in the privacy of the Dakota, perhaps the wonderful foolishness of John's mirror-freaking teen narcissism could be re-enacted to accompaniment, "enabling you," felt Cloud Nine, one of many New Age labels, "to feel as though you are starring in your own movie in a space mapped by the emotions".

Do you buy it with the same discrimination as you would a few pounds of spuds or can it only be appreciated by the finest minds? Is it rock'n'roll's most piquant form – or merely irritating aural wallpaper with even Sound Waves, newsletter of the New Age Music Association, irked by conveyor-belt creation of "bleeping whale music"?

Perhaps Lennon was turned onto it by David Bowie, whose 1977 album *Low* – described by an *NME* reviewer as 'the first modern rock'n'roll album' – and its follow-up, *'Heroes'*, each containing the murky instrumentals that Bowie called his 'dreamy stuff'. Moreover, old beat groups often peep out from beneath the pervading backwash. The mainstay of Stairway – probably the best-loved British New Age outfit – is ex-Yardbird Jim McCarty. Other New Age denizens have included former Monkee Mike Nesmith, Rod Argent, whose Zombies' trademark was a minor key contradiction of enjoyable melancholy, and Matthew Fisher of

Procol Harum, whose 'A Whiter Shade Of Pale' was never off Lennon's turntable. Some hedged their bets with two or three tartly arranged songs per album.

BRIAN POOLE

Once, Brian Poole & The Tremeloes were accorded a foot-note in pop history as the group Decca chose instead of The Beatles when both groups auditioned on New Year's Day 1962. "That's a complete myth," protested Brian in a 1996 interview. "Our studio test was sometime in 1961 – not New Year's Day 1962 when The Beatles did theirs. How did that story get around? Maybe one of our publicists made it up.

"You check the release dates. Our first album was *Big Big Hits Of 1962* – so we had to have been recording quite a bit before that to be allowed to do an album in those days. Also, George Martin told me later that The Beatles were still in Germany when two of The Tremeloes and I were recording as a backing vocal group for Decca at EMI studios."

PUSSYCATS

In 1974, John was in the throes of producing the Harry Nilsson album, *Pussycats*, at Los Angeles' suburban Burbank Studios, whilst taping demos back at Santa Monica. "We picked songs off the top of our heads and just did them," he shrugged. This strategy was very much in force when Paul McCartney, staying at the Beverley Hilton Hotel, looked in – with Linda, his first wife – at what were becoming fiascos at Burbank on Thursday, March 28, 1974. Paul helped in trying to salvage an arrangement of traditional 'Midnight Special', once in The Quarry Men's skiffle repertoire, and was invited to a musical evening the following Sunday at Lennon's house.

Present too would be Nilsson, guitarist Jesse Ed Davis – Eric

Clapton's understudy at The Concerts For Bangla Desh – 'supersideman' saxophonist Bobby Keyes, and blind singing multi-instrumentalist Stevie Wonder, Tamla Motown's former child-star, who'd notched up his first US hit, 'Fingertips', in 1963.

As there were so many distinguished participants at Santa Monica, it was decided to keep a tape rolling for posterity – and the inevitable bootlegs – on equipment borrowed from Burbank. With McCartney choosing to beat the drums, they cranked out an interminable quasi-reggae version of Ben E. King's much-covered 'Stand By Me' (later, re-made as a Lennon A-side), a slow and raucous 'Lucille' and, with Wonder to the fore, a medley of Sam Cooke's 'Cupid' and 'Chain Gang'.

These were punctuated by various meanderings during which were heard the intermittent strains of Bobby Byrd's 'Little Bitty Pretty One' – revived later by The Jackson Five – and, beneath improvised lyrics by Paul, Santo and Johnny's 'Sleepwalk' instrumental from 1959, as well as blues-derived chord cycles over which Lennon – who belly-ached throughout about the low volume of his voice in the headphones – kicked off an extrapolation that touched on his immigration woes.

During the making of *Pussycats* too, John thrummed chords. Harry sang backing vocals and Jack Bruce plucked bass as Mick Jagger emoted ribald 'Too Many Cooks', a Chicago blues opus by Willie Dixon. A one-sided 10-inch acetate of the result surfaced in 2002, amid much speculation about the high bids it might attract if auctioned.

LONG JOHN LENNON

One evening in 1960, John Lennon 'sat in' with Cass and the Cassanovas at the Jacaranda, Allan Williams's late-night coffee bar. Afterwards, John mentioned to leader Brian Cassar that his own group was thinking once more of changing its name. Buddy Holly had his Crickets, and Gene Vincent had been backed by The Beat Boys on a recent visit to Britain, so, with Stuart Sutcliffe, he'd come up with 'Beetles', 'Beatles' or 'Beatals'. As an adherent to the 'Somebody & The Somebodies' dictate of the Fifties, Cassar howled with derision.

A much-repeated vocal affectation then was the ooo-arrr West Country used by Robert Newton in his swaggeringly overplayed and utterly unforgettable role as Long John Silver in the Walt Disney film adaptation in 1950 of Treasure Island. Lennon and Cassar had picked up on it when the enthralling Newton-as-Silver's shiver-me-timbers pirate villainy was extended into a long-running series on children's television, dominated by the actor's manic, eye-rolling facial expressions and his grindingly slow and brandy-slurred intonations: "Aaaahhhh, me old pal, me old beauty . . ." There had also been a classic edition of *Hancock's Half-Hour* – 'The Knighthood' in March 1959 – in which the comedian delivered excerpts from Shakespeare in the style of Newton in *Treasure Island*, while getting into arguments with the fake parrot on his shoulder.

What about Long John & His Pieces of Eight?, suggested Cassar. Warming to his theme, he next put forward Long John & The Silver Beatles. Neither was acceptable to Lennon. However, Brian stopped being facetious long enough to help secure John the drummer that the group – whatever they called themselves – had been lacking since Colin Hanton's departure from The Quarry Men. A forklift truck driver at Garston Bottle Works, Tommy Moore started rehearsing at the Jacaranda with what was now The Silver Beatles.

DO YOU WANT TO KNOW A SECRET?

A composition that was far more Lennon than McCartney, the lyrics of 'Do You Want To Know A Secret' were inspired, apparently, by a song from a Walt Disney movie – though more than a touch of Frank Ifield prevailed in its tune.

After John demo-ed it in a toilet (for echo) with just voice and acoustic guitar on a 78 rpm acetate, it was granted to George Harrison as his only lead vocal on the *Please Please Me* LP. Conscious that John would knowingly warp the melodies of others to his own ends, it dawned on George that this particular opus was "actually a nick, a bit of a pinch" from Liverpool vocal group The Chants' arrangement of 'I Really Love You' by The Stereos, a US ensemble, which had reached number 29 in the Hot 100 in October 1961.

'Do You Want To Know A Secret' was given to Harrison because, in Lennon's lordly estimation, "it only has three notes, and he wasn't the best singer in the world." Whereas Frank Ifield might have yodelled lustily its 'I am in love with yooooooooou' hookline, George got by with a thin falsetto, boosted by reverberation.

Before his calculated retreat from the pop mainstream, Shane Fenton (later, Alvin Stardust) was to decline a management offer from Brian Epstein, who used John's demo of 'Do You Want To Know A Secret' as bait. It went instead to Billy J Kramer & The Dakotas, the third act in Epstein's stable to reach number one. It had been Lennon, incidentally, who had advocated dividing 'Billy' and 'Kramer' with a non-signifying J. John also accepted a commission to provide Kramer and his boys with another made-to-measure smash in 'Bad To Me'.

'I Really Love You' would be revived in 1982 by George Harrison as a spin-off single from his *Gone Troppo* album.

LENNON LEAD VOCALS ON BEATLES BRITISH B-SIDES, 1962–1970

'Ask Me Why'

'Thank You Girl' (duet with Paul McCartney)

'I'll Get You' (duet with Paul McCartney)

'This Boy'

'You Can't Do That'

'Yes It Is'

'Dizzy Miss Lizzy' (import)

'Drive My Car' (import: duet with Paul McCartney)

'Rain'

'Baby You're A Rich Man'

'I Am The Walrus'

'Revolution'

'Don't Let Me Down'

'You Know My Name (Look Up The Number)' (duet with Paul McCartney)

YOKO AND THE FAB THREE

After her husband's death, Yoko would remain to the surviving ex-Beatles – who she described as "the in-laws" – roughly what the embarrassing 'Fergie', the Duchess of York, is to the British Royal Family.

There was a fiscal debacle as early as 1981 when Paul McCartney was presented with the opportunity to acquire The Beatles' catalogue, Northern Songs, from ATV as Lord Grade's company had had its fingers burnt by *Raise The Titanic!*, a movie that had cost 40 million dollars but had taken only seven. Over the main course one expensive lunchtime, McCartney persuaded Grade, against his better judgement, to sell Northern Songs as a separate entity from the rest of a huge ATV job-lot. Over dessert, his Lordship said Paul could regain his and John's compositions for

£20,000,000 – with a week to make up his mind.

Determined upon the utmost correctness, Paul telephoned Yoko to emphasise that, as he didn't want to be appear to be stealing Lennon's half of the portfolio, Yoko ought to be in on the deal too. In any case, he wasn't sure if he could lay his hands instantly on the full amount. Yoko, however, felt that £20,000,000 was too much. She'd consider the proposal if it was a quarter of that.

Grade wouldn't wear it, and thus the wheels were set in motion for Northern Songs to be acquired by the Australian entrepreneur Robert Holes A'Court who in turn would sell out to Michael Jackson, the precocious youngest member of The Jackson Five and now solo star, who outbid McCartney, Ono and all other interested parties for the publishing rights to Northern Songs in 1986. "He snatched them from under Paul's nose," chuckled Adam Faith, then writer of a weekly financial column in a national newspaper.

Moreover, whether Paul, George and Ringo liked it or not, she was also an equal partner in Apple Corps – as she'd been de facto for as John's business representative throughout his house-husband years. Indeed, Lennon had so washed his hands of such matters that he couldn't bring himself so much as to put his head round the door the last time his three former colleagues were head-to-head with Yoko in the Dakota.

With him unavailable physically as well as spiritually, the first major discussion over the division of the empire took place in January 1984 when the four financiers locked them-selves away with champagne and a continuous running buffet in an eighth-floor suite at the Dorchester, overlooking Hyde Park. One of Yoko's gofers observed that "nothing was accomplished", and that when she wasn't around, the three who'd travelled a longer road with Lennon loosened up with

matey abuse, coded hilarity and selective reminiscences
about the struggle back in Liverpool and Hamburg when the
world was young.

THE LENNON-GENTLE SONGWRITING TEAM

While atypical of the prevalent mood of stoic cynicism
during Johnny Gentle & The Silver Beatles' trek round Scotland, there was a creative diversion involving Lennon and
Gentle.

A year younger than Lennon, Gentle's surname had been
Askew when he was a merchant seaman who sang semi-
professionally before he was spotted and re-christened by
Larry Parnes. Beginning with 1959's 'Boys And Girls Were
Meant For Each Other', this square-jawed hunk's 45s all
missed the UK chart but he was often seen on British television pop series such as *Oh Boy!* and *Drumbeat* and was,
therefore, guaranteed a period of well-paid one-nighters
with pick-up groups, who'd mastered mutually familiar
rock'n'roll standards and the simpler sides of Johnny's four
singles – such as self-penned 'Wendy', a four-chord ballad
that repeated the words 'Wendy, Wendy, when? 'Wendy,
Wendy, when?' ad nauseum – that must have made Lennon
and McCartney wonder what they were doing wrong.

Whatever they thought of him, Johnny was delighted with
The Silver Beatles, and said as much when he rang Parnes
with progress reports. Furthermore, as each backing musician's small wage dwindled, the spurious thrill of 'going professional' manifested itself in John, purportedly, assisting
Johnny with the composition of a song entitled 'I've Just
Fallen For Someone' one Sunday afternoon in an Inverness
guest house. Lennon's principal contribution was the lyrics
to the chorus, in which he borrowed a line from Barrett

Strong's 1959 single, 'Money' – to be recorded by The Beatles on their second UK album in 1963.

That same year, John was uncredited when 'I've Just Fallen For Someone' was issued – by Parlophone of all labels – when Gentle had assumed yet another nom de song, 'Darren Young'. It was also recorded by Adam Faith on his eponymous debut long–player two years earlier.

TAKING THE BISCUIT
During one of the sessions for *Abbey Road*, Yoko Ono provoked a row by eating a digestive biscuit that George Harrison had left on top of a speaker cabinet.

FEEDBACK
Straight in at number one in Britain during 1964's cold, wet December, 'I Feel Fine' began with a buzz like an electric shaver: mid-range feedback. The following summer, The Kinks would approximate this at the start of 'I Need You', B-side to 'Set Me Free' the following summer. At the same time, The Who were enjoying their second hit, 'Anyway Anyhow Anywhere' – and, lubricated with feedback too would be The Yardbirds' 'Shapes Of Things' and its flip-side 'You're A Better Man Than I' in 1966. Each made a most effective melodrama of what was merely implicit in the mild gimmick had that kicked off 'I Feel Fine', a rival group's idea that The Beatles had picked up so fast that – as was often the case – the general public assumed that they'd thought of it first.

Months before 'I Feel Fine', The Yardbirds, The Kinks and The Who had all been featuring guitar feedback on the boards as a deliberate contrivance to sustain notes, reinforce harmonics and, when necessary, create severe dissonance. This strategy had been logged by Lennon when The Kinks were low on the bill to them at Bournemouth's Gaumont Cinema on August 2, 1964. In the teeth of audience chants of 'We want The Beatles!', Dave Davies, The Kinks' lead guitarist, began 'You Really Got Me', their recent chart breakthrough, by turning up his amplifier to feedback level, "and the high-pitched frequency cut right through the screams of The Beatles' fans," his brother was to write in his 1994 autobiography, *X-Ray*. Ray Davies noticed, too, that John Lennon was watching from the wings.

Come Christmas, and Lennon had composed 'I Feel Fine'. "That's me completely," he was to insist. "The record with the first feedback anywhere. I defy anyone to find a record – unless it's some old blues record in 1922 – that uses feedback that way. So I claim it for The Beatles before Hendrix, before The Who, before anyone – the first feedback on any record."

Incidentally, though John played the tricky ostinato of 'I Feel Fine' on the record, George learnt it parrot-fashion for regurgitation on the boards.

THE MIKE SAMMES SINGERS

With first refusal on innumerable recording dates in London studios from the mid-Fifties until the early Eighties, this vocal ensemble were hired for two Lennon numbers with The Beatles, and proved equally at ease with Lennon's psychedelic 'I Am The Walrus' as his valedictory 'Goodnight' – "possibly over-lush," thought the composer – on the *White Album*. This lullaby to John's neglected first-born son bore the removal of a spoken preamble – of "toddle off to beddie-byes, kiddles!" persuasion – but lead singer Ringo's plaintiveness rather than John's simmering inflection better conveyed the necessary air of over-tiredness before the last run-out groove.

SHORT NOTICE

Months before the formal dissolution of Messrs. Harrison, Lennon, McCartney and Starkey as a business enterprise, John had slipped a teasing ". . . when I was a Beatle" into a November 1969 interview with *Disc And Music Echo*. Long before Paul did sp formally on April 11, 1970, John announced his own departure from the group – but this had been hushed up, mainly for fear of it cramping Allen Klein's re-negotiation of a higher royalty rate with Capitol Records.

NORWEGIAN WOOD

The second track on *Rubber Soul*, 'Norwegian Wood (This Bird Has Flown)' was John's smokescreening of an extra-marital affair – most likely with a well-known journalist from a British tabloid. It was also the first Beatles recording to feature a sitar.

FREEING THE BIRD

At January 1994's Rock'n'Roll Hall Of Fame extravaganza at the Waldorf-Astoria, Paul McCartney was the only ex-Beatle to show up. He was there to make the induction speech when his late and most famous songwriting partner received a lifetime achievement. As the ovation unfurled, the widow climbed the podium for the statuette. She and Paul then obliged hovering snap-shotters and the cream of the US music industry with a seemingly conciliatory, even affection-ate embrace as if all their feuding and furies of the past 20-odd years were spent.

It gets better. When Yoko and Sean visited England the following year, they sampled hospitality chez McCartney in Sussex for a weekend that might have seemed more like a fortnight for some members of the household. The stay cul-minated with a session at Paul's home studio in which he,

Linda and their children accompanied seven minutes of Aunt Yoko's screech-singing of a one-line lyric entitled 'Hiroshima Sky Is Always Blue' (also known as 'Hiroshima, It's Always A Beautiful Sky'), a remembrance of the 50th anniversary of the nuclear bombs falling on Japan.

The creation of this hitherto-unreleased opus was, smiled Yoko, the final confirmation of a new understanding between her and McCartney: "It was a healing for our families to come together in this way. That feeling was very special." While she – and Paul – may have insisted that there was no ulterior motive, for the more cynical amongst us, the sub-text of this and the more public all-pals-again encounter at the awards ceremony might have been McCartney oiling the wheels of Ono's co-operation on a planned CD anthology of Beatles tracks from the vaults to be supplemented by her donation of stark voice-piano tapes of 'Free As A Bird', 'Real Love' and other latter-day Lennon compositions for Paul, Ringo and George to use as they thought fit.

As 'Keeper Of The Wishing Well' – her phrase – Yoko had opened these archives – which also embraced several hundred hours of out-takes, in-concert performances, alternate mixes et al. – a few winters earlier for broadcast as *The Lost Lennon Tapes* for a US radio series that stretched out for four years.

Isn't it marvellous what they can do these days? Precedents had been set by the respective superimposition of backing onto musical sketches by Buddy Holly and Jim Reeves. In 1981, Nashville producer Owen Bradley's skills with vari-speed, editing block and sampler had brought together Reeves and Patsy Cline on disc with a duet of 'Have You Ever Been Lonely'. A decade later, there arrived a global smash with 'Unforgettable', a similar cobbling together of Nat 'King' Cole and daughter Natalie's voices over a state-of-the-art facsimile of Nat's original 1951 arrangement.

With Jeff Lynne as console midwife, 'Free As A Bird' took shape as near as dammit to a new Beatles record as could be hoped, complete with a bottleneck passage from George, Ringo's trademark 'pudding' drums, and both George and Paul emoting a freshly composed bridge as a sparkling contrast to John's downbeat verses. The result was not unlike a mordant 'Hard Day's Night'. It was certainly better than certain A-sides issued by The Beatles when Lennon was still amongst us.

TONY AND BERT

The Beatles were backing Tony Sheridan at Hamburg's Top Ten club when Alfred Schlacht, a publisher associated with Polydor, a subsidiary of Deutsche Grammophon, dropped by. At his urging, record producer Bert Kaempfert looked in too. In his late 30s, Kaempfert had enjoyed recent acclaim as co-writer of Elvis Presley's 'Wooden Heart', and, conducting his own orchestra, via a US chart-topper in 'Wonderland By Night'.

"He'd been trying rock'n'roll with young German artists," recounted Sheridan, "but it had sounded ludicrous – because you can't sing anything approaching rock'n'roll in German. He was impressed, therefore, with what he thought was our authenticity – which was, of course, second-hand American music infused with elements of our own which were authentic. On stage, it was a free-for-all. I was doing most of the lead guitar – though if, say, John wanted to take a solo, he'd be halfway good because it came out of the rawness in him. Bert made no comment on this."

Soon afterwards, the artists were hastened by taxi to "the British Army Radio Station," said Tony, "which was in a big assembly hall within the Friedrich Ebert Halle, a school in

Harburg, just outside Hamburg. There being no afternoon lessons in Germany, Polydor used it for their pop acts. We used the same equipment at the back of the stage that was there when the British occupied Germany in 1945."

While 'Wonderland By Night' might not have been to John's taste, he was in awe of a man who'd breathed the air round Elvis. Yet Bert acknowledged freely that he was more at home with light orchestral outings, and, remembered Sheridan, "was quite happy to leave it all to us to play live – like we did at the club – after discussing the choice of material with him."

Tony Sheridan was the man of the moment in 1961, and The Beatles merely one of two outfits, both to be called The Beat Brothers. Nevertheless, Kaempfert wondered about The Beatles' rocked-up 'Ain't She Sweet' as a single in its own right. Conversely, after 'My Bonnie (Mein Herz Ist Bei Dir Nur)', attributed to Sheridan alone, was behind German counters by summer 1961, it would be incorporated into The Beatles' act – with Lennon assuming Tony's lead vocal – to emphasise the group's association with a disc that had lodged itself in Hamburg's Top 10 of Twist singles. For whatever reason, disc-jockeys in other areas started spinning the Sheridan 45 too, and cash changed hands for 20,000 copies within a fortnight.

It was Tony's correct assertion that "the initial success of 'My Bonnie' had nothing to do with The Beatles, but it was a stepping stone for Brian Epstein to come into the picture." Liverpool fans were to ask for 'My Bonnie' in the department store where Epstein was sales manager. His clout as a major record retailer in northern England was to impel Polydor's UK outlet to release 'My Bonnie' – by 'Tony Sheridan and The Beatles' – in January 1962. The *New Musical Express* reviewer was generous ("worth a listen for the above-average ideas") but, un-aired on national radio, the disc died its death – just like it did that same month when it appeared in the USA where a three-line news snippet in *Cashbox* made a lot of the 'Wonderland By Night' hitmaker's part in it.

GOOD MORNING GOOD MORNING

The Shadows aside, Kent's Sounds Incorporated were the only nationally popular instrumental unit of the mid-Sixties beat boom. Yet they did not sell millions, but earned Musicians Union-regulated tea breaks as session players, most famously when the horn section was hired for 'Good Morning Good Morning' – the work of Lennon, but, as he confessed, "throwaway, a piece of garbage" – on what became *Sgt. Pepper's Lonely Hearts Club Band*.

Nevertheless, with Brian Epstein's entrepreneurial muscle behind them, Sounds Incorporated entered the chart in their own right at last when 1964's 'The Spartans' teetered on the edge of the Top 30. Thanks to Epstein too, the ensemble supported The Beatles in North America – including Shea Stadium and the Hollywood Bowl.

FLANGER/PHASER

While US console engineers prefer to say 'phaser', their British opposite numbers call this electronic strategy a 'flanger' – a term that, according to George Martin, was first coined by John Lennon when two signals in a slightly out of time alignment were deployed as automatic double tracking to enhance The Beatles' vocals, especially – at his own insistence – Lennon's.

This operation is more conspicuous when applied to instruments. In 1958, Don Bonham designed a phase shift device to create vibrato on electric organs – though, 13 years earlier, Les Paul stumbled on the 'whooshing' effect via two tape recorders fractionally out of synchronisation when recording 'Mamie's Boogie'. However, flanging is better instanced by Kenny Jones' effervescent drumming on The Small Faces' 'Itchycoo Park'. Other examples of like psychedelic cast are heard on Eric Burdon's 'Sky Pilot' and throughout Captain Beefheart's *Strictly Personal*. In the Seventies, a gadget that reproduced studio quality phasing/flanging onstage was marketed by Gibson.

MCCARTNEY-LENNON

After *Anthology*, business between Ono and McCartney was by no means concluded. Indeed, the weather vane of rapprochement lurched back to the old thinly veiled antagonism when it came to Yoko's attention that, wherever he could – in tour programmes and on disc – Paul ensured that composing credits read 'McCartney-Lennon' rather than, as it had been fleeting before, Parlophone and everyone else made it the more alphabetically correct 'Lennon-McCartney', even on *Anthology*.

This was nipped in the bud by Yoko and her legal team, but you could understand Paul's attitude. On the basis of mostly song-by-song break-downs by Lennon during one of his last interviews, BBC Radio Merseyside presenter Spencer Leigh figured out that, statistically, McCartney was responsible for approximately two-thirds of The Beatles' output of originals, including 'Yesterday', subject of over a thousand cover versions.

This was borne out by implication, too, in John's remarks to an aide in 1979: "Paul never stopped working. We'd finish one album, and I'd go off and get stoned, and forget about writing new stuff, but he'd start working on new material right away, and as soon as he'd got enough songs, he'd want to start recording again." McCartney corroborated this 23 years later in a weighty and widely circulated press statement, grousing too that, "Late one night, I was in an empty bar, flicking through the pianist's music book when I came across 'Hey Jude' written by 'John Lennon'. At one point, Yoko earned more from 'Yesterday' than I did. It doesn't compute – especially when it's the only song that none of the other Beatles had anything to do with."

SUN KING

"I like that Fleetwood Mac instrumental," John told *Disc & Music Echo* in January 1969, referring to 'Albatross', the chart-topper that triggered the overall lush ambience of his 'Sun King' – all warm latitudes and dreamy sighs – on Abbey Road.

SUCCESS . . .

SHUT UP
SHUT UP AND LISTEN!: THE THOUGHTS OF CHAIRMAN JOHN was the banner headline of an interview with Lennon in *Record Mirror* in spring 1970.

LENNON SOLO SINGLES THAT PEAKED AT NUMBER SIX IN BRITAIN
'Imagine' (1975)
'Nobody Told Me' (1984)
'Too Late For Goodbyes' (Julian Lennon, 1984)
'Saltwater' (Julian Lennon, 1991)

SUPERSTAR
Early in December 1969, it was reported in the *Daily Express* and then several other domestic newspapers that John was considering an offer to play the title role in a forthcoming musical, *Jesus Christ Superstar*, but only on condition that Yoko Ono star too as Mary Magdelene. All this was a surprise to composer Andrew Lloyd-Webber and his lyricist, a former EMI production assistant named Tim Rice, who issued a terrified denial straightaway.

When they had once passed on the stairs at Abbey Road studios, Lennon had spoken to Rice briefly 'in what seemed like fluent Spanish. I suspect now that it might have been stoned Jabberwockian.'

LET IT BE
Given that even a mediocre offering by The Beatles would have sold well, 1970's *Let It Be* album was successful in a

statistically commercial sense in that it outsold several previous Beatles LPs – despite a then-forbidding UK retail price (albeit with a glossy book thrown in) – topped the US Hot 100, and won a Grammy award.

VOTES VOTES VOTES

In the run-up to the post-Profumo general election, a *Daily Express* cartoon had Britain's two main political figures, Prime Minister Alec Douglas-Home and Harold Wilson, Leader of the Opposition, soliciting the Fab Four for their support, thus lending credence to the homily, "I care not who makes a nation's laws as long as I can compose its songs."

THE FIRST NUMBER ONE?

In the first instance, sales of The Beatles' first 45, 1962's 'Love Me Do', were limited to Liverpool – where it went directly to number one in the *Mersey Beat* list.

After national airplay commenced with a Radio Luxembourg spin one night, the record inched into the *New Musical Express* Top 30 at number 21 on December 8, and lingered on the frontier of the Top 20 until the New Year, outselling on aggregate a revival of 'Love Me Tender' by Richard 'Dr Kildare' Chamberlain, and the latest by domestic heart-throb Mark Wynter. At number one was 'Lovesick Blues', a revival of a 1949 country-and-western million-seller, by Frank Ifield, a yodelling balladeer at the height of his fame with no fewer than three singles concurrently in the Top 20.

The January edition of *Mersey Beat* proclaimed the forthcoming issue of 'Please Please Me', the second Beatles single. On February 2 it entered at number 16 in *Record Mirror* – and *Record Retailer* – jumping 13 places by the following week. This position was held for a further seven days before reaching its apogee one place short of the top, obstructed by Frank

Ifield's latest, 'The Wayward Wind'.

A fortnight later, it had slipped to number three, but was back at two on March 16 with only 'Summer Holiday' from Cliff Richard blocking the way. Then it began a downward spiral out of the list.

'Please Please Me' followed a similar trajectory in the charts of the other pop newspapers – except that *Melody Maker* had it shutting down 'The Wayward Wind'. Thus, The Beatles were, technically, the first Mersey Beat act to achieve a number one in Britain at large – as announced by compere Bob Wooler at the Cavern one lunchtime.

Nonetheless, the first single by a Merseyside outfit to dominate all Britain's national charts was Gerry & The Pacemakers' 'How Do You Do It' in 1963's late spring.

WALLS AND BRIDGES

John's solo album *Walls And Bridges* was recorded in New York during the summer of 1974. Attributed to 'John Lennon (with the Plastic Ono Nuclear Band)', it topped the US charts for one November week. In Britain, it reached number five.

It was not Lennon's favourite album. "There was no inspiration," he commented, "and it gave it an aura of misery."

FAR EAST MEN

The Beatles gave two performances on July 4, 1967 at the Rizal Memorial Football Stadium in Manila, capital of Luzon, the largest island of the Philippine archipelago.

After a fashion, these appearances were totally successful in that 30,000 turned up for the afternoon, 50,000 in the evening. At a press conference shortly after the matinee, however, certain of the local media took umbrage because

John Lennon seemed vague about what country The Beatles were actually visiting, having longed ceased to care about the glimpses they caught of the places where their blinkered lives had taken them.

Meanwhile, back at the hotel, Brian Epstein had received an invitation for his charges to be guests of honour at a party to be thrown by Imelda, wife of Philippines' autocratic President Ferdinand Marcos, at Malacanang Palace on the morning after the Rizal shows. Not appreciating that it was less an invitation than an order, Epstein let the weary entourage slumber through the arrival and ireful departure of presidential underlings who had been directed to bring them to the waiting Imelda and her 300 other guests, exclusively the families of the totalitarian government and military junta.

This unwitting snub to the First Lady of the islands was avenged the following day when the expected crowd of fans at Manila International Airport were puzzled that no security measures had been laid on. Close enough to be touched, their agitated idols lugged their baggage up static escalators a few steps ahead of a jeering mob of adults, apparently assured of official leniency and even commendation no matter how they behaved.

Naked malevolence stopped just short of open assault when their prey threaded slowly and in a cold sweat through a customs area resounding with pushing, shoving, jack-in-office unpleasantness and every fibre of red tape that Philippino bureaucracy could gather. "You will be treated like ordinary passengers," screamed an official who aimed a kick at John. "Is this how you treat ordinary passengers?" he replied.

Sent on their way by the boos and catcalls of the dictator's creatures, never had arguments for The Beatles' discontinuation of touring made more sense.

DAVE DEE & THE BOSTONS

By 1962, Liverpool groups were so rife in Hamburg that bar staff's pidgin English was infused with Scouse slang, and there were rumblings that once you'd heard one Merseybeat group, you've heard 'em all.

On learning that yet another outfit from north-west Lancashire was about to begin a season at the Star-Club, Dave Dee, leader of Salisbury's Dave Dee & The Bostons, then resident at the Top 10, enquired, "And what are they called?" . . . The Beatles . . . "What a bloody silly name that is!"

"You make a statement like that, and you always remember it," Dave rued later. "Then, of course, we ended up with a name like Dave Dee, Dozy, Beaky, Mick and Tich."

They were still Dave Dee & The Bostons – and perhaps Hamburg's most adored musical attraction – while, as 'Love Me Do' lost its tenuous grasp on the British charts, The Beatles were second-billed at the Star-Club to Johnny & The Hurricanes, a saxophone-dominated combo from Ohio, whose hits had dried up in 1961.

Nevertheless, it seemed Dave and his gang were unintentional ambassadors of Beatle music. "We learnt all the songs off *With The Beatles*," he recalled, "and all President Kennedy's fleet were coming into the Top 10 – it was the year he went to Germany and did his Ich bin ein Berliner line – and they said to us, 'What is this music you are playing?' We told them it was Beatle music, and they said, 'Gee, why don't you play it in America?' I guess they were the first Americans that ever heard of The Beatles and Beatle-type music."

RIGHT

On March 23, 1964, John Lennon's first book, *In His Own Right*, was published in Britain.

CAVERN CHAOS

Formerly a jazz haven, the Cavern in central Liverpool followed the nearby Iron Door's example by allowing pop and traditional jazz groups to share the same bill. Inevitably, it hosted its first all-pop event in May 1960.

Though John had played there in 1957 with The Quarry Men before Paul and George joined, The Beatles first appeared at the Cavern during a lunchtime session in February 1961. Nights were still devoted mainly to jazz with the main concession to pop being every Tuesday's Swinging Blue Genes' Guest Night – and it was on one of these that The Beatles made an evening debut performance in the Cavern on March 21, 1961. The 60 fans they attracted loudly voiced their preferences. In their uniform striped blazers and denim hosiery, the headliners – and the club's manager Ray McFall – failed to see how anyone could like a group that had almost been refused admission for their slovenly turn-out.

CRY FOR A SHADOW

The first Beatles original composition to be released on disc was an instrumental attributed to 'Lennon-Harrison'. Recorded during the session in Hamburg with Tony Sheridan in May 1961, it was constructed to fool Rory Storm into thinking that it was the latest by The Shadows. Homing in on a simple phrase, and with generous employment of the tremolo arm – the note-bending protrusion on some electric guitars – George and John's joke sounded much like a Shadows out-take.

As it was more in keeping with current trends than anything McCartney and Lennon had to offer, producer Bert Kaempfert permitted The Beatles to tape it as one side of a possible single in their own right. Given a title and enlivened with barely audible background yelling, 'Cry For A Shadow' – or 'Beatle Bop', as it was known informally – first appeared in June 1962 on Sheridan's Germany-only *My Bonnie* LP.

'Cry For A Shadow' was not issued outside the Fatherland until it had acquired historical – and expediently commercial – importance. In 1964, it was released as the A-side of an Australian single that reached the national Top 10.

FATE
On December 10, 1980, a *Daily Express* editorial conjectured that Lennon had had "the look of fated youth" about him, and then thanked fate that Mark David Chapman hadn't killed the "much more talented" Paul McCartney instead.

RANDOM REVIVALS
'You've Got To Hide Your Love Away' by Tim Rose
'Please Please Me' by David Cassidy
'Eight Days A Week' by Procol Harum
'A Day In The Life' by Eric Burdon and War
'I Wanna Be Your Man' by Adam Faith
'I Wanna Be Your Man' by Suzi Quatro
'I Wanna Be You Man' by The Rezillos
'Nowhere Man' by Tiny Tim
'Ticket To Ride' by Fifth Dimension
'Daytripper' by The Ramsey Lewis Trio
'Tomorrow Never Knows' by 801
'It's Only Love' by Bryan Ferry
'Help!' by The Damned
'Help!' by Tina Turner
'Come Together' by Tina Turner
'Gimme Some Truth' by Generation X
'Eleanor Rigby' by Ray Charles

'Eleanor Rigby' by Blonde On Blonde
'Eleanor Rigby' by Dozy, Beaky, Mick and Tich
'Working Class Hero' by Marianne Faithfull
'I Want To Hold Your Hand' by Frank Zappa
'I Am The Walrus' by Frank Zappa
'I Am The Walrus' by Oasis
'A Day In The Life' by The Portsmouth Sinfonia
'Dear Prudence' by Siouxie and the Banshees
'Cold Turkey' by U2
'I'm Only Sleeping' by Suggs
'Power To The People' by Ringo Starr
'Happy Xmas (War Is Over)' by The Pop Idol 12
'Mother' by Carol Grimes

OPEN YOUR BOX

In June 2002, the once-risque 'Open Your Box', the self-written B-side of 'Power To The 'People' was remixed in electro-pop fashion, with an undercurrent of dub-reggae, in an endeavour to reinvent Yoko Ono as a disco diva. A poster campaign infiltrated underground railway stations in London, New York and other major cities, and the disc found its way onto club turntables.

Not quite a year later, a similar overhaul of 'Walking On Thin Ice', courtesy of The Pet Shop Boys, eased to number one in *Billboard*'s dance charts.

KINGSIZE

Released by Allan Williams in 1977 on a costly vinyl double-album, *The Beatles Live At The Star-Club, Germany, 1962*, reared up again 20 years later when a record company called Lingasong announced its intention to reissue it on CD. Reviewing it the first time around, the now-defunct UK pop journal *Sounds* had noted contemporary implications in the back cover photograph depicting 1962 teenagers congregating beneath the club's attributive neon sign, Treffpunkt Der Jugend ('Youth Rendezvous'), before concluding waspishly, "The Beatles couldn't play either."

That's as may be, but Billy Childish, then a leading light of a Medway Towns group scene of agreeably retrogressive bent, had considered it "their finest LP". The artists concerned, nonetheless, lacked Billy's objectivity about both the alcohol-fuelled performance and the atrocious sound quality – despite expensive studio doctoring of what Liverpool singer Edward 'Kingsize' Taylor had taped with a hand-held microphone onto a domestic machine.

So it was that on a mid-week day in May 1998, the surviving Beatles forced Lingasong before the High Court in London. Leaving his Southport butcher's shop to take care of itself for the day, Kingsize Taylor would swear that he'd been granted verbal permission by John Lennon to immortalise the group's late shift at the Star-Club, "as long as I got the ales in". Lennon-as-leader's go-ahead meant – so Kingsize had assumed – that it was OK by the other Beatles too. The judge decided that it wasn't, and the mutton-dressed-as-lamb press-packs of the CD that had been distributed by Lingasong in wrong-headed anticipation of victory became instant prized rarities.

MIDLAND BEAT

The main feature of the first edition of *Midland Beat* in October 1963 was an interview with "John Lennon, one of The Beatles, but otherwise the entire content is restricted to Midlands items" for, according to editor Dennis Detheridge, "Liverpool started the ball rolling. Now the Midlands is ready to take over."

BILLBOARD

In 1981, Lennon was voted third Top Male Vocalist post-humously in *Billboard*'s annual poll. That 'All Those Years Ago', his Lennon tribute, had been a hit that year may have helped George Harrison to be tenth.

THE TOP OF THE POPPERS

The British budget label Pickwick specialises in albums containing carbon-copies of then-current hits. In 2003, it compiled from its archives *The Long And Winding Road: A Tribute To The Beatles* and *When They Was Fab: A Tribute To The Solo Beatles*, attributed to an amorphous and anonymous combo called *The Top Of The Poppers*.

Only the occasional misjudged timbre of the lead vocals make one or two tracks on these two so-bad-they're-good. What's more, neither package contains pictures of the usual scantily clad females, epitomised by the blonde gripping a phallic fishing rod on the front cover of a *Hot Hits* collection. Therefore, apart from extreme Beatles completists, at what sort of lunatic were these products targeted?

While these perky, workmanlike efforts are as much a cultural summary of the late Sixties as the actual smashes the anonymous participants are ghosting, certain famous acts were once so desperate that they were willing to record on such second-rate terms; among them John Lennon's mate, Elton John, whose lack of individuality as a vocalist was – and still is – ideal for duplicating the music of others.

If you've the inclination, there might be sport in listening out for Elton, and speculating on other guilty secrets within the grooves of albums that sounds like a resident band on Radio One Club, removed to the sterile surroundings of a studio with a pound-sign hanging over every note.

FROM ME TO YOU

A break in US vocalist Del Shannon's itinerary on a tour of Britain – backed by a Bristol unit, The Eagles – allowed him to book a London studio for a crafty cover of 'From Me To You', purely for the US market. He hoped thereby to steal a march on The Beatles before they invaded North America.

Issued on the Big Top label, Del's version slipped into the Hot 100 at Number 86 on July 6, 1963, climbing nine places over the next fortnight. Thanks in a perverse way to this chart penetration, The Beatles' 'From Me To You' crept by association to number 116 towards the end of the summer.

'Runaway', one of Shannon's biggest hits, was reputed to have inspired 'I'll Be Back', a Lennon ballad on 1964's *A Hard Day's Night* long-player.

THE FIRST SOLO HIT

Among the more conspicuous signs that The Beatles were sundering prior to the formal split in 1971 were John Lennon's hat-trick of hit 45s with his Plastic Ono Band splinter group. 'Give Peace A Chance' (with a debatable 'Lennon-McCartney' composing credit), 'Cold Turkey' and 'Instant Karma' all reached the Top 30 on both sides of the Atlantic. Yet, even as *Let It Be* overtook such as *Andy Williams' Greatest Hits*, *Led Zeppelin II* and offerings by Simon-and-Garfunkel, The Who and Crosby, Stills, Nash & Young in May 1970's album charts, Ringo Starr's *Sentimental Journey* and Paul McCartney's eponymous solo debut were edging up too – though neither contained a spin-off single.

However, Paul's non-album A-side, 'Another Day', slipped into the British list on February 27, 1971, and the US Hot 100 a week later. Slightly over a month earlier, 'My Sweet Lord', the biggest-selling single from George Harrison's *All Things Must Pass* triple-LP, knocked 'Grandad' by Clive

Dunn from number one in the UK within two weeks of its release on January 23. The following month, it was at the top more or less everywhere else too – and 'Isn't It A Pity', its North American flip-side, made the domestic Top 40 too.

'Another Day' and 'My Sweet Lord' were still in the charts after the March 12 cut-off point. Otherwise, the first smash by an official former Beatle was John's 'Power To The People' – at number 11 in the Hot 100 in April 1972, number seven in the Britain a month earlier. Yet, if you're one of these dogmatists who argues that, as the artist credit on the disc's label read 'John Lennon and the Plastic Ono Band', it wasn't a solo single in the strictest sense, then the honour goes to 'It Don't Come Easy' by Ringo which, unleashed on April 17, rose rapidly to number four in both the USA and at home.

PETULA CLARK
Petula Clark's translation of 'Please Please Me' for the French market was titled 'Tu Perds Son Temps' ('you lost your chance').

OASIS
Liam Gallagher of Oasis and actress Patsy Kensit named their eldest child 'Lennon'. Liam has also inherited a singing style that crosses that of John Lennon and Allan Clarke, once of The Hollies.

JACK PAAR
A film short of The Beatles performing 'She Loves You' at Bournemouth's Winter Gardens on November 16, 1963, was shown on NBC's *Jack Paar Show* on January 3, 1964, three weeks before 'I Want To Hold Your Hand' made its US Hot 100 debut.

TOP VOCALIST

In 1969, John Lennon won a *New Musical Express* poll in which other famous vocalists had each been asked to nominate their own three favourites. Paul Rodgers of Free was runner-up, and Bob Dylan, third. Mick Jagger and Maggie Bell (of Stone The Crows) tied in fourth place.

Lennon was, debatably, as adept as he'd ever get by the late Sixties – as illustrated by the coda of 1968's 'Happiness Is A Warm Gun' when he swerved cleanly into falsetto, having already built from muttered trepidation to strident intensity earlier in the song, tackling its surreal lyrics without affectation.

Yet self-doubt about his singing skills was to persist as an ex-Beatle who allowed US producers Phil Spector and, later, Jack Douglas to smother his vocals in what became a trademark echo, not only in the mix but even as he sang them onto tape, refusing to open his mouth unless this was so. "After he left me, he did all his own distortion to his heart's content," lamented George Martin, "and I didn't like that. After all, the raw material was so good."

ROLLS-ROYCE

In 1964, when a road manager was remonstrating with fans who were defacing the exterior of The Beatles' getaway car with affectionate scratched and lip-sticked messages, Lennon shouted from a theatre window two storeys up, "Leave them alone! They paid for it!"

CONVENIENCE

On the Christmas edition of the BBC2 satire programme, *Not Only But Also*, presented by Peter Cook and Dudley Moore, John Lennon was the guest star as a uniformed commissionaire in a sketch that began outside a public convenience. He directs Cook to the urinals with the instruction, "Just follow your nose."

JOHN LENNON MBE

Britain's new Labour government disguised vote-catching as acknowledgement of The Beatles' contribution to the export drive when it recommended that the sovereign invest Messrs Lennon, McCartney, Harrison and Starr as Members of the British Empire on October 26, 1965. Prime Minister Harold Wilson – also Member of Parliament for a Merseyside constituency – seemed to have heeded a headline in *Melody Maker* the previous spring that read, 'Honour The Beatles!' No honours list has ever been so controversial, before or since. "I didn't know you got that sort of thing," gasped George, "just for playing rock'n'roll music."

Neither did the disgusted retired admirals and senior civil servants who returned their medals to the Queen. The *Daily Express* printed a suggestion that, if the group had to be so honoured, they ought to subject themselves to a "decent" short-back-and-sides before setting off for Buckingham Palace. How many among these protesters would have remained silent had they known how one Beatle in particular had steeled himself to accepting MBE like a dog to a bath. "Taking the MBE was a sell-out for me," Lennon glowered later, "one of the biggest jokes in the history of these islands."

John would later insist that he had several spliffs – marijuana cigarettes – about his person when, soberly attired, he, Ringo, Paul and George were driven in a black Rolls-Royce through cheering masses to the palace. While waiting to be presented to Her Majesty at 11.10 a.m., he and the other three retired to a washroom to light up and pass round one of his joints. Yet either Lennon's memory was playing him false or, more likely, he was attempting to beef up his image as a rebel rocker, as his story was later refuted by George Harrison, who maintained that nothing more narcotic than tobacco was inhaled.

Certainly, none of the national treasures appeared noticeably under the influence of marijuana's short-lived magic when either in the royal presence or during a press conference afterwards in the Saville Theatre up the West End.

Nevertheless, nearly two years later, The Beatles would affix 'MBE' after their signatures to lend respectability to a petition calling for marijuana's legalisation.

The only other serious use any of them made of the decoration was Lennon's renouncement of it – accompanied by a slapdash and facetious letter to the Queen – as a political gesture in 1969.

MUCH MISSED MAN

At a John Lennon Memorial Concert at Liverpool's Philharmonic Hall in 1981, Gerry Marsden was present but not participating beyond a brief cameo at the end. Nonetheless, the Philharmonic's resident orchestra helped him do his bit in 2001 with 'Much Missed Man', a remarkable CD that, clocking in at just over 20 minutes, hung on a title requiem for Lennon with lyrics by Joe Flannery, once Brian Epstein's friend and business associate.

Within weeks of December 8, 1980, Flannery had written 'Much Missed Man' with Marsden in mind. "I felt it was too soon for a tribute from me then," thought Gerry. "However, when the anniversary of John's 50th birthday was coming up in 1990, Joe rang and asked me to give it another listen as he felt that the time might be right for me to record it – and he was right. The words said what I thought about John. People who like John will like the record."

Most of the playing time, however, would consist of a

chronologically illogical collage of John holding forth amid a recitation of one of his poems and interruptions by Yoko and persons unknown (among them a "street corner evangelist" that I suspect might be McCartney). There's fun to be had dating these excerpts which seem to stretch from final interviews back to the 'Jesus' press conference in Chicago in 1966.

As for 'Much Missed Man' itself, a fragment of dialogue by the Lennon and an 'Imagine'-esque piano figure segued into a lush and adventurous arrangement behind a heartfelt serenade from one who still earns good money as an entertainer. He certainly has as warm a rapport with the audience as he did way back when, even if the rehearsed jokes told by both him and the latest edition of the Pacemakers about his age, weight and love life are received nearly as well as 'How Do You Do It', 'Ferry Cross The Mersey' and all the rest of them.

CHRISTMAS CARD
A pencil sketch – of a man holding a leaf of holly beneath a woman's chin – by John Lennon was donated for use as the front design of a 1966 Christmas card to raise funds for the charity Action For The Crippled Child.

UP AGAINST IT
When The Beatles were debating a follow-up movie to *Help!*, John was earmarked to be the main character in *Up Against It*, a rejected development by playwright Joe Orton of *Shades Of A Personality*, a script in which a single person has four separate personalities.

APPLE AND ZAPPLE
Crosby, Stills & Nash were, apparently, intending to be contracted by Apple Records, but negotiations foundered, as did those with another up-and-coming act, Fleetwood Mac.

Awaiting his destiny as a chartbusting post-Woodstock singer-songwriter, James Taylor, was taken on, but 20-year-old David Bowie slipped through The Beatles' fingers. So also did Freddie Garrity – after an interview with Yoko Ono (!). Furthermore, though a one-shot Apple single – a reggaefied 'Give Peace A Chance' – by Hot Chocolate was issued in 1969, did The Beatles miss a commercial opportunity by auditioning and then rejecting Bamboo, a Swedish outfit that would connect genealogically with Abba?

Certain North American literary celebrities – including Richard Brautigan, Allen Ginsberg and Ken Kesey (of The Merry Pranksters) – were sounded out to recite their works on Apple's subsidiary label, Zapple, intended as a platform for the spoken word and experimental music. Other Zapple projects considered were an album of existing monologues from US night-club raconteur Lord Buckley, and another of children's stories told by movie actress Hermione Gingold. With laudable honesty, George Harrison admitted, "both of the Zapple albums that did come out were a load of rubbish" – namely his own *Electronic Sounds* and John and Yoko Ono's *Unfinished Music No. 2: Life With The Lions*.

Lennon and Harrison's standings as Beatles ensured that these self-indulgencies shifted sufficient quantities to make them profitable, and Lennon's 45s with his Plastic Ono Band all reached the Top 40 in both Britain and the States. Nevertheless, after Mary Hopkin, Billy Preston and Badfinger's respective chart runs ground to a halt, all that remained were The Beatles, together and apart, whose Apple product continued to sell by the mega-tonne.

1960s TRIBUTE DISCS

John was singled out as 'leader' in the lyrics of 'We Love The Beatles', a 1964 single by The Vernons Girls, recruited originally from employees of the Liverpool football pools firm. Yet, until his death, there were few Beatles tribute discs relating to him alone, partly because 'John' wasn't a name of comparable individuality as 'Ringo'. "It's had a lot to do with my success and acceptance," Starr would admit. "It might sound mad, but people remember it." Cornered for autographs by some French Beatles fans in Cannes in 1965, Lennon dryly signed himself 'Ringo Starr', and they went away quietly.

'Ringo I Love You' and 'Santa Bring Me Ringo' were among anthems of adoration issued after the group's conquest of North America, but there were others such as 'To Kill A Beatle', a 45 of unconscious prescience, by someone called Johnny Guarnier. Its lyric was from the perspective of a US teenager, insanely jealous because every other girl at high school had lost her marbles over the new sensations from England.

The ordinary fan's shocked reaction to the sleeve photographs of 1968's *Unfinished Music No. 1: Two Virgins* was articulated in the topical disc 'John You Went Too Far This Time' by Rainbo, alias Sissy Spacek, who was then a struggling starlet awaiting a starring role in the 1976 horror flick, *Carrie*. Her love, she sang, would never be the same. Well, he had a penis, hadn't he? Who'd have thought a Beatle could ever possess one of those?

Even more unrecognisable from the yeah-yeah-yeah moptop of old, Lennon, bearded to the cheekbones, was in the VIP enclosure at the second Isle of Wight Festival on 1969's August bank-holiday weekend. Among the acts he saw was Tom Paxton, a US singer-songwriter who ran in the same folksy pack as Judy Collins, Phil Ochs, Peter, Paul & Mary and the like. He gave 'em a track – and spin-off single – from his just-released Tom Paxton 6 entitled 'Crazy John'. It was, he explained, "about the media trashing after he came out strongly for peace in Vietnam. Bob Dylan introduced us backstage, and John nodded, and, very Liverpudlianly, said, 'Crazy John'. It made my day."

As arranged, when the show was over, Dylan boarded a helicopter to spend the night with the Lennons at Tittenhurst Park.

US BREAKTHROUGH

The Beatles' headway in the United States was negligible until 'I Want To Hold Your Hand' penetrated the Top 40 on 1964's New Year's Day – though everything released previously was repromoted to sell consequent millions.

Yet, the first four singles and the *Please Please Me* album (minus two tracks and re-titled *Introducing The Beatles*) were not considered worthy of release by Capitol as, so senior executive Jay Livingstone pontificated, "We don't think The Beatles will do anything in this market."

So it was that 'Love Me Do' was issued by Tollie, a company of no great merit; 'Please Please Me', 'From Me To You' and the album by Vee-Jay, a Chicago-based label that dealt generally in black music by such as Betty Everett, Jimmy Reed and Billy Boy Arnold; and 'She Loves You' by something called Swan. Yet within months of the success of 'I Want To Hold You Hand', 'Love Me Do', 'Please Please Me' and 'She Loves You' had all topped the national chart. Even the B-sides of the first two also made the Top 40, though 'From Me To You' stopped one position short.

REQUIEMS

George Harrison was sufficiently inspired – or thick-skinned – to start work on a Lennon tribute disc within days of the shooting. While it's futile to hypothesise about John's beyond-the-grave verdict on 'All Those Years Ago', George's first big hit since 1973 – not to mention 'It Was Nice To Know You John', 'Elergy For The Walrus' and like chart-shy efforts by others – he might have shared the disappointment of Sean's godfather, Elton John, whose 'Empty Garden (Hey Hey Johnny)' climbed no further than Number 51 in 1982. Though procrastinating for even longer, Mike 'Tubular Bells' Oldfield – with sister Sally on lead vocals – slummed it on *Top Of The Pops* with 1983's 'Moonlight Shadow' which addressed itself to the horror outside the Dakota on the night it happened. The principal subject of Oldfield's po-faced ditty was not John but Yoko.

I like to think that Lennon would have preferred Roxy Music's overhaul of 'Jealous Guy' of all the immediate post-December 8 efforts. Lennon was, after all, an artiste with whom their Bryan Ferry, via a *Melody Maker* feature, expressed a wish to collaborate. Bryan may have told the man himself when, in 1974, he dined with Lennon, Harrison and Starr in New York. Touring Germany with Roxy Music, the week after the slaying, Ferry closed performances with 'Jealous Guy'. A German record company executive suggested that it might be a sound choice for the next Roxy Music 45, but Ferry felt it might seem tasteless. Nonetheless, following further deliberations, the group tried an arrangement during an exploratory studio session. With an oblique 'A Tribute' printed on its picture sleeve, 'Jealous Guy' scudded all the way up the British charts, the only Roxy Music single to do so, by March 1981.

As deserving too of a chart placing was the title song of The Downliners Sect's *A Light Went Out In New York*, a 1993 album that mingled overhauls of some of the reformed Sixties British rhythm-and-blues combo's old tracks with Beatle obscurities. It's not unreasonable to suggest that the

Sect actually improve on 'I'll Keep You Satisfied', 'That Means A Lot' and so forth? Indeed, 'A Light Went Out In New York' – written by the Sect's own Paul Tiller – may be the most moving Lennon tribute of them all, certainly riding roughshod over the likes of 'All Those Years Ago', 'Empty Sky' and 'Moonlight Shadow'.

FURY

After Lennon granted the magazine a frank, unashamed and circulation-boosting two-part interview, *Rolling Stone* surmised that his singing on 'God' – fifth track, side two of *John Lennon: Plastic Ono Band* – "may be the finest in all rock", and that the entire album was "a full, blistering statement of fury". Overall, the reviewer seemed to like it.

OVERLANDER

By the mid-Sixties, it would be a strange week if a version of a Lennon-McCartney opus wasn't among the flotsam-and-jetsam that washed up around record reviewers' typewriters.

Vocalist Paul Friswell contended that his Overlanders "did Lennon and McCartney a favour" via a faithful if unsolicited reproduction of 'Michelle', the bilingual ballad on *Rubber Soul*. Friswell's cheek was mitigated when, for three weeks, beginning in January 1966, The Overlanders' 'Michelle' became the first xerox of a Beatles album track to top the UK singles chart. While it eclipsed a version by David & Jonathan, it was to be The Overlanders' only hit.

In the Top 30 that same month were 'Girl', by both The Truth and St. Louis Union, as well as 'If I Needed Someone', The Hollies' crack at another *Rubber Soul* track, though missing the charts completely were Jan & Dean and Frankie Vaughan's respective covers of 'Norwegian Wood' and 'Wait'.

NIGHT

In 1974, John's 'Whatever Gets You Through The Night', Ringo Starr's 'You're Sixteen' and 'Band On The Run' by Wings all spent exactly one week at number one in the US Hot 100. Lennon's single, however, was the only one of the three not to make the British Top 30.

MISERY

The first cover of a Lennon-McCartney song was of 'Misery'.

Helen Shapiro was the principal attraction on the bill of the round Britain package tour with The Beatles, Kenny Lynch, Danny Williams, The Kestrels and others in February 1963. Knocked together by John and Paul as the tour bus braved the icy tundra of the country's worst winter for a century, 'Misery' was in the shops by the final night at Hanley Gaumont – not by Shapiro, who was given first refusal, but Kenny Lynch, who didn't need asking twice.

Spiced with strings, it also featured veteran guitarist Bert Weedon's period twanging – to which John took exception – which replaced George Martin's piano ostinato on The Beatles' *Please Please Me* album version. "Kenny solos and self-duets excellently," exclaimed *New Musical Express* critic Keith Fordyce. "The song is very attractive with a medium-paced beat."

The Beatles also left their mark on Kenny's own song-writing – as exemplified by another of his 1963 singles, 'Shake And Scream', modelled on 'Twist And Shout' and beefed up with canned berserk audience reaction.

The Kestrels were to Xerox another *Please Please Me* track, Lennon's introspective 'There's A Place'.

ANTHOLOGY

After the flush of 'sympathy' million-sellers in the aftershock of December 8, 1980, the next time Lennon made the charts was in 1982 when 'Beatles Movie Medley' reached number 10 in Britain and 12 in the USA. In interviews, George Harrison in particular underlined his boredom with the endless interest in The Beatles, an interest that was to escalate with the runaway success in 1994 of *Live At The BBC*, a compilation of early broadcasts. This prefaced official news of an upcoming anthology of further items from the vaults. These were to be hand-picked by George, Paul and Ringo themselves for issue over the period of a year on nine albums (in packs of three) as companion records to a six-hour documentary film to be spread over three weeks on ITV, and presented likewise on foreign television.

Then came talk of the Fab Three recording new material for the project. The general feeling, however, was that it wouldn't be the same without John. Yet, after a fashion, a regrouping of Harrison, Starr and McCartney – the 'Fab Three' – in the mid-Nineties wasn't without Lennon. Their labours in George's and Paul's respective private studios yielded the grafting of new music onto demos by their former standard bearer.

Yet for all the amassing of anticipation via no sneak previews, a half-hour TV special building up to its first spin over a remarkable video, and the multitudes willing it to leap straight in at number one as usual, 'Free As A Bird' stalled in second place in Britain's Christmas list when up against 'Earth Song' by Michael Jackson and an easy-listening cover of Oasis's 'Wonderwall' by The Mike Flowers Pops.

The follow-up, 'Real Love', reached the Top 10 more grudgingly, having been dogged by exclusion from BBC Radio One's playlist of choreographed boy bands, chart ballast from the turntables of disco and rave, and – despite evidence that they'd been fed Beatles music from the cradle –

Britpop executants like The Bluetones, Supergrass, Ocean Colour Scene and, most pointedly of all, Oasis.

ENGELBERT

Proving that schmaltz was very much alive, Englebert Humperdinck's 'Release Me' prevented The Beatles' double-sided meisterwerk 'Strawberry Fields Forever'/ 'Penny Lane' from going straight in at number one in Britain on March 2, 1967. In most British charts, The Beatles' offering progressed no further than number two, checkmated further by 'Something Stupid' by Frank and Nancy Sinatra and then Sandie Shaw's Eurovision Song Contest winner, 'Puppet On A String'.

BEATLES FAN CLUB CLOSES

Three years after *Beatles Monthly* magazine ceased publication, falling membership led to the closure of the fragmented group's official fan club in March 1972. In Britain, much of the blame lay in the ex-Beatles' individual images and vinyl output which, if still commercially potent, embrace elements that were anathema to the current 'glam-rock' trend. Moreover, to even the most optimistic fan, the quartet's reformation was no longer inevitable despite newspaper headlines shrieking 'Beatlemania Sweeps A City!', 'The Beatles Are Back!' and the like after George Harrison and Ringo Starr reunited on a New York stage for Harrison's Concerts For Bangladesh in 1971. Since then, monetary inducements for the four to play together just one more time multiplied to no effect.

FLOOD STREET

The Beatles arrived at photographer Michael Cooper's studio in Flood Street, Chelsea on March 30, 1967 for a session that resulted in the front cover for *Sgt. Pepper's Lonely Hearts Club Band*. Dressed as pantomime militia and clutching brass and woodwind instruments, the four fronted a life-size photo collage mounted on hardboard, consisting mostly of the images of each Beatle's all-time heroes, together with a few suggested by designer Peter Blake and London art dealer Robert Fraser.

It was possible to guess individual choices. John Lennon was responsible principally for Oscar Wilde, Lewis Carroll, H.G. Wells, Edgar Allen Poe and other literary figures. Of only a handful of icons from the world of pop, the most poignant was that of the late Stuart Sutcliffe, the group's first bass guitarist. The Beatles also acknowledged likewise the influence of Bob Dylan, The Rolling Stones (whose name was displayed on a doll's pullover) and their earlier selves via wax models borrowed from Madame Tussaud's. Further details included a hookah, a row of nursery plants and The Beatles' name spelt out in crimson flowers.

SLADE
In March 1973, Slade's 'Cum On Feel The Noize' entered the UK chart at number one, the first single to so do since The Beatles. The previous year, Slade's 'Look What You Dun' – which singer and co-writer Noddy Holder confessed had been inspired by John Lennon – had reached number four.

TOP OF THE POPS
The Beatles made an in-person debut on BBC television's *Top Of The Pops* on March 25, 1964. On the broadcast from a converted church in Manchester, they mimed their newly released single, 'Can't Buy Me Love' and its 'You Can't Do That' B-side. With unprecedented advance sales of over one

million copies in Britain alone, this disc was destined to enter both the UK and US charts at number one.

SMOKIN'

In Abbey Road's number 2 studio, Noel Gallagher (of Oasis), Paul Weller (once of The Jam) and Paul McCartney reworked Lennon's 'Come Together' for *Help!*, a 1995 various artists album to raise funds to alleviate the war in Bosnia's aftermath of homelessness, disease and starvation.

RUSSIA

The first Beatles disc to be issued in Soviet Russia was a 1966 single of 'Girl', coupled with Sandie Shaw's 'Long Live Love'. An unlikely scheme for a 1966 trip to the republic that might have re-awaken the group's enthusiasm for the stage was thwarted by an immovable world tour in which The Beatles would visit many other territories for the first and only time.

March 1990 saw the publication of a survey conducted amongst Russian teenagers that revealed that the western rock acts they'd most like to see in concert were Michael Jackson, Pink Floyd – and The Beatles.

BY THE BOOK

As well as the millions generated by *Anthology*, dividends from 1996's renovated *Yellow Submarine* were to benefit Pete's successor in The Beatles – and McCartney and Harrison. More was to come via the publication of the *Anthology* autobiography in 2000. Several years in gestation, it was a "Beatles story told for the first time in their own words and pictures". Whereas Ringo, George and Paul's were from turn-of-the-century taped reminiscences, with no anchoring narrative, John's were from media archives and, therefore, not influenced by hindsight. He came over, therefore, as less of a straightforward, unspoilt Merseyside lad than any of the other three.

With its weight on a par with a paving slab, this amassed enough advance orders to slam it straight in at number one in *The Sunday Times* book chart, a feat duplicated across the world.

The *Anthology* book remained a best-seller while EMI co-ordinated its biggest-ever marketing campaign. Eight million copies of *1*, a compilation of The Beatles' 27 British and US chart-toppers were shipped around the world. The fastest-selling compact-disc ever, *1* was just that in Britain, Japan, Germany and Canada within a week of its issue.

YOKO ON THE ROAD

While a North American public looked as if it might have been receptive to a coast-to-coast tour a decent interval after her famous husband's death, Yoko chose instead a water-testing 32-date trudge round Europe's concert halls in 1985 that didn't even break even, not even out of sympathy or morbid inquisitiveness. While a night in Budapest closed on an emotional high with a jubilant 15,000 – almost all of them Beatles diehards – blasting up a rowdy singalong finale of 'Imagine', in Vienna, the auditorium was less than half full. That was typical – as was the painfully transparent fact that the older you were, the louder you clapped, and that all the customers wanted was some ersatz Beatles magic.

Yoko seemed to have gone off the boil in the States too. Attempting to fill venues that were the domain of those in the higher league of the "adult-orientated rock" hierarchy, she shifted only a quarter of the tickets in the Universal Amphitheatre in Los Angeles. In the 20,000 seaters in the mid-west too, while Yoko was received with some affection by those whose life had been soundtracked by The Beatles, turn-out was so poor that cancellation of the remaining shows was the only way to staunch further financial haemorrhaging.

CUBA

Cuban pop music developed over decades of cultural isolation. This was encouraged by the revolutionary government's official disapproval of subversive rock'n'roll until quite comparatively recently – as exemplified by the erection in a Havana public park of a statue of John Lennon.

STAND BY ME

Following a US hit with the evocative 'Spanish Harlem', Ben E. King's self-penned 'Stand By Me' was initially only a moderate seller when first issued in 1961 – though it inspired many covers. The most successful of these were by Kenny Lynch, Cassius Clay(!) and John Lennon. As the single from 1975's *Rock 'N' Roll* LP, it reached number 27 in Britain, and number 20 in the States. As a solo artist, it was his only chart entry with a non-original.

Julian Lennon also recorded a version of 'Stand By Me'.

MARMALADE

The high summer of Glaswegian pop was evidenced in 1968 by Marmalade's shrewd Yuletide copy of Lennon-McCartney's 'Ob-la-di Ob-la-da' (from The Beatles' *White Album*) to which John, by his own admission, contributed only "a couple of lyrics". It was inspired, however, by the Jamaican patois of Georgie Fame's percussionist, Speedy Acquaye.

The third (and last) Beatles cover to reach number one in Britain, Marmalade celebrated by miming it on *Top Of The*

Pops in national costume, the Clydeside boys in sporrans, gorgets, clan tartans et al. with their English drummer in redcoat gear as a reminder of Culloden.

THE WAY HE WOULD HAVE WANTED IT?

On January 20, 1988, The Beatles were inducted into the third Rock And Roll Hall Of Fame. Amid the murals and mosaics in New York's deluxe Waldorf-Astoria Hotel, what was left of the group was represented by George, Ringo, Julian Lennon and Yoko, who was coaxed to the podium's microphone to say a few words, viz "I am sure that if John was alive, he would have been here."

Two years later, she compered a televised and international concert spectacular for charity she'd arranged at Liverpool's Pier Head, that although several months in advance, was to mark what would have been John's fiftieth birthday. A relatively minor landmark on rock's road to respectability, it still attracted the likes of Ray Charles, Lou Reed, Roberta Flack, Kylie Minogue, Christopher 'Superman' Reeve and other disparate big-names-in-good-cause, even if some bickered over billing.

While they declined to show up in person, Paul and Ringo each sent a filmed piece, with Starr's "Hi, Liverpool!" and "supergroup" overhaul of a Beatles track from 1964 bridging a gap between Philadelphian duo Hall & Oates and Welsh guitarist Dave Edmunds' John Lennon Tribute Band. George, however, elected to have nothing to do with an event he considered to be "in poor taste".

At least Harrison had been approached by Ono to participate. No Merseybeat groups – "who'd got drunk with him," muttered one disgruntled member – had been requested even to warm up for her star turns or to muscle in amongst the assembled cast for the big finish with 'Give Peace A

Chance', lately re-made by Yoko and Sean with lyrics revised as a searing indictment of the Gulf War between the USA and Iraq.

PRAGUE

In Prague, a mural of John Lennon was painted in his memory on the garden wall of the Grand Priory of the Knights of Malta by authorised city graffiti artists. It has since been disfigured to the point of almost total obliteration by unofficial graffiti.

WOODSTOCK

Woodstock Music and Arts Fair took place in the squelching mud of lakeside meadows in upstate New York in August 1969. It would be viewed from a distance of years as the climax of hippy culture, and a vote of no confidence in President Nixon.

John Lennon volunteered to perform there with Yoko Ono and a Plastic Ono Band, as he would at Toronto Rock & Roll Revival Show the following month, but the organisers, who had written to him requesting The Beatles, rejected the offer, even though Lennon, assuming otherwise, was intending to billet himself with Bob Dylan, who lived in the nearby village of West Saugerties.

JOHN LENNON AIRPORT

Yoko Ono was conspicuous at the official opening and unveiling of an honorific plaque on the wall of Mendips, John's childhood home in Woolton, in March 2003. That same month too, she'd been there to view a seven-foot statue of her late husband in the presence of the Queen when Liverpool displayed its pride in him by renaming its principal air terminal John Lennon Airport in the teeth of certain civic objections that Lennon, though an admirable young man in many ways, had more than his share of young man's vices. Yoko was also pragmatically supportive of the John Lennon Memorial Scholarship at the University of Liverpool, which was to benefit talented local youngsters, just as the Jimi Hendrix Memorial Foundation had been doing for boys and girls in seats of learning in and around his home city of Seattle since 1971.

WATCH OUT

While she gave her blessing to a Broadway musical based on his life in 2003, Yoko Ono allowed a John Lennon watch to be marketed for 1996's Christmas sell-in – but rather than his face, it portrayed his naked buttocks.

Bibliography

Such is the volume of literary spin-offs both before and after his death that someone ought to write a book about books about John Lennon. These have ranged from scurrilous trash to well-researched, scholarly works that any historical figure of his stature deserves. There surfaced too countless volumes containing minutiae and raw information that only the most crazed devotee would not find too insignificant to be totally intriguing.

Therefore, rather than attempt a long – and probably incomplete – list of dry titles for further reading, it makes more sense to compile a selection with brief commentary of items that either I found helpful or are prototypical of specific aspects of John Lennon and The Beatles.

Shout! The True Story Of The Beatles by Philip Norman (Elm Tree, 1981)

Despite factual errors, this is still accepted by most as the standard work on the group.

The True Story Of The Beatles by Billy Shepherd (Beat Publications, 1964)

Neither a triumph of linguistic ability nor a penetrating insight into the human condition, this assignment was, nevertheless, the first of more Beatles biographies than anyone in 1964 could have ever comprehended.

Revolution In The Head by Ian MacDonald (Fourth Estate, 1994)

A track-by-track study of The Beatles' recorded output, regarded as the late MacDonald's magnum opus, even when he dared, for instance, to suggest that John Lennon, during his eye-stretching peace campaign in the late Sixties, "unwittingly put himself in a position in which he was obliged to defend things that, deep down, he cared nothing about".

The Day John Met Paul by Jim O'Donnell (Hall Of Fame, 1994)

After eight years of committed research, the author has tried hard to be unfailingly accurate in his account – minute-by-minute at times – of the 1957 day that kicked-off one of the most crucial partnerships in pop, setting it in the context of local, national and global events that were occurring even as The Quarry Men mounted the stage at Woolton village fete.

The Beatles' London by Piet Shreuders, Mark Lewisohn and Adam Smith (Hamlyn, 1996)

With maps and full index, this lists by postcode every significant Beatle location in London and the Home Counties, from the Decca audition on January 1, 1962 to Paul McCartney's Royal Court of Justice application for receivership in February 1971 which legally broke up the group.

Backbeat – Stuart Sutcliffe: The Lost Beatle by Alan Clayson and Pauline Sutcliffe (Pan-Macmillan, 1994)

If, ostensibly, a film tie-in, this serves as an insight into the social and academic atmosphere from which The Beatles emerged.

The Beatles After The Break-Up by Keith Badman (Omnibus, 1999)

This most comprehensive reference work provides comprehensive facts about Lennon's life as an ex-Beatle as well as those of the other personnel.

Every Sound There Is: The Beatles' Revolver And The Transformation Of Rock And Roll ed. Russell Reising (Ashgate, 2002)

Born of symposiums and dialectic gymnastics, this is a series of meticulous and scholarly essays that cut, dry and dissect an album released when The Beatles had the means to turn their every whim into audible reality. From the pens of college academics from across the globe, titles like 'A Flood Of Flat-Sevenths', 'Premature turns: thematic disruption in the American version' and 'Re-arranging base and superstructure in the rock ballad' telegraph that you might need to have a dictionary of musicological terms close to hand and undergo a crash course in sight-reading.

The Lives Of John Lennon by Albert Goldman (William Morris, 1988)

Intricately researched muck-raking, this must be read on the understanding that the good doctor disliked Lennon, The Beatles and pop, and that he did it for the money.

John Winston Lennon Volume 1 1940–1966 and John Ono Lennon Volume 2 1967–1980 by Ray Coleman (Sidgwick and Jackson, 1984)

The antithesis of the Goldman job, these are very much the sort of books that John himself might have approved – with all that that implies.

Beatles Guide To Hamburg by Ulf Kruger (Europa Verlag, 2001)

A very slim volume in German and slightly dodgy English concerning the group's visits to Germany between the season at the seedy Indra in 1960 through the Star-Club period ("which extremely improved the quality of music of the different bands") to their scream-rent concert at the Ernst-Merck-Halle six years later. It should prove useful if you wish to visit such Golgothas as the Fischmarkt (where "rumour has it that the Beatles bought a young pig") or the Bambi Kino ("where Paul and Pete lit a condom that hung from a nail off the concrete wall in the hallway"). This myth and others are compounded by Kruger in a text enhanced by a map of the area, a foreword by Astrid Kirchherr and a selection of photographs, mostly new ones of buildings and people with bit-parts in the saga, and old ones of the Fab Four (once, Fab Five) and their intimates that you've seen in a hundred other books.

First Of The True Believers: The Autobiography of Theodore Hennessy by Paul Charles (Do-Not Press, 2002)

Subtitled *A Novel Concerning The Beatles*, a Liverpool lad, Theo's protracted courtship of a local girl – and his membership of an also-ran Merseybeat outfit, The Nighttime Passengers – merges with the fairy tale of John, Paul, George, Ringo and their fellow travellers, embracing chatty regurgitations of many of the old errors.

The British Invasion by Bill Harry (Chrome Dreams, 2004)

If marred by minor errors and omissions, this chronicle is laced from the beginning with a shot of justifiable autobiography. Indeed, Harry traces the phenomenon in question back to 1960 and a discussion in a Liverpool pub between himself and three fellow art students. These included John Lennon, whose Beatles spearheaded what has passed into myth as the 'British Invasion' of North America.

Arthur Ballard by Peter Davies (Old Bakehouse, 1998)

A life of the late Ballard, the painting lecturer and general tutor at Liverpool College of Art for over 30 years, who defended Lennon against those who wanted his expulsion, and fine-tuned star pupil Stuart Sutcliffe's output. Accessible to both Beatle devotees and those with a general interest in the history of British fine art, this is a fluid and workmanlike account.

The Art & Music Of John Lennon by Peter Doggett (Omnibus Press, 2005)

A first-rate critical analysis of Lennon's output from The Beatles to his death, and not only the music as Doggett chronicles Lennon's movies, painting, poetry, pose and conceptual art.

John Lennon And The FBI Files by Phil Strongman and Alan Parker (Sanctuary, 2003)

The thrust of this account is that Mark David Chapman was programmed by the Reagan administration to slay one whose return from artistic slumber might also have meant the resumption of anti-government activism. There are also well-argued comparisons of Chapman's deeds and personality with those of the assassins of President Kennedy, his brother Robert and Martin Luther King. Compilation of macabre coincidences can occupy many hours of enjoyable time-wasting, but, over and over again I was convinced that Parker and Strongman might be telling me something – possibly a truth – that I don't want to believe.

The Best Years Of The Beatles by Pete Best and Bill Harry (Headline, 1996)

In this second account of the sacked drummer's tenure with The Beatles, a treasury of archive illustrations accompany a text divided between the sometime editor of *Mersey Beat*'s briefer personal reminiscences and anchoring historical perspectives, and transcriptions of Pete's taped telling of quite a few unfamiliar anecdotes and his meditations on old yarns.

The Playboy Interviews With John Lennon And Yoko Ono by David Sheff, ed. by G. Barry Golson (New English Library, 1982)

One of the final interviews – and perhaps the lengthiest ever – it delves into many important areas, including recollections about nearly every song he ever composed.

The Beatles From Cavern To Star-Club by Hans Olof Gottfridsson (Premium/Turnaround, 1999)

The most thoroughly investigated work ever undertaken on the group's pre-Parlophone recording career – certainly more so than my own *Backbeat* with Stuart Sutcliffe's sister – and better even than Gareth Pawlowski's excellent *How They Became The Beatles* (Penguin, 1989).

Borrowed Time (Xanadu, 1991) by Frederic Seaman
One of the more compassionate 'insider' efforts.

John Lennon Encyclopedia (Virgin, 2000) by Bill Harry
Written by an art school crony of John Lennon, founder of *Mersey Beat* and pal of The Beatles up to and beyond their disbandment, this vast and detailed tome remains the reference work for both the longtime fan and that Tibetan monk who still hasn't heard of the wretched fellow.

There Are Places I'll Remember Volumes 1 & 2 by Ray O'Brien (Ray O'Brien, 1999)
These self-published guides concern the venues The Beatles played in and around Merseyside and North Wales up to 1963. An entertaining commentary is enhanced by maps and a vast selection of photographs of apposite buildings and people with at least bit-parts in the saga as well as all manner of memorabilia.

The Encyclopaedia Of Beatle People by Bill Harry (Blandford, 1997)
The author is justified entirely in letting a picture of himself be used in a front cover montage that also embraces 15 other selections from a cornucopia of co-stars and bit-part players vast and detailed enough to almost completely satisfy the most obsessed Lennon lunatic or Beatlemaniac's craving for new characters and twists in the plot of the old, old story.

If you wanted to start nit-picking, there's no passage on the Hideaways – Cavern regulars liked by George's Mum – or Brute Force that recorded an Apple 45 entitled 'The King Of Fuh'. A much more conspicuous omission is that of Kenny

Lynch, the most frequent guest on the UK tours, and the first to cover a Lennon–McCartney composition.

Conversely, where can it end? By including all the acts on the same label? Everyone who ever recorded a Beatles song? The foresters who felled the trees to make the paper on which they were written?